MICHAEL CHABEREK, O.P.

AQUINAS AND EVOLUTION

THE CHARTWELL PRESS

Published by Thomas D. Hamel
"The Chartwell Press"
thechartwellpress.com

Second Edition, Revised and Updated
Copyright © 2019 Michael Chaberek
Printed in the United States of America
All rights reserved.
ISBN: 978-0-9919880-6-8

"I, Mark Padrez O.P., Prior Provincial of the Western Dominican Province, hereby grant the Nihil Obstat and Imprimatur to Aquinas and Evolution by Michael Chaberek O.P.

The Nihil Obstat and Imprimatur are official declarations that this book is free of doctrinal or moral error. No implication is contained herein that I, who granted the Nihil Obstat and Imprimatur, agree with the contents, opinions, or statements expressed. Given in Oakland, CA October 17, 2016"

www.aquinasandevolution.org

TABLE OF CONTENTS

Foreword	5
Chapter I: *Status Quaestionis*	11
1. The older and the newer Thomists	11
2. The problem of "commensurability"	17
3. Preliminary definitions	20
4. The two questions to be answered	30
5. *Modus procedendi*	33
6. Ordering the arguments	35
Chapter II: Aquinas and the Origin of Species	39
1. It seems that Aquinas's teaching does not exclude theistic evolution (objections)	39
2. The origin of species according to Aquinas (*corpus*)	51
3. Replies to the objections	62
Chapter III: Aquinas and the Augustinian Interpretation of Genesis	96
1. Augustine and the six days of creation	96
2. Augustine and the *mode* and *order* of creation	102
3. Thomas and the Augustinian "seminal reasons"	104
4. Augustine in the contemporary debate	117
Chapter IV: Aquinas and the Origin of Man	125
1. The context of the contemporary debate	125
2. Aquinas and the origin of the human body	132
3. Aquinas and the origin of woman	145
Excursus 1: Human Origin in the 1992 Catechism ...	151

Chapter V: Aquinas and Intelligent Design 161
   1. It seems that Aquinas's teaching excludes ID
      (objections) 162
   2. Aquinas and intelligent design (*corpus*) 173
   3. Replies to the objections 187

Chapter VI: Thomists versus Thomas 213
   1. Aquinas and the progress of science 213
   2. Why do Thomists adopt theistic evolution? 218
   Excursus 2: Could God have used evolution? 232

Bibliography 249

Endorsements 257

FOREWORD

Though I had heard for years about the writings of a certain Polish Dominican with a doctorate in theology, I first had the privilege of meeting Fr. Michael Chaberek at Ave Maria University in early 2015. We had been invited to attend a small discussion of diverse viewpoints on Thomism, evolution, and intelligent design. After observing Fr. Chaberek's keen mind and kindly disposition, I am absolutely convinced that his voice is an essential ingredient for getting a handle on current debates about whether the thought of Thomas Aquinas can be squared with evolution in general and Darwinian evolution in particular.

Few people (in recent times, anyway) have devoted serious and sustained attention to the obvious *prima facie* conflict between Thomism and Darwinism. An older generation of Thomists saw the conflict. But today the issue is mostly glossed over—even by well-trained Thomists. They sweep the problem under the rug and proceed as if God creates wholly through 'secondary causes.' If this were so, there might indeed be no conflict after all. Theology tells us *that* God creates; the sciences tell us *how*.

But this is far too superficial. How is it, then, that leading Catholic intellectuals propound such a view? Culturally it has been easy to dismiss worries about Darwinian evolution as a 'fundamentalist' Protestant problem. Additionally, we Catholics have a Galileo Complex. This neurosis might be cured with a better understanding of the Galileo affair, but as things stand Catholic intellectuals want any apparent conflict between faith and contemporary scientific theories resolved as quickly as possible—and in a way that never appears critical of science. This is obviously not a recipe for careful thought.

It is in this context that we can see the courage of Fr. Chaberek and the importance of his work. Fr. Chaberek understands that we live in intellectually exciting times in the life of the Church. As he shows in his first book, *Catholicism and Evolution: A History from Darwin to Pope Francis* (Angelico Press, 2015), the Church's views of evolution simply aren't settled. There he took on the now-enshrined myth that the Church never saw any difficulties with Darwin. He described two distinct periods of the Church's interaction with evolution. The first, from 1860–1909, he described as an "inefficient rejection of evolutionism." Unlike many others, he made no attempt to downplay or minimize the thought of this period; its concerns have not been addressed so much as forgotten. The second, from 1950–2015, he described as a "moderate acceptance of theistic evolution." He laments the large number of influential theologians who treat Darwinian evolution or evolution in general as if it were simply a matter of long-established dogma. A plurality of opinion, he maintains, is allowed by the Church at this point in history. This is good news for academics. There is important work to be done.

At the end of *Catholicism and Evolution* Fr. Chaberek seemed to be looking ahead to a third period in the history of the Church's engagement with evolution. Real Protestant fundamentalism has had its heyday, and for the first time in a century Catholics can re-think Darwinian evolution without that monkey on their backs. Regardless of whether any particular argument of the intelligent design movement succeeds, Phillip Johnson and current ID theorists have changed the terms of the debate and opened up a window on stale intellectual space.[1] They have shown one way in which Christians

---

[1] See, for example, Phillip Johnson, *Darwin on Trial*, 2nd ed. (Downers Grove, IL: InterVarsity Press, 1993); Michael Behe, *Darwin's Black Box: The Biochemical Challenge to Evolution* (New York: Touchstone, 1996); William Dembski, *The Design Inference: Elimi-*

might fruitfully engage in science from a theistic point of view. In the face of heated opposition—after all, people can't stand having their easy categories of 'backwards fundamentalists' and 'enlightened Darwinians' upset—ID theorists have taught us that we need not simply accommodate Christian theology to Darwin or accept a facile we-can't-tell-how-but-God-uses-evolution view. The ID movement has not only (negatively) poked holes in current materialist theories but (positively) revealed that much of the best of current science points to theism. For this all theists should be grateful. The project is in its infancy. But at last a satisfying and positive synthesis of modern biological science and theistic belief seems at least possible.

At the same time, there has been a revival of Thomistic metaphysics. In the twentieth century we saw Etienne Gilson, Jacques Maritain, and others not only pass along the tradition but deepen our understanding of it. Numerous Thomistic schools have thrived, and analytic Thomism was born.[2] Thomistic philosophy is no longer in a ghetto but is now in constant conversation with mainstream Anglo-American philosophy. We have yet to see the full fruit of this movement, but this is undoubtedly a healthy development.

To those interested in the revival of Thomistic thought and tired of the same old platitudes about Christianity and evolution, the present volume will prove stimulating. Fr. Chaberek rightly treats Darwinian theory as a substantive hypothesis with metaphysical implications (he speaks of "Darwinian metaphysics"). This is a breath of fresh air, for many Christians today dismiss the very possibility of conflict

---

nating Chance Through Small Probabilities (New York: Cambridge University Press, 1998); Stephen Meyer, *Signature in the Cell: DNA and the Evidence for Intelligent Design* (New York: HarperOne, 2009); and Douglas Axe, *Undeniable: How Biology Confirms Our Intuition that Life Is Designed* (New York: HarperOne, 2016).

[2] See R. Cessario, O.P., *A Short History of Thomism* (Washington, D.C.: The Catholic University of America Press, 2005).

between Darwinism and the faith by claiming that metaphysics (and philosophy generally) can be hermetically sealed off from science. They think that if the Richard Dawkinses of the world would just stick to science all would be well. But as Jay Richards writes:

> ... The problem here isn't merely that science has transgressed its proper boundaries, as one often hears. The problem is that materialism has entered into the foundations and content of the science itself.
>
> This materialist infection of science is distinct from scientism and requires a different response. Failure to tread carefully here leads many well-meaning Catholics to take the scientific claims of Darwinists for granted, and then to find a theological excuse for not looking at the actual scientific evidence.[3]

Some theories will be both scientific and metaphysical (or will, at least, have philosophical and/or theological implications). Fr. Chaberek understands this and treats Darwinian theory without the typical naïveté.

If Christianity is true, as both Fr. Chaberek and I believe, then nothing that we observe in the natural world will ultimately conflict with the truths of theology. But it is a leap in logic to assume that good theology will never conflict with (even well-meaning) scientific theories. Scientific theories can be mistaken; they are not handed to us from above but are inventions of finite minds to describe observed phenomena (or their causes) from within a worldview. And our worldview can be mistaken. The positivistic days of seeing scientists as men in white lab coats who simply 'find' scientific theories as

---

[3] *God and Evolution: Protestants, Catholics, and Jews Explore Darwin's Challenge to Faith*, ed. Jay W. Richards (Seattle: Discovery Institute Press, 2010), p. 268.

though they are just lying about on the ground are, I hope, behind us.[4]

While well aware of the scientific debates surrounding Darwinian theory, in this book Fr. Chaberek is primarily concerned with the philosophical and theological adequacy of Darwinism according to the thought of St. Thomas. Many Thomists have (surprisingly) argued that Darwinian theory fits quite well with the metaphysics of St. Thomas—or at the very least does not conflict with it in any important way. Finally giving the issue the book-length treatment it deserves—instead of the usual quote-mining and weak extrapolations—Fr. Chaberek piles on reason after reason to doubt that this is so, not merely repeating the arguments of others (such as Robert Koons and myself) but making his own novel contribution.[5] And the results are stimulating.

Fr. Chaberek deftly replies to the most serious arguments of Thomistic Darwinians using the structure of the medieval *quaestio*. He argues that theistic evolution is excluded by some of Aquinas's basic principles: that no being can convey more act than it possesses; that the natures of living beings cannot be transformed via accidental changes; that God created distinct levels of perfection in nature; that Scripture indicates a literal and historical direct creation of Adam and Eve; that secondary causes are not responsible for the creation of species (i.e., the appearance of new kinds of substantial form); and more. He further shows that St. Augustine's writings, despite advancing ideas with superficial resemblance to evolution, do not support contemporary theistic evolution. But more than this, arguing from a traditional understanding of

---

[4] The *locus classicus* for understanding the role of worldviews in shaping scientific thinking is Thomas Kuhn, *The Structure of Scientific Revolutions* (Chicago: University of Chicago Press, 1962).

[5] Robert C. Koons and Logan Paul Gage, "St. Thomas Aquinas on Intelligent Design," in *Proceedings of the American Catholic Philosophical Association*, Vol. 85 (2011), pp. 79–97. See also Jay Richards's chapters in the aforementioned *God and Evolution*.

the division of the disciplines Fr. Chaberek shows that the theory of intelligent design does not, *contra* many Thomists, conflict with Aquinas's metaphysical principles or Thomistic natural theology.

Whether Fr. Chaberek will convert other Thomists is still to be seen. But what is clear is that his arguments are thoughtful and challenging. All serious future discussion of this issue will have to grapple with this text. While this is the most thorough reply to Thomistic *evolutionists* to date, of its very nature one book could never settle forever all of the complex issues at play between Thomism and Darwinism. Much more work needs to be done. But Fr. Chaberek is at the vanguard; and his contribution is vital. Let's hope that many more follow him in taking up these important questions in the spirit of *fides quaerens intellectum*.

Logan Paul Gage, Ph.D.
Assistant Professor of Philosophy
Franciscan University of Steubenville (Ohio)

CHAPTER I:
STATUS QUAESTIONIS

1. THE OLDER AND THE NEWER THOMISTS

Our inquiry into the question of compatibility between Thomas Aquinas's philosophy and the modern theory of evolution should begin by recognizing the current state of opinion on the subject.

Today the majority of "Thomists" assert that Aquinas's theology/philosophy can be reconciled with the evolutionary origin of species. Most of them make some reservations as to what kind of "theory of evolution" can be reconciled with Aquinas's principles, but hardly any would claim that the two are entirely incompatible. Virtually none of the Thomists would phrase the problem in "either/or" terms—namely, that either you accept Aquinas along with the principles of classical metaphysics and then you need to say "goodbye" to Darwin, or you embrace biological evolution and then you need to say "no" to Aquinas. This is where we are today—the "compatibilist" party rules.

This was not the case in the past. Even as recently as the 1940s and 1950s (already nearly a hundred years after Darwin), one could still find prominent Catholic scholars who rejected the idea of evolutionary origin of species based on principles of classical metaphysics (e.g., E. Ruffini, R. Garrigou-Lagrange). And at the end of the nineteenth century, the situation was exactly opposite to the present—Thomists universally rejected the Darwinian theory of origins. They based their position on revealed doctrine and sound philosophy. By sound philosophy they meant a broad heritage of classical metaphysics found in the Aristotelian-Thomistic as well as Platonic-Augustinian schools. Both of the schools seemed to exclude what Darwin taught. This fact leads us to the following question: Darwin's ideas have not substantially changed over the past 150 years. Neither have the teachings of Aquinas. How is it therefore possible that the Thomists of the late nineteenth century excluded Darwin's theory based on Thomistic principles, whereas the contemporary Thomists do not see any substantial incompatibility between the two? Who is right? The old school Thomists of over a century ago, those educated in the spirit of the Neo-Thomistic renewal implemented by Pope Leo XIII, or, perhaps, the contemporary ones who grew up in the post-Teilhardian culture pervaded by a broad worldview we might call "evolutionism"?

To see the problem more sharply, let us refer to a few examples. After scholars such as St. George Mivart, Raffaello Caverni, Dalmas Leroy, and John Augustine Zahm developed the first versions of "Catholic evolutionism," their works encountered opposition among the scholastics of the Roman School. The three priests (Caverni, Leroy, and Zahm) were denounced to the Congregation of the Index and several experts were asked to file their opinions regarding the books of those first Catholic "theistic evolutionists." The opinions of the Roman experts, along with a number of critical papers published in journals such as *La Civiltà Cattolica*, accounted for a goodly portion of the Catholic apologetics of that time, the edge of which was aimed against the Darwinian theory, or—in more general terms—the theory of the evolutionary origin of species.

Among the more spicy assessments we can find that of the Jesuit, Francesco S. Seewis, who called Darwinism "a tissue of ridiculous suppositions, intolerable analogies, and patent errors."[1] Or, on another occasion: "evolutionism can

---

[1] This and the following quotations come from M. Artigas, T. F. Glick, and R. A. Martínez, *Negotiating Darwin: The Vatican*

only be deemed a tissue of vulgar analogies, arbitrary suppositions, not sustained but proven wrong by the facts, fantastic adages and subterfuges that render indecent the seriousness of science."[2] In the same tenor Salvatore Brandi, S.I., claimed that the theory of evolution "is a fantastic edifice and there is no better way to describe it than as a tissue of vulgar analogies and arbitrary suppositions which are not supported by the facts."[3] Another Jesuit, Pietro Caterini, published a series of thirty-seven papers against Darwin-friendly theories. The whole project concluded with the following assessment: "In sum, transformism considered theologically is a gross and manifest error contrary to faith. Examined philosophically it is a plainly absurd variant of materialism. Assessed scientifically, it is a fantastic dream, a strange a priori system, opposed to observations and facts of nature."[4] One of the leaders of the Neo-Thomistic movement, Tommaso M. Zigliara (later declared Cardinal), in his evaluation of Caverni's work claimed that the Darwinian theory of evolution was "metaphysically absurd" and did not differ from Hegelian pantheism.[5]

For its part, the Congregation of the Index stated that "Darwin destroys the bases of revelation and openly teaches pantheism and abject materialism."[6] Another great Thomist of the time, Luigi Tripepi (who also became Cardinal) claimed that "the doctrine which teaches that animal and plant species can change from one to another through a slow transformation, viewed scientifically and independently of its consequences, is a false doctrine that must be rejected, because it contradicts: 1. experience and observed facts; 2. history; 3. paleontology; 4. common sense; 5. the most important

---

Confronts Evolution 1877–1902 (Baltimore: Johns Hopkins University Press, 2006), p. 37.

[2] Ibid., p. 138.
[3] Ibid., p. 228.
[4] Ibid., p. 38.
[5] Ibid., pp. 43–44.
[6] Ibid., p. 47.

naturalists."[7] According to Tripepi, "the system (of transformism) is contrary to great and firm philosophical principles and to facts which show that specific types [species] are absolutely irreducible, and varieties of a species should not be confused with transformation of species."[8] Still another Thomist of the Roman School, Enrico Buonpensiere, had no doubts that "Evolutionism, as all Catholic philosophers teach, is resolutely condemned by *ontological* and *empirical* science... evolutionism, opposed by all philosophical science, cannot even be called a *hypothesis*: it is a simple, more or less Platonic, *desideratum* of materialism." He added, "To attribute evolutionism to Saint Augustine is to defame a saint. Neither was Aquinas an evolutionist."[9] Consequently, Buonpensiere claimed, "I do not see how a Catholic writer could defend the system of limited evolution, even though limited to Adam's body only."[10]

The list of evidence could be continued, but the point has been made: Thomists of a hundred and more years ago deemed the theory of evolution incompatible with Thomistic philosophy. Even though the arguments of those scholars fell into oblivion, they should not be ignored. Those people had something important to say, and had concerns that remain directly relevant. They were the best-educated Catholic churchmen of their time and to them (not to their opponents) the hierarchy entrusted the duty of assessing publications promoting a "Catholic" version of evolution. Their judgment was unanimously negative, and this fact leaves us with an alternative: Either they were fatally wrong, or they grasped some part of truth that has since been lost, even in Thomist circles.

It is important to highlight here two facts about the early reaction to modern evolutionary theory among the Thomists. First: They did not oppose just the *materialistic* or *atheistic*

---

[7] Ibid., p. 84.
[8] Ibid., p. 84.
[9] Ibid., p. 148.
[10] Ibid., pp. 92–93, 111.

version of evolution. On the contrary, all of the quoted opinions refer to the *theistic* type of evolution, proposed by Catholic authors, where evolution is considered a process somehow directed, started or influenced by God. Second: Those Thomists were not ignorant of science or different theological interpretations of Genesis. They firmly claimed that scientific evidence, along with theology and philosophy, excludes the Darwinian interpretation of the facts. Their claim that the theory of evolution is absolutely incompatible with the principles of sound philosophy flowed from the breadth of their knowledge in science, theology and philosophy. Hence, their worldview was coherent. It was not a "religion against science" argument, but rather the clash of one coherent worldview against another that claimed coherence.

A great number of today's Thomists also believe that their worldview is coherent—they do not see a problem in accepting evolutionary origin of species, either from a theological or a scientific perspective. In fact, it is precisely the strong, fundamental conviction that *science has proved evolution* that makes the contemporary Thomists believe that evolution must be compatible with philosophy. After all, if something is a "fact" (and these Thomists believe that biological macroevolution is a "fact") it cannot contradict the realist philosophy of Aquinas. The starting point for today's Thomists is their conviction, derived from supposedly scientific evidence, of the truth of the transformation of species and universal common ancestry. Thomists deem it their task to show how Aquinas's teachings are compatible with that assumption derived from science. In this sense, today's Thomists judge Aquinas in the light of science, or rather, a scientific theory. In contrast, the older Thomists asked what Aquinas's (and the Church's) position on the origin of species was, and from there they assessed the theory of Darwin. In our opinion the latter approach is correct, not because we lack scientific evidence against the theory of evolution, but because this is the proper way to address questions of origins, including the origin of species.

These fundamental questions, by their very nature, cannot be answered by empirical science. They belong primarily to philosophy and theology.

As we noted, it is not the understanding of Aquinas or evolution that has changed over the last century or so. It is rather the change of the paradigms—from roughly speaking "Biblical" or "creationist" to "naturalistic" or "evolutionary." This change of paradigms explains why a great number of today's Thomists greatly differ from those of a century ago. In our opinion, the "evolutionary" paradigm, as opposed to the "Biblical" one, is not the proper context in which the problem of origins should be addressed. For this reason we believe that not today's but the previous Thomists were closer to the truth regarding both—the interpretation of Aquinas's metaphysics and the assessment of the evolutionary theory of origins.

This does not mean, however, that a simple return to the older positions would correctly resolve the issue today. An older historical situation should not be embraced as a rigid blueprint for current problems and questions. Perhaps our times, with all the astounding discoveries in biology and physics, give us an opportunity to build a new science-faith synthesis, one that neither Aquinas himself nor his nineteenth-century followers could have imagined. Our goal in this book, however, is much more modest. In what follows we will show that the teachings of Thomas Aquinas—and indeed, of any sound philosophy (*sana philosophia* or *philosophia perennis*) are not just *incompatible* with the Darwinian theory, but *exclude* it in principle. By showing this we want to achieve another objective, namely, to help contemporary Thomists to realize some of the difficulties, inaccuracies, or even flat-out errors in their interpretation of Aquinas when it comes to the question of the origin of species and man. In this sense, we will side with the older Thomists, who—despite their sometimes somewhat naive Biblical interpretations and the state of science in their day—interpreted Aquinas more adequately than their contemporary counterparts.

2. THE PROBLEM OF "COMMENSURABILITY"

One of the objections that might be filed right at the outset of our project concerns the problem of the so-called commensurability of the different levels of discussion involved in the question of origins. We already noticed that it is possible to counter the idea of universal common ancestry or the transformation of species with principles of sound philosophy (in our case we talk specifically about Thomistic philosophy). This was the approach of a number of Thomists of the past. But is it correct at all to counter one level of knowledge with another? Does it not lead to a confusion of methods, discourses and conclusions?

Since Aquinas was not a scientist (in the modern sense of the word) any discussion regarding the compatibility (or the lack thereof) between Aquinas and modern evolutionary theories assumes that the juxtaposition of science, philosophy and faith is possible. Many skeptics say it is not. In their opinion science, philosophy and theology constitute completely different realms that cannot be compared or juxtaposed without falling into methodological errors. One of the examples of such an approach is the concept of NOMA presented a few decades ago by Stephen J. Gould. NOMA stands for "non-overlapping magisteria," which means that science and faith constitute two completely different realms that have nothing to do with each other. Both realms should be kept within their confines. According to NOMA, a conflict between science and religion does not happen, in fact, is not even possible, because they speak about different things. Thus, one can maintain a completely coherent Biblical view of creation and at the same time accept the Darwinian theory as a scientific explanation of the origin of species. In this context, science gives us a realistic picture of the history of the universe, whereas religion adds some kind of a "deeper," "more profound" or "theological" insight into the issues settled by scientific theories. NOMA was originally proposed to resolve the apparent conflict between science and faith regarding the question of origins. It was proposed by the *compatibilists* (those who believe that evolution does not exclude creation), but it resolves the problem in such a way that compatibilists become *isolationists*.[11] It is true that if science and faith have completely different scopes (magisteria) conflict is avoided, but this comes at a cost: Dialogue between the two is only apparent and no real science-faith synthesis is possible.

We agree that the three levels of knowledge (science, philosophy, theology) differ regarding subject matter, method, and scope of possible conclusions. However, there are some spheres where their magisteria do overlap. This happens specifically when the subject matter of these disciplines is the same. For example, a primary subject matter of theology is God and the invisible reality, whereas for science[12] it is the material universe. Yet, theology has also the material universe as a secondary subject matter. And this is where their competences overlap—both science and theology make statements about the material universe. To expand and gain new knowledge science uses the experimental method and systematic observation, whereas theology employs the premises that are supernaturally revealed by God about the material universe. The denial of the supernaturally revealed truth about the universe is called naturalism. Christianity excludes naturalism and accepts that some part of knowledge about the material universe cannot be derived from scientific scrutiny alone. This part of knowledge is unattainable to human reason

---

[11] A good example of this approach is found in the work of G. M. Verschuuren. The author essentially follows W. E. Carroll and other Thomists who distinguish and separate the realms of theology and science to the point of isolation. See Verschuuren, *Aquinas and Modern Science: A New Synthesis of Faith and Reason* (Angelico Press, 2016), pp. 103–105, 144–145.

[12] For the sake of communicability we use the word "science" in the modern sense as an equivalent of "natural science." By this usage, theology and philosophy are not sciences. It does not follow, however that they are less reliable or coherent disciplines of knowledge.

without divine help that comes in the form of special revelation. Examples of this knowledge are supernatural events in the history of salvation, such as the virginal conception of Jesus or the Resurrection. These events are unique, transcend the order of nature and cannot be known just from history or archeology. Other truths concerning the material universe that humans cannot know by studying the material universe alone are: the first beginning of the universe (*creatio ex nihilo*), the miracles, and the truths about the supernatural formation of the universe. All of these cannot be explained by science, even though these things happened (or still happen) in the physical order.

We see that both theology and science can speak about the universe. They do it from their own perspectives and they achieve their own knowledge. However, the subject matter of both disciplines in this case is the same and this is why their conclusions may be juxtaposed, compared or even refuted by one another. Surely, if we adhered to and respected the proper limits of both disciplines the conflict should never arise. But we do not readily know the proper limits of science when addressing the questions of origins or the limits of theology when speaking about the material universe. It takes time and requires progress both in theology as well as in science to establish the limits of both disciplines. And very often we learn about their proper limits when we encounter apparent conflicts. The case of Galileo is a good example when we learnt something about the limits of theology. Today it seems necessary to learn about the limits of natural science based on the case of Darwin.

As we said, one condition to fruitfully juxtapose science, philosophy and theology is the common object of their inquiry. All three disciplines can address the question of the origin of species. Hence, in this case, the subject matter is identical for all. If science asks about the origin of biodiversity this refers to the same biodiversity that is the object of philosophy and theology. When the Bible speaks about the origin of "kinds" (Hebrew *mîn*) of plant and animal life, it is the same reality that philosophy understands as different "substantial forms" and biology as different natural species. (This will become clear when we will narrow down our definitions in the next section.) But there is also another indispensable condition to make the juxtaposition of different disciplines possible: The notions of evolution and species must be understandable by each discipline on its own terms, within its own conceptual framework. Confusion arises when one attempts to transfer the biological understanding of species into theology (for example), or when the philosophical definition of evolution is confused with the scientific one. Thus both conditions must be met simultaneously: the identity of the subject matter (or reality) described by each of the disciplines and the communicability of the notions describing this reality within its own discipline. As we will see, both criteria are met by the definitions proposed below.

3. PRELIMINARY DEFINITIONS

In recent decades more than a few Thomists have elaborated on the compatibility of Aquinas and evolution. Unfortunately, many of their works lack clear definitions of the terms, such as *evolution* and *species*. But these are two crucial terms employed in the debate and its outcome will entirely depend on how one defines the terms.[13] Aquinas was a precise author

---

[13] For example, a recent book by a group of Thomists entitled *Thomistic Evolution* is probably the most complete work on the topic. It opens with the definition of evolution as "the scientific claims that all the living organisms on our planet have a common biological origin and that these diverse organisms arose through a process of natural selection acting on genetic diversity" (p. 1). As much as the definition is clear it nevertheless contains a problem—if all life was to arise through natural selection working on genetic diversity, then genetic diversity must have preceded the diversity of life. But this leads to the question: Where did the genetic diversity (on which natural selection supposedly

and we should emulate his precision, lest a small mistake at the beginning emerge as a huge error at the end.[14] Moreover, once we clarify the definitions we will stick to them consistently throughout the book unless indicated otherwise. Let's begin with "species."

---

worked) come from? The genetic diversity is contained in the diversity of life, therefore, the proposed definition ends up in the logical fallacy called *petitio principii* (begging a question). Usually, evolutionists say that "genetic diversity" is produced by natural selection working on random genetic mutations. This postulate, however, is not included in the proposed definition. Still there is another, more fundamental problem with the use of the word "evolution" in the book. Upon careful reading one may identify transitions between at least five different meanings of "evolution," including: universal common ancestry (p. 1); struggle for life and survival of the fittest (p. 103); microevolution, i.e., environmental adaptations or changes within one family (p. 205); devolution (p. 103); and merely change over time (p. 200). Throughout the book the arguments and evidence for one type of evolution are arbitrarily extrapolated to a substantially different understanding of evolution. Yet, the argument for evolution taken in one sense may not be an argument or evidence for evolution in a different sense. And similarly, a compatibility of Aquinas's teachings with one type of evolution (for example, "change over time") does not necessitate a compatibility with another type of evolution (for example, "universal common ancestry"). Moreover, *Thomistic Evolution* lacks an explanation of the concept of species. If all biodiversity is supposed to have descended from a single ancestor (the thesis defended in the book) then species should be understood as taxonomical genera, families, or phyla. But in at least one case the authors speak of merely a hybrid within the horse family, such as the mule (p. 205). A mule is typically used as an example of microevolution, and as such does not play any role in the controversy over biological macroevolution. (Cf. In Met. Lib. 7, Lect. 7, No. 1433). See: N. P. G. Austriaco, J. Brent, Th. Davenport, and J. B. Ku, *Thomistic Evolution: A Catholic Approach to Understanding Evolution in the Light of Faith* (Tacoma, WA: Cluny Media, 2016).

[14] Cf. Thomas Aquinas, *De Ente et Essentia*, Prooemium.

SPECIES

Many skeptics over the last two centuries have claimed that discussions about evolution in biology are impossible because we do not have a clear idea what a species is. This argument is commonly raised when it comes to the distinction between *microevolution* and *macroevolution*. Since we do not know where another species begins, we cannot say if a given difference is already on the level of species, or perhaps merely on the level of varieties or races. Typically the environmental adaptive changes, the interbreeding between populations, or the breeding of new races within populations would be called microevolution, whereas changes crossing the limits of genera or families (according to classical taxonomy) would be called macroevolution.

The argument of the skeptics originates in Darwinian theory. Darwin had to blur the concept of species in order to introduce the idea of transformation of species. Before Darwin, naturalists deemed species constant and definable. This made the idea of gradual change of one species into another quite unlikely. But if one thinks that life forms constitute a continuum, where we cannot point out where one species ends and another begins, the idea of evolution looks more plausible. This is why Darwin preferred to see all biodiversity as a continuum. There is, however, a twofold misunderstanding in Darwin's and the skeptic's approach to the concept of species.

First of all, Darwin's claim about our inability to distinguish species[15] is clearly against our common experience. Of course, when Darwin speaks about species that are "fluid" he

---

[15] In *On the Origin of Species* Darwin claims: "No line of demarcation can be drawn between species" (p. 485). "There is no infallible criterion by which to distinguish species and well-marked varieties" (p. 57). "No one can draw any clear distinction between individual differences and slight varieties; or between more plainly marked varieties and subspecies, and species" (p. 470). C. Darwin, *The Origin of*

usually gives examples of what we call today biological species. But when he develops his argument he gradually extrapolates this limited idea of species onto the entire biodiversity. The very sense of his theory is the claim that all biodiversity comes from one or a few ancestors. But his argument fails due to the unjustified extrapolation. Within lower taxonomical groups there may be problems with classification and transitions between species may be possible, but this does not mean that there is the same problem on the higher taxonomical levels. The fact that from the earliest times people classified organisms confirms that there is something objective in reality that makes us think that cat is not a cow, is not a dog, is not a horse, and that each of these constitute separate species. Moreover, all classical taxonomies have more in common than not. Hence, classification is not an arbitrary activity for the hobbyists, but rather stems from the very reality of biological beings. After all, if species did not exist, or if their recognition were impossible (as Darwin suggests), then writing books on their origin, including Darwin's own work *On the Origin of Species*, would be pointless. This is why—no matter how much Darwin tries to obscure the concept of species—he cannot avoid distinguishing "true species" from "intermediate species."[16] If we apply to this Darwinian distinction classic taxonomy, the first category would mean taxonomical genus or family and the latter would refer to varieties, races, or biological species. Then, even within the purely Darwinian framework one can distinguish between microevolution (i.e., changes leading to

---

Species (London: John Murray, 1859). All following quotations come from this first edition.

[16] Darwin uses also a few other words, such as "parental," "distinct," "aboriginal," "aboriginally distinct," "independent," "dominant," "well-marked," "well-defined," and "original species." The linking forms he calls "doubtful species," "incipient species," "sub-species," or "intermediate species." The number of different names to describe the same thing seems to serve Darwin to further blur the idea of species, which he cannot outright reject, since it is the very thing whose origin he seeks to explain.

the "intermediate" species) and macroevolution (i.e., changes establishing the "true" species).

Secondly, Darwin, as well as other species-skeptics, demands more than is needed to conduct a fruitful debate. The argument of the skeptics goes more or less like this: "No one knows where a new *well-defined* species begins, therefore we cannot distinguish between microevolution and macroevolution." Yet, skeptics who employ this argument usually do not have a problem with distinguishing a coyote from a wolf, from a dog, from a fox, and they also admit that the differences between these animals are of a different kind than the differences between, let's say, an ape and an elephant, or a crocodile and a snake. Their argument rests on a few examples of organisms that are harder to classify. But, if this is the case, the difficulty with distinguishing micro and macroevolution applies to only those few cases. And even if the problem with biological classification in these few cases were truly insurmountable, there are still thousands, even millions of other cases that do not create any difficulty. My point here is that we do not really need the type of "mathematical" precision that skeptics require to have a conclusive debate about the origin of species. To avoid both mistakes (that of the skeptics, who claim that species are impossible to define, and that of some Thomists, who do not provide any definition of species) we will distinguish here four meanings of "species."

1) *Logical species*—the idea of species taken as a logical subcategory of the broader category of genus. In this sense, species can be attributed to individuals quite arbitrarily, simply by projecting new working definitions on different classes of beings. Species, taken in merely a logical sense, is a relative term that simply maintains a distinction between classes and sub-classes of a specified group of objects or organisms.

2) *Metaphysical species*—a species predicated with respect to a substantial form. Metaphysical species includes beings that possess the same substantial form.

3) *Natural species*—kinds of living organism such as dogs, cats, cattle, and horses. From a theological perspective, natural species could be identified with the "kinds" mentioned in Genesis 1. From a metaphysical perspective, a natural species includes organisms that share the same nature. In this context "nature" is defined by Aquinas as "the essence of a thing as it is ordered to the proper operation."[17] From the same, metaphysical perspective, natural species can be seen as living beings (composites of form and matter) that share the same substantial form. From the biological perspective these are organisms that belong to one taxonomic group of family or genus.

4) *Biological species* (or *modern scientific notion of species*)—according to one modern definition by Ernst Mayr, a biological species signifies all populations in which individuals are prospectively able to interbreed in their natural environment and produce fertile offspring.[18]

We said before that one precondition to make fruitful the interdisciplinary debate on the origin of species is to define one concept that refers to one reality within each discipline separately on its own terms. Our third definition of species (natural species) has a scientific (biological), a philosophical, as well as a theological meaning. Thus, we defined natural species separately for each discipline; still, each of the disciplines

---

[17] "And so the Philosopher says in V *Metaphysicae* that every substance is a nature. But the term nature used in this way seems to signify the essence of a thing as it is ordered to the proper operation of the thing, for no thing is without its proper operation" (*De Ente et Essentia*, cap. 1).

[18] E. Mayr, *Systematics and the Origin of Species from the Viewpoint of a Zoologist* (New York: Columbia University Press, 1942). We are aware of the fact that Mayr's definition is not the only one accepted in contemporary science. Scientific literature abounds in definitions, and the debate on how to define biological species is far from ended. However, here we deal with natural species, and need not await a consensus on what makes a biological species.

refers to the same reality. And this is the understanding of species that is relevant in the debate on origins. We should notice that skeptics who claim that species "do not exist," as well as nominalists, understand species according to the first definition, i.e., just as a logical category. Those who accept the second or the third definition are realists. The controversy between nominalists, who consider "species" merely an organizing concept imposed by the investigator, and realists, who hold that species exist in every individual, has a long history which is not quite relevant to our topic. The bottom line is that Aquinas was not a nominalist. He viewed species as really existing, not just in the mind, but in the physical world. In fact, Aquinas employed the term "species" many times—sometimes according to the first meaning (logical species), sometimes according to the second (metaphysical species), or the third (natural species). We will account for these differences when presenting further arguments in this book. At this point we conclude that in the debate on the origin of species we ask about the origin of *natural species*. And this is the main meaning of species adopted in our book.

EVOLUTION

Evolution can be observed in two distinct realms: nature and culture. Our focus is on *nature*, that is, the material reality on which man acts, and which he transforms. Culture can be defined as an entirety of rational activity of man, whereas nature is all that man receives in the material order. Hence, we are not concerned here with the evolution of human laws, languages, sciences, philosophical concepts, etc., because these are all products of typically human (rational) activity and, as such, they follow somewhat different rules of development than those found in nature. For the same reason any argument "proving" evolution in culture (like evolution of languages or the progress of civilization, the development of

Teilhardian *noosphere*) is not an argument supporting evolution in nature.

Evolution in nature can be applied to the origin of the galaxies and planetary systems (cosmic evolution), the origin of stars (stellar evolution), the origin of chemistry or the origin of life (chemical and biochemical evolution). Our focus is on *biological evolution,* or the changes in the realm of living beings. But not all types of biological changes are of our interest—we are concerned with the origin of biodiversity, that is, different forms of life. This, however, does not refer to the origin of varieties or races. We are talking about the origin of forms of life on the level of new genera, families, phyla and kingdoms. This kind of evolution is called "biological macroevolution." Based on our previous definition of species, we understand biological macroevolution as the *theory of origins that attempts to explain the origin of new natural species.* Biological macroevolution consists of two grand claims about the natural world:

1. All species share common ancestry, i.e., there was one living organism at the beginning of the history of life (LUCA—Last Universal Common Ancestor) who is a natural progenitor of all living creatures—those who underwent extinction as well as those existing today.

2. The process of evolution is *natural,* i.e., it does not require any *supernatural* activity of God to bring about the visible effects in the form of biodiversity.

In science (biology), the concept of biological macroevolution is combined with a mechanism that would explain in material terms how the new species arise. Thus the biological understanding of evolution consists of two elements: (1) an *overarching claim* about universal common ancestry and (2) a particular *mechanism* constituting the proper object of scientific scrutiny. Currently a commonly accepted mechanism of evolution is the Neo-Darwinian one. This means that the whole of biodiversity is the effect of natural selection acting on random genetic mutations. The preservation of the so-called "beneficial" mutations (combined with the cancellation of the detrimental mutations, genetic drift and other factors) supposedly leads to the emergence of biological novelties, such as new organs, and ultimately new genera, families, etc.

Our definition of biological macroevolution does not include any specific *mechanism* such as the Lamarckian, the Darwinian, the Neo-Darwinian one, or any other. This is important, because this means that our definition is more philosophical than scientific in nature. We are concerned with the first element of evolutionary theory in biology, that is, the overarching claim about universal common ancestry. It also follows that it is irrelevant for our discussion what kind of mechanism a given scholar would attach to evolution. Consequently, it is irrelevant for us whether science yields any support to a given mechanism or not. We are concerned here with the *effect* of the evolutionary process in the form of different species rather than with the *cause* in the form of a mechanism.

Even though most scholars would readily classify biological macroevolution as a concept belonging to science, the actual status of this theory is not so obvious. In fact, only the mechanism of evolution is strictly speaking scientific, and hence the proper object of scientific scrutiny in biology. In contrast, the grand claims about universal common ancestry and the idea of transformation of species are more philosophical than scientific in nature, even if they are commonly embraced by scientists. Since only those grand claims are of interest for us, we can say that we are going to discuss the philosophical aspects of biological macroevolution.

In theology, biological macroevolution is defined according to different roles that God is supposed to play in the evolutionary process (or a lack thereof). Hence, materialistic, atheistic and theistic evolution. According to *materialistic evolution,* the origin of biological forms is a purely natural process, which biology is competent to fully explain, and which doesn't demand any supernatural influence of any kind. Proponents of materialistic evolution do not need to deny the existence of God, they simply leave the question aside. Charles Darwin, Thomas H. Huxley and Ernst Haeckel were the first to introduce materialistic evolution in modern times. Materialistic evolution could also be called *agnostic evolution* as Huxley coined the term "agnostic" to describe the religious position of Darwin and his first followers. In this context *atheistic evolution* is just one form of materialistic evolution, which assumes that God does not exist and so deduces that all natural phenomena must be reducible to underlying physical causes. The first prominent scholars to introduce atheistic evolution in modern times were Ernst Mayr, Julian Huxley, George Gaylord Simpson and Jacques Monod. Today one of the most widely renowned atheistic evolutionists is Richard Dawkins.

Theistic evolution is the idea that God somehow participates in the evolutionary process. The most popular view among theistic evolutionists is that God "uses" evolution as a secondary (precisely, an instrumental) cause in the process of production of new species. Some authors deem it a "co-operation" between nature and God, while others say that God works as a "final cause," or that he simply "pre-planned" or "guides" all evolutionary development. Different authors have different accounts of how this works, but the common point is that God doesn't work directly or supernaturally, but, at least in natural history, operates entirely through natural causes. It is this definition of theistic evolution that we will employ in what follows. (As a result, any theory that invokes God's direct or supernatural causality in the history of life will not be theistic evolution.) It is important to realize that theistic evolution is a theological, not a scientific concept. It speaks about the role of God in the formation of the universe and—as such—is a matter of belief rather than scientific evidence. In this sense, theistic evolution is an alternative concept to the classical theological concept of creation understood as the separate creation of species. To summarize, we understand theistic evolution according to its three essential tenets:

1. Evolution cannot happen without God, but it is still a natural process, which doesn't demand any supernatural or direct divine causality (except for the incessant maintenance of the universe in existence).

2. Evolution is understood as biological macroevolution, which means that all living beings have one or a few (polyphyletic evolution) common ancestors, which are natural progenitors ("parents") to all organisms inhabiting the earth.

3. This process is continuous, i.e., it has never finished and new forms of living beings can still arise through the same biological processes.

4. THE TWO QUESTIONS TO BE ANSWERED

Previously we defined biological macroevolution as a theory of the origin of species claiming that all life comes from a single ancestor through natural generation over vast periods of time. We said that this general idea is present in biology (science), philosophy and theology. Since we are not concerned here with a mechanism of evolution, the biological concept of evolution boils down to the philosophical idea of universal common ancestry. In theology, biological macroevolution takes a form of theistic evolution which is an alternative to the classic Christian concept of special creation. Now is the time to ask, what is the exact problem which we will address when discussing the compatibility of Thomas Aquinas and evolution?

Aquinas, of course, was neither an atheist nor an agnostic and we may be sure that he would reject materialistic, agnostic or atheistic type of evolution. In fact, any process or theory that would exclude God's providence or operation in the universe would be rejected by Aquinas at the very outset.

For this reason we will not address the question of whether materialistic or atheistic types of evolution are compatible with Aquinas's views. We limit our inquiry only to the question of whether his views are compatible with the *theistic* type of evolution. Since biological macroevolution consists of universal common ancestry and natural transformation of species, we can break down the problem to three questions: Would Aquinas allow universal common ancestry? Would he allow transformation of species due to accidental changes? And, is his own understanding of the origin of species compatible with modern theories of evolution? These three are included in one precise question which we formulate as follows:

What is the relation of Thomas Aquinas's teaching on the origin of species to the concept of theistic evolution?

Theoretically there can be four answers to this question:

1. Aquinas's teaching is generally compatible with and even supportive of the idea of theistic evolution. There may be a certain degree of incongruence regarding some secondary issues, but there are no fundamental conflicts and the two can be reconciled in a more general synthesis.

2. Aquinas does not provide any specified concept of the origin of species and thus he is neutral to theistic evolution—his thought neither supports it, nor excludes it. If this is the case, his position is compatible with any other theory of origins, even those contradictory to theistic evolution such as progressive creation or young earth creationism.

3. Aquinas did not know about the modern idea of biological evolution, therefore his views cannot constitute any argument in the debate. Medieval philosophy and modern science speak about completely different things. It is a methodological fallacy to compare Aquinas's views with those of contemporary evolutionists. By doing so one either

ends up in a confusion of theology and science, or commits an anachronism.

4. Aquinas's teaching is *substantially incompatible* with theistic evolution even if some secondary elements of his doctrine may superficially resemble some elements of theistic evolution.

Out of these four positions the third one was excluded when we discussed the problem of "commensurability." We have shown that as long as we follow a few criteria we are able to correctly juxtapose ideas from different levels of knowledge (natural science, philosophy and theology). If we define concepts in permanent philosophical categories, the time distance that divides them does not play any significant role. For example, philosophical concepts of "species," "form," "substance" or "act" have the same meaning today as they had two millennia ago. Therefore, contrary to what skeptics say, we can compare and contrast doctrines from different times and levels of knowledge, as long as they speak about the same reality. Thus there remain three other possible answers. A majority of contemporary Thomists support the first answer, few argue for the second. The goal of this book is to provide evidence that only the fourth answer is true.

Still, our treatment of the topic would not be complete if we did not ask about a compatibility of Aquinas's teaching and the theory of intelligent design (ID). ID is a scientific theory and a paradigm of doing science that is opposite to the scientific theory of Neo-Darwinism and the Neo-Darwinian paradigm currently dominating biological sciences. We can therefore say that both intelligent design and Neo-Darwinism have scientific as well as philosophical aspects. The core of the ID criticism against Neo-Darwinism pertains not to the idea of biological evolution as such, but to the proposed mechanism of macroevolutionary changes that consist of random (genetic) mutations and natural selection. In this sense, ID challenges the supposed *mechanism* of evolution rather than the grand claim about universal common ancestry. In particular, ID rejects the idea that random events (such as random genetic mutations) can provide adequate "material" for natural selection to produce all kinds of information (specifically new genes) that are absolutely necessary for life to diversify into species. At the same time ID provides positive scientific evidence for the need of intelligent causality to bring about new biological information. Thus, the controversy between ID and Neo-Darwinism pertains primarily to the role of chance in biology: Can chance bring about biological design? Can random events create new functional organs and new species? Is design detectable? Are biological structures designed? Or do they only appear to be designed, when in fact they were created by the interplay of chance and necessity? ID and Neo-Darwinism provide mutually exclusive answers to these and similar questions.

It seems that no other modern idea has challenged the scientific materialism of our era as directly and effectively as it has been done by intelligent design. Even so, most Thomists contend that Aquinas's teaching is not compatible with ID while it is reconcilable with Neo-Darwinism. Since this Thomistic claim may sound somewhat bold and even surprising to a Christian ear it requires thorough examination. Hence, the second question:

What is the relation of Aquinas's philosophy/theology to the modern scientific claims of intelligent design?

5. *MODUS PROCEDENDI*

To answer the two proposed questions we will apply the classical scholastic method that Aquinas followed in his *Summa* which involves a dispute between two parties. Chapter II contains a response to the first question (Aquinas and theistic evolution) whereas Chapter V answers the second question

(Aquinas and intelligent design). In Section One of Chapter II (II,1) we gather the arguments occurring in writings of theistic evolutionists. Note that we do not address only the arguments of the Thomists who are proponents of theistic evolution, but also the objections proposed by any type of theistic evolutionists, as long as their views pertain to the teachings of Aquinas. Needless to say, not every theistic evolutionist agrees with each of the objections in the same degree. Our goal is to formulate the arguments of the opponents in their strongest and most synthetic form (this was also Aquinas's method, so that in many instances he presented the position of his opponents better than they had themselves). In the footnotes the Reader will find references to the actual writings where the arguments can be found. Section Two (II,2) constitutes the *corpus* of the *questio* containing Aquinas's positive doctrine on the origin of species. Section Three (II,3) contains responses to the objections presented in section one.

In the *Commentary on Peter Lombard's Sentences, Book II*, Aquinas provides a summary of the two great traditions of interpreting Genesis in Christianity. This part of his writings contains a thorough discussion of his own views on creation (the origin of species). Hence, we devote the whole of Chapter III to presenting the content of Aquinas's *Commentary*.

Given that man is the only physical creature capable of knowing God, Catholic theologians have always considered the problem of the origin of man more important than the origin of species. The origin of species was usually considered a matter of "sound philosophy," whereas the origin of man had both philosophical and theological implications. Also the explanation of the origin of man entertained greater theological certainty than the origin of species. For this reason, we devote a separate chapter (Chapter IV) to present Aquinas's teaching regarding the origin of the human body and how it relates to modern evolutionary concepts.

Next, in Chapter V we take up the problem of Aquinas in relation to the modern scientific theory of intelligent design

(ID). Here we again follow the scheme of the medieval *questio*: first, the objections against compatibility of Aquinas and ID (V,1); second, the comparison between Aquinas and ID (V,2): and third, the responses to the objections (V,3). In the last chapter (VI) we present possible reasons why contemporary Thomists engage in defending theistic evolution while rejecting intelligent design. This last chapter contains some conclusions regarding the current situation as well as possible perspectives for the future development of Thomistic thought.

Everything in this book should be kept within our intended boundaries, that is, the problem of the origin of species and man. If we present critical remarks concerning contemporary Thomists, it does not follow that Thomists are wrong on any other issues, or that they do not understand any part of Thomistic metaphysics. Generally speaking there are many knowledgeable and wise Thomists out there. However, some have become vocal in their defense of the evolutionary paradigm in science and theology. The thrust of our criticism is directed neither against these individuals personally, nor against the totality of their thought, but only against parts which are mistaken regarding the problem of biological origins.

6. ORDERING THE ARGUMENTS

The quantity of publications online and in print regarding Thomistic understanding of evolution has been growing over recent decades. As we observed above, the vast majority of them promote the compatibilists' view that Aquinas's teaching does not present difficulties for theistic evolution. Unfortunately, the self-confidence of the authors promoting this thesis is rarely accompanied by any strength of their arguments. Our goal is to answer to all the arguments proposed by the compatibilists. The problem is, however, that only a small portion of their arguments is relevant in this debate. Thomists promoting theistic evolution usually spend a lot of time on issues that do not actually address the compatibility of Aquinas and evolution. For example, they discuss the Thomistic understanding of the reason and faith relation. But the problem of Aquinas and evolution is the problem of science and philosophy (or theology), not the problem of reason and faith. They spend time on proving God's existence, defining the four Aristotelian causes, God's attitude towards the created universe, the problem of *creatio ex nihilo*, the origin of evil, the goodness of creation, etc. But all of this is perfectly compatible with any answer to the problem of Aquinas and evolution. In other words, no matter what one thinks about theistic evolution and its compatibility with Aquinas, one may fully accept all of Aquinas's teachings on those other issues. Yet, they may constitute as much as 70% of a paper supposedly treating the topic of Aquinas and evolution.[19] In this book we are not concerned with the arguments that do not pertain to the issue of biological macroevolution.

Another problem with the argumentation of theistic evolutionists is that they blend together the arguments derived from Aquinas with those that have nothing to do with the Angelic Doctor. For example, the authors of the book *Thomistic Evolution* have a chapter on the interpretation of Genesis. Yet, while promoting the thesis that Thomistic reading of Genesis is fully compatible with the evolutionary origin of species, they back up their thesis with sources such as the Second Vatican Council, the writings of then-Cardinal Ratzinger, and "modern Biblical exegesis."[20] As far as all of them could be

---

[19] For example, P. Lichacz devotes 70% of his paper "Does Creation Exclude Evolution?" to problems such as the possibility of proving the existence of the first cause, the first beginning of the universe, whether or not an unchangeable being can act, etc. See P. Lichacz, "Czy stworzenie wyklucza ewolucje?" [Does Creation Exclude Evolution?], in *Teologia sw.Tomasza z Akwinu dzisiaj* [*Theology of Thomas Aquinas Today*] (Poznan: Uniwersytet Adama Mickiewicza, Wydzial Teologiczny, 2010), pp. 71–94.

[20] Austriaco et al., *Thomistic Evolution* (cited in note 18 above), pp. 113, 127, 134, 156–164.

compatible with evolutionary exegesis, it is not an argument for the compatibility of Aquinas's reading of Genesis with theistic evolution. The fact that, let's say, "modern exegesis" makes room for evolution ("modern exegesis" makes room for pretty much anything) does not mean that Thomistic exegesis does the same. In another chapter of the same book entitled *A Thomistic Response to the Intelligent Design Proposal*, there is not a single reference to any Thomist, let alone Thomas Aquinas himself.[21] Hence a large portion of the argument is irrelevant and only blurs the topic. In this book we are not concerned with the arguments coming from outside of Aquinas's writings.

The third problem is the use of a type of an argument that we can call a "De Koninck argument." (The name "De Koninck" can be replaced with the name of any other theistic evolutionist who liked or read Aquinas, or even used Aquinas to promote his personal opinions on evolution.) This argument takes more or less the following form: "Charles De Koninck was an excellent Thomist of the twentieth century. De Koninck did not see a problem with the evolutionary origin of species. Therefore, Aquinas's doctrine can be reconciled with evolution." The *non sequitur* of this argument is obvious: The fact that someone is generally considered an excellent Thomist does not mean that the person is infallible in all his reading of the Medieval Doctor. Galileo was an excellent astronomer, but his theory of tides was completely mistaken. Aquinas was a theological genius, but his explanation of Blessed Mary's sinlessness differs from the one established by the dogma of the Immaculate Conception. Hence, even the greatest minds may err. It means that we cannot blindly trust De Koninck regarding his interpretation of evolution just because he was a "great Thomist." At the same time, if we prove that Aquinas's teaching excludes theistic evolution, the high rating of De Koninck as a "great Thomist" should significantly

---

[21] Ibid., pp. 236–241.

decrease. (See the eight and tenth argument and the responses to them in the next chapter). In this book we do not address such "De Koninck" arguments from authority. Instead, we will respond to those arguments that make an explicit use of Aquinas's thought to either promote theistic evolution or refute intelligent design, or claim compatibility of biological macroevolution with the doctrine of the Angelic Doctor.

CHAPTER II:
AQUINAS AND THE ORIGIN OF SPECIES

1. IT SEEMS THAT AQUINAS'S TEACHING DOES NOT EXCLUDE THEISTIC EVOLUTION (OBJECTIONS)

1. From secondary causation
God's causality doesn't exclude natural causality in the world. Thus, evolution is simply a secondary or instrumental cause, which God used to form different species. This complies with Aquinas's understanding of secondary causation, and explains how new species can emerge through natural processes. God acts through nature in order to bring about biological novelty.[1]

---

[1] F. Ryan, "Aquinas and Darwin," in *Darwin and Catholicism*, ed. L. Caruana (NY: T & T Clark, 2009), pp. 54–55; F. J. Beckwith, "Intelligent Design, Thomas Aquinas and the Ubiquity of Final Causes," The Biologos Foundation, http://biologos.org/uploads/projects/beckwith_scholarly_essay.pdf (accessed 10 Dec. 2012), p. 6; W. E. Carroll, "Creation, Evolution and Thomas Aquinas," http://www.catholiceducation.org/articles/sc0035.html (accessed 10 Dec. 2012); W. Tkacz, "Aquinas vs. Intelligent Design," in *This Rock*, Nov. 2008, available at http://www.catholic.com/magazine/articles/aquinas-vs-intelligent-design (accessed 9 July 2016). See also the statement of Dodds: "God's causality does not constitute a miraculous intervention; nor does it negate the real causality of all the natural agents involved in the evolutionary process. In this way, God is most intimately involved in the process of evolution, acting through the natural causes that science studies." (Michael J. Dodds, *Unlocking Divine Action* (Washington, DC: Catholic University of America Press, 2012), pp. 201–202, cf. 204.)

2. From the sufficiency of secondary causes

Natural secondary causes, such as mutations, natural selection, biological generation, genetic drift, etc., are sufficient to bring about higher effects, such as new species of living beings, because:

(a) Secondary causes in this case are merely instrumental, which means that God brings about effects unattainable for those causes by their own power. Similarly, chalk cannot make any signs by itself. When moved by another body, it can act as a secondary cause by leaving marks on a surface. But when man uses chalk to write, the effect in the form of intelligible message transcends the capacity of chalk as secondary cause. In the same way God transcends the abilities of nature when using evolution as the instrumental cause of the production of new species.[2]

(b) The effect is contained in all its causes, not in just one of them. Although one secondary cause cannot produce a new species, a set of different causes working together toward one effect can do it. Thus, even though random mutations and natural selection may not be sufficient, combined with many other causes (including unknown ones), they cause the production of new species.[3]

---

[2] "It would seem philosophically impossible to say that this ontologically more perfect organism is the evolutionary effect of less perfect organisms... We can resolve this possible dilemma between philosophy and science by using the notion of instrumental causality... So higher species may be brought forth from lower species if the natural causes of this process are also instrumental causes of a higher principal cause." (M. Dodds, op. cit., pp. 201–202.)

[3] B. Ashley tries to resolve the problem of lack of an adequate cause in biological macroevolution by referring to a set of multiple causes: "If we ask how this greater comes from the less, modern evolutionary theory gives a clear answer. The proportionate cause of the emergence of new types or organisms of increasingly complex organization and independence of the environment is not a single law or force but a concurrence of many causes in an evolutionary *event*, or better, a *history*" (p. 215). Yet, the reader cannot avoid an impression of incoherency in Ashley's argument. First he claims that "There is

(c) Aquinas teaches that "the same effect is not attributed to a natural cause and to divine power in such a way that it is partly done by God, and partly by the natural agent; rather, it is wholly done by both, according to a different way, just as the same effect is wholly attributed to the instrument and also wholly to the principal agent" (ScG III,70,8). Hence, evolution acting as secondary cause can generate new species because their emergence is caused by God as much as it is caused by evolution.[4]

3. From the "better picture of God"

The power of God is manifested by the fact that He gives the power for some causes to be secondary causes of creation.

---

a precise, objective, and empirical sense in which an atom is a more complex and integrated system than an electron... a mammal than a protozoan, the human brain than a bird brain" (p. 200). This fact brings him to saying that "we must identify... a proportionate cause, a sufficient agent of evolutionary emergence." But when it comes to biological macroevolution, he concludes that "The plant kingdom and the animal kingdom are superior to each other in different respects, so that it is impossible to classify them in an absolute hierarchy of forms" (pp. 213–214). It seems that for Ashley species constitute hierarchy only when it is required by metaphysics, and they cease to be hierarchical when it comes to explaining their supposed evolutionary origin. The same applies to the principle of proportionate cause: the author accepts it when speaking about metaphysics and abandons it when justifying evolution. Interestingly, Ashley acknowledges that Aquinas excludes secondary causation in creation and (in this respect) he explicitly distances himself from Aquinas's doctrine (pp. 229–230). See B. Ashley, "Causality and Evolution," in *The Thomist*, 36(2), pp. 199–230. Marie George believes that new species arise thanks to the carefully orchestrated combination of "[those causes] acting by tendency and those acting by chance." (M. George, "What Would Thomas Aquinas Say about Intelligent Design?," *New Blackfriars*, Vol. 94 (1054), Nov. 2013, p. 698.)

[4] M. Heller and J. Zycinski, *Dylematy ewolucji* [*The Dilemmas of Evolution*] (Tarnow: Biblos, 1996), pp. 158–159; F. J. Beckwith, "Intelligent Design, Thomas Aquinas, and the Ubiquity of Final Causes" (cited above), p. 6; M. Dodds, op. cit., p. 192.

The more perfection God conveys to nature, the more God's perfection is manifested through the working of secondary causes. Thomas argued: "The perfection of the effect demonstrates the perfection of the cause, for a greater power brings about a more perfect effect. But God is the most perfect agent. Therefore, things created by Him obtain perfection from Him. So, to detract from the perfection of creatures is to detract from the perfection of divine power. But, if no creature has any active role in the production of any effect, much is detracted from the perfection of the creature" (ScG III,69,15). Moreover, a created being that is endowed with causality has more dignity and value than the one that doesn't cause anything: "According to St. Thomas, it is a greater perfection, and therefore, more fitting, for God to share his causality with his creatures, making them authentic causes that can cause by their own natures, than for God to remain the sole cause acting within creation."[5] Thus, although God could have produced species directly, He chose to produce causes of species, by creating an evolving nature.[6]

4. From *reductio ad absurdum*

On the other hand, Aquinas says, "The universe in its beginning was perfect as regards the species of things" (De Pot. q.3, a.10, ad2). If everything was created immediately by God right from the beginning, there would be no room for secondary causation, which goes against Aquinas's teaching. Therefore "this teaching, which speaks of perfection [of creatures in

---

[5] Austriaco et al., *Thomistic Evolution* (see Ch. 1 n. 18 above), p. 186.

[6] F. Ryan, op. cit., p. 54; Austriaco et al., *Thomistic Evolution*, pp. 182–191; P. Lichacz, "Czy stworzenie wyklucza ewolucje?"; M. George, "What Would Thomas Aquinas Say about Intelligent Design?," p. 700. George also quotes S.Th. I,103,6 to support the same thesis (p. 684). See also footnote 34 on page 688.

the beginning], does not necessarily preclude the addition of new species through the agency of secondary causes."[7]

5. From *creatio continua*

Although God created the world in the beginning, He never ceased to create it and still maintains it by His power, which is called continuous creation (Lat. *creatio continua*). Thus, the emergence of new species in the evolutionary process is easy to justify within the concept of continuous creation.[8]

6. From the existence of chance events

Accidental changes, such as random genetic mutations, are the main driving forces behind the formation of new species in the majority of evolutionary theories, including modern theistic ones.[9] Aquinas argued that in the visible world there are not only planned events, but also events that are truly "random" or "chance." God, in exercising providence over the world, can

---

[7] F. Ryan, op. cit., p. 55. This argument can be presented also in a different way: If all forms were created in the beginning it would mean that nothing new appeared in natural history. But we know that many new species appeared successively in the long history of earth. Therefore, either we interpret Aquinas in such a way that he allows emergence of new substantial forms by natural causation in the course of time, or his teaching contradicts facts.

[8] J. F. Haught, *God After Darwin* (Westview Press, 2008), p. 37; R. J. Schneider, "Essay II: Theology of Creation: Historical Perspectives and Fundamental Concepts," http://community.berea.edu/scienceandfaith/essay02.asp (accessed: 12 Nov. 2014); M. W. Tkacz, "Aquinas vs. Intelligent Design." Tkacz writes: "God creates without taking any time to create: He creates eternally. Creation is not a process with a beginning, a middle, and an end. It is simply a reality: the reality of the complete dependence of the universe on God's agency." Even though Tkacz does not use the term "continual creation," he understands the creative divine act as a continual creation of the whole being by God. See http://www.catholic.com/magazine/articles/aquinas-vs-intelligent-design (accessed 21 June 2016).

[9] Cf. M. Ryland, "What is Intelligent Design Theory?," *Second Spring*, 2012(15), pp. 46–57, esp. p. 48.

use both planned and random events to achieve pre-planned results. Thus, Thomas's teaching can accommodate the role of chance in producing different natural species.[10] "God designs with chance."[11]

7. From matter tending toward higher form

Aquinas taught that all matter tends toward "the furthest and most perfect actuality to which it can attain, as to the ultimate end of generation… Hence the last stage of the whole process of generation is the human soul, and matter tends to this, as to its ultimate form" (ScG III,22,7). Thus, according to St. Thomas, matter is subjected to the natural desire to achieve the most perfect form. This premise supports theistic evolution, which also says that all living beings are to acquire ever new forms of higher organization with the rational soul as the end.[12]

---

[10] A document by the International Theological Commission of July 23, 2004, *Communion and Stewardship*, no. 69; S. M. Barr, "Chance, by Design," *First Things*, Dec. 2012, pp. 25–30, esp. 28; M. George, "On Attempts to Salvage Paley's Argument from Design," in *Science, Philosophy, Theology*, ed. J. O'Callaghan (South Bend, Indiana: St. Augustine's Press, 2002); M. George, "What Would Thomas Aquinas Say about Intelligent Design?," *New Blackfriars*, Vol. 94, Issue 1054 (Nov. 2013), esp. p. 698: "Chance is a means used by an intelligent being to get novelty"; Austriaco et al., *Thomistic Evolution*, pp. 83–101; M. Dodds, op. cit., p. 221; W. Newton, "A Case of Mistaken Identity: Aquinas's Fifth Way and Arguments of Intelligent Design," *New Blackfriars*, Volume 95, Issue 1059, Sept 2014, pp. 569–578, esp. 575; G. M. Verschuuren, *Aquinas and Modern Science*, pp. 143–145.

[11] Austriaco et al., *Thomistic Evolution*, pp. iii, 200.

[12] E. C. Messenger, *Evolution and Theology* (NY: The Macmillan Company, 1932), p. 94; F. Ryan, op. cit., p. 53; Charles De Koninck, "The Cosmos: The Philosophic Point of View," in *The Writings of Charles De Koninck*, ed. and transl. by R. McInerny (Indiana: University of Notre Dame Press, 2008), Vol. 1, pp. 256–321, esp. 289; J. Maritain, "Toward A Thomist Idea of Evolution," in *Untrammeled Approaches: The Collected Works of Jacques Maritain, Vol. 20* (South Bend: University of Notre Dame Press, 1977), pp. 85–131; R. J. Nogar, *The Wisdom of Evolution* (New York: Mentor-Omega, 1966), p. 260.

8. From the concept of *dispositio materiae* employed by Aquinas

Every composite being (this includes living organisms) consists of properly disposed matter and form. Even though evolutionary mechanisms cannot produce new forms, they act upon matter in such a way to dispose it to accept a new form. Hence, biological macroevolution is possible due to changes in matter, because once matter achieves an adequate disposition, it receives or assumes—as if automatically—a new form which is a new species.[13]

9. From the possibility of an eternal universe

Aquinas taught that natural reason cannot prove the temporal beginning of the universe and that this truth is known to us only by Revelation. According to Aquinas, the created universe could exist eternally. Therefore, it is not *the temporal beginning of the world* that is important in the doctrine of creation, but *the fact that the world is still maintained in existence by God*. So the core of Aquinas's doctrine on creation is the *dependence* of the universe for its being rather than its

---

[13] De Koninck, "The Cosmos: The Philosophic Point of View,," pp. 278–283. M. J. Bolin pushes the argument to its limits when he believes that once matter achieves the proper disposition, God directly induces a new form into the being. Bolin's idea of direct induction of forms whenever matter is properly disposed should be called "materialistic occasionalism." See M. J. Bolin, *"And Man Became a Living Being": The Genesis of Substantial Form*, a lecture delivered at Wyoming Catholic College, October 25, 2013, https://sancrucensis.files.wordpress.com/2015/01/and-man-became-a-living-being.pdf (accessed 10 April 2017). The argument presented by M. Dodds is a blend of the previous one (the seventh) and the current one: "We can understand God's involvement as primary cause in the process of evolution using the analogy of God's involvement in any act of generation... As parents are instrumental causes of the being and substantial form of their offspring, so previous generations may be seen as instrumental causes, gradually disposing primary matter for the eduction of a new form in a given generation that might also constitute a new species," M. Dodds, op. cit., p. 204.

beginning in time. This is compatible with theistic evolution which also emphasizes the world's *dependence* on God and not its *temporal beginning*.¹⁴

10. From the reduction of the number of species

Accidental change cannot bring about new species. But there are only four species in nature: man, animals, plants, and the inorganic. The substantial change that required divine supernatural action would happen only in transitions between those four species. Therefore, evolution, which consists of accumulation of accidental changes in species, can bring about everything within those four species.¹⁵

---

¹⁴ S. E. Baldner and W. E. Carroll, *Aquinas on Creation* (Toronto: Pontifical Institute of Mediaeval Studies, 1997); G. M. Verschuuren, *Aquinas and Modern Science*, p. 100. J. Salij, "Pochodzenie czlowieka w swietle wiary i nauki," [*The Origin of Man in the Light of Faith and Science*] in *Kontrowersje wokol poczatkow czlowieka*, ed. G. Bugajak i J. Tomczyk (Katowice: Ksiegarnia Swietego Jacka, 2007), pp. 277–286; J. Zycinski and M. Heller, *Dylematy ewolucji*, p. 154.

¹⁵ "The ensemble of beings constituting nature is divided into four species: men, animals, plants, and the inorganic... These four species are the only ones philosophically definable. The canine species is not a species in the philosophical sense." (De Koninck, op. cit., p. 258.) N. Luyten suggests that the only distinct and definable essence among living beings is the human. Thus, in his view there would be three essences—inanimate, animate, and human. (N. Luyten, "Philosophical Implications of Evolution," *New Scholasticism* 25(1951), pp. 303–304.) While defending theistic evolution, Maritain goes as far as saying that "There is only one ontological species which we are sure of knowing and encompassing, and that is the human species." (J. Maritain, "Toward a Thomist Idea of Evolution," in *Untrammeled Approaches*, p. 112.) Mortimer J. Adler, even though skeptical of macroevolution, supports the idea that there are only five irreducible species: man, animal, plant, mixture, and element (See his *Problems for Thomists: The Problem of Species* (New York: Sheed & Ward, 1940). According to the Polish Thomist, M. A. Krapiec, supernatural creative acts must have taken place at least in the transitions between inanimate and animate matter, then between vegetative and sensory life, and then between sensory and intellectual life. See Krapiec's *Wprowadzenie do filozofii* [*The Introduction to Philosophy*] (Lublin: RW KUL, 1996),

11. From the separation of faith from science regarding the origin of the universe

"Creation" for Aquinas does not mean the temporal beginning of things but "dependence of the existence of all things upon God." On the other hand, science speaks about changes in things and not about their dependence upon God. Therefore, there can be no contradiction between biological evolution and Aquinas's teaching on creation.[16]

12. From Aquinas's commentary on Peter Lombard's *Sentences*, *Book II*

Aquinas taught that there are two different types of truth contained in Revelation: the first type of truth pertains to the essence of the faith, and the second type pertains to faith only accidentally (Super Sent. lib.2, d.12, q.1, a.2, co). The mode or order of creation of the world belongs to the latter category. Thus, "what is essential to Christian faith according to Aquinas is the *fact* of creation, not the *manner* or *mode* of the formation of the world."[17] Therefore, evolution can be the mode of creation of species.

---

pp. 256–265. Feser defends macroevolution by claiming that "every species is essentially just a variation on the same basic genetic material." If this were the case, there would be only one species of living beings, namely the one containing the genetic material. For Feser this is also evidence that in evolution lower cause does not produce higher effect. See Edward Feser, *Scholastic Metaphysics* (Piscataway NJ: Transaction Books, 2014), p. 158.

[16] W. E. Carroll, "Creation, Evolution and Thomas Aquinas." The same argument is found in *Thomistic Evolution*: "Thomas Aquinas does not hold a historical account of creation, and he does not think of creation merely as a past fact that is now over and done. Rather, he holds a metaphysical account of creation. To say that God creates the world is to say that God gives being to contingent things: *to create properly speaking, is to cause or produce the being (esse) of things* (S.Th. I,45,6)." See Austriaco et al., *Thomistic Evolution*, op. cit., pp. 65–66.

[17] W. E. Carroll, "Creation, Evolution and Thomas Aquinas"; P. Lichacz, op. cit.; Austriaco et al., *Thomistic Evolution*, p. 148; M. George, "What Would Thomas Aquinas Say about Intelligent Design?," p. 683.

13. From Aquinas's preference of the Augustinian interpretation of Genesis over the Ambrosian one

There is nothing against theistic evolution in Augustine's writings. Aquinas says that he prefers (*plus mihi placet*) Augustine's concept of emergence of natural species from seminal reasons to Ambrose's doctrine of special creation of different species over time (Super Sent. lib.2, d.12, q.1, a.2, co). Therefore, Aquinas's teaching must be compatible with theistic evolution.[18]

14. From the fact that nature does not require miracles for its operation

Thomas Aquinas quotes Augustine's convictions about the origin of the world: "It is our business here to inquire how God has constituted the natures of His creatures, not how far it may have pleased Him to work on them by way of miracle (S.Th. I,68,2, ad1)." Thus, Aquinas didn't require miracles in the formation of the world, which is consistent with the fact that theistic evolution does not require or allow miracles in the formation of species.[19]

15. From the continual creation of human souls

God creates each human soul directly at every act of conception. It follows that His creative work has never finished. If the souls are created every day, then new species of animals and plants may also be created, even after the work of creation was completed on the sixth day.[20]

---

[18] W. E. Carroll, ibid.; P. Lichacz, ibid.; *Thomistic Evolution*, op. cit., pp. 153–154.

[19] E. McMullin, "Darwin and the Other Christian Tradition," *Zygon*, Vol. 46, No. 2 (June 2011), pp. 291–316, 298, 301.

[20] A different argument is N. Luyten's claim that as human souls are continually created, in the same way the first human being could have been created, from matter disposed to "humanity" by a previous animal. Luyten's argument does not challenge the temporal completeness of creation but rather seeks for sufficient cause in the generation

16. From spontaneous generation

Aquinas believed in spontaneous generation, which means that living beings can originate from unanimated matter. Therefore his teaching is consistent both with the contemporary theory of abiogenesis, and with the possibility of the emergence of new species after creation was completed. We find confirmation in the following passage: "Species, also, that are new, if any such appear, existed beforehand in various active powers; so that animals, and perhaps even new species of animals, are produced by putrefaction by the power which the stars and elements received at the beginning. Again, animals of new kinds arise occasionally from the connection of individuals belonging to different species, as the mule is the offspring of an ass and a mare; but even these existed previously in their causes, in the works of the six days" (S.Th. I,73,1, ad3).[21]

17. From the Bible

According to Aquinas, there are two senses in the Holy Scripture—the literal and the spiritual. The literal sense may be further divided into historical, etiological, analogical, and parabolical (metaphorical). The spiritual sense includes allegorical, tropological, and anagogical. Only the literal sense can be used to make a theological argument.

Now, the first creation account must be read in the context of the second creation account. The second creation account, however, presents an order of creation different from that found in the first account (in the first, the order is: earth, plants, animals, man; in the second, the order is: garden,

---

of a human from an animal. There are at least two problems with his argument. First, Aquinas excludes any active co-operation of the secondary causes in the origin of man (which could not be the case if an animal was generating the first human). Second, his argument would explain only the emergence of man, yet he extends his conclusions to all species. See N. Luyten, "Philosophical Implications of Evolution," *New Scholasticism*, 25(1951), pp. 290–312, 306–309.

[21] F. Ryan, op. cit., p. 55–56; R. J. Nogar, op. cit., pp. 259–260.

Adam, animals, Eve). Hence, if they were read historically, the two creation accounts would contradict each other. Therefore, the meaning of the creation accounts intended by the author cannot be literal and historical, but must be literal and metaphorical (the literal sense includes metaphors and figures of speech if such was the intention of the author). This is additionally confirmed by other Scriptural passages, showing that the intention of the Biblical author is not to give us an astronomical or a zoological record of the events, but to reveal something "deeper and greater" about creation, for example, that everything comes from God, and that God intended the whole creation. But this message is entirely compatible with theistic evolution. Hence, according to Thomistic principles of exegesis, the Genesis accounts of creation should not be read historically and thus do not pose any difficulty for accepting the evolutionary origin of species.[22]

18. From the progress of knowledge

Aquinas taught separate creation of species because he didn't know modern biology. Had he known it, he would have adopted (theistic) evolution.[23]

Sed contra:

The Mother of the seven sons says: "Look upon heaven and earth, and all that is in them, and consider that God made them out of nothing, and mankind also" (2 Macc 7:28). It follows that heaven and earth are not the only things that God made out of nothing.

---

[22] *Thomistic Evolution*, pp. 119–135. Interestingly, E. McMullin attributes this argument to Augustine; however, he does not support it with any quotations. See E. McMullin, "Darwin and the Other Christian Tradition," pp. 293, 302, 306.

[23] M. George, "What Would Thomas Aquinas Say about Intelligent Design?," op. cit., pp. 690–691. Cf. G. M. Verschuuren, op. cit., p. 147.

2. THE ORIGIN OF SPECIES ACCORDING TO AQUINAS (*CORPUS*)

I answer that,

The answer can be given in two ways: One is to show that Aquinas's teaching excludes theistic evolution—and this is an explicit answer (A). Another is to show that Aquinas teaches the supernatural and direct formation of species—and this also excludes theistic evolution, although not explicitly but *a fortiori* (B). This latter answer can also be given in two ways: First by showing Aquinas's understanding of the history of creation, i.e., how things happened in time (B.1.) and this is a *historical* approach; another is by showing his positive doctrine about how new species are produced, and this is a *systematic* answer (B.2.).

A. There are five reasons why Aquinas' teaching excludes theistic evolution. First, according to theistic evolution the lower (i.e., less perfect) cause can lead to the higher effect (i.e., more perfect). But in Aquinas's view, no being can convey more act than it possesses.[24] Here "act" is understood as

---

[24] "Every imperfect thing is caused by one perfect" (S.Th. I,44,2 ad2); "The perfection of the effect demonstrates the perfection of the cause, for a greater power brings about a more perfect effect" (ScG, III,69,15); "The effect is not more powerful than its cause" (S.Th. I,45,8, 2). Someone could argue that in the modern understanding of biology and evolution the notion of perfection does not play any role. But theistic evolutionists recognize different levels of perfection in biology (cf. M. Dodds, op. cit., p. 202). All the more does Aquinas: "In natural things species seem to be arranged in degrees; as the mixed things are more perfect than the elements, and plants than minerals, and animals than plants, and men than other animals; and in each of these one species is more perfect than others" (S.Th. I,47,2 co). Even if biological evolutionists do not recognize different grades of perfection in biological realm, it doesn't follow that they do not exist. It is impossible to coherently maintain that no grades of perfection exist in biology. Even the notion "the fittest" employed in evolutionary biology implies existence of different grades of fitness, which—in terms of

any kind of perfection or realization. Indeed, although theistic evolution has a final cause, since God governs this process with His omniscience, still it maintains that more perfect beings can be produced through natural generation and propagation of less perfect ones.

The second reason why theistic evolution contradicts Aquinas's doctrine is that it presupposes that the nature (or the substantial form) of a living being can be changed into a different nature by an accidental change. This, however, is impossible in Aquinas's view, for accidental change can lead to only accidental differences, whereas a change of nature requires substantial change. That is why transformation of species, by any kind of natural generation, indeed, by any physical process, is not possible. Evolutionary process (as well as any other physical process) may change the accidents of a living being, but it will never produce a new substantial form.

There are two possible errors in the understanding of this argument. The first thrives on confusion between the substantial and the individual form. Someone could say that killing a chicken brings about substantial change, but the act of killing the chicken is an accidental change. Hence, the accidental change results in the substantial change. But in this example, killing this particular chicken annihilates the substantial form of this particular chicken which is nothing else but the individual form of this chicken. The substantial form (or species) of chicken as such is neither annihilated nor altered by this accidental change. Moreover, no accidental change could ever produce a totally new substantial form (species), one that has never existed, which would be the case if theistic evolution were true. Thus, even though an accidental change may

---

underlying metaphysics—means the same as "more perfect." Therefore, evolutionary biology also recognizes some levels of perfection.

substantially change an individual it cannot change the species of a thing or produce a new nature.[25]

The second error thrives on the misunderstanding of what substance is. Someone could say, if I take salt and water and dissolve salt in water, I make salt solution, which is a different substance than water or salt. The act of adding salt to water is an accidental change, therefore the accidental change of one substance brings about another substance. Hence, the accidental change results in the substantial change. In this example, however, we do not deal with substances but merely with elements and compounds. Substance is an analogous term, which means that it is predicated about different things with regard to one. Substance is something that is the most self-contained, separated, unified, and distinct. Hence, the only true substance is God, because He is the most individual, the most indivisible, and simply the most "Is." Everything else is a substance only by participation. There is a hierarchy of substances that descends from angels, to humans, to animals, to plants, to compounds and elements. Therefore, the highest substance among the composites of matter and form are humans followed by animals and plants. Living beings constitute substances in a much stronger sense than non-living beings, to the point that the latter should not even be called substances but elements and compounds. And if we consider a true substance there is no way to transform it into another substance by an accidental change. For example, hybrids of different natural species are impossible (mixing a cat and a dog does not bring any effect), and for the same reason evolution cannot transform one animal or plant species into another.

---

[25] One of the best attempts to reconcile biological macroevolution with Thomistic philosophy is George P. Klubertanz's paper, "Causality and Evolution." However, the author ends up in precisely this error—he takes production of a new accidental form for the production of the new substantial form. See "Causality and Evolution," *The Modern Schoolman*, Vol. 19, issue 1 (Nov. 1941), pp. 11–14.

The third reason why theistic evolution contradicts Aquinas's doctrine is that theistic evolution presupposes that one nature can be a cause of another nature. In contrast, according to Aquinas no "perfect thing" produces its own nature, but only participates in the nature that it inherits. A "perfect thing," in Aquinas's thinking, is a being that has a highly specified substantial form or essence. Good examples of "perfect things" are different species of living organisms. Aquinas himself invokes a human being as it is the most perfect among composite things. Thus, a man cannot be a cause of mankind, a dog cannot cause dog's nature, a cat, cat's nature, and so on. But if a being is not a cause of its own nature, much less it can produce a different nature.[26] And this is why Thomas says that "generation of nothing except a man results from the semen of man" (ScG III,69,co), which means that species of living beings are fixed and never change into different species by generation.

The fourth reason why theistic evolution contradicts Aquinas's doctrine is that it gives an inadequate account of causation. According to Aquinas (following Aristotle) every composite thing has four causes: final, formal, efficient, and material. In theistic evolution, two of the four causes are missing, the efficient and the formal. Regarding the first: In theistic evolution the efficient cause of the production of new species is the power of generation combined with an evolutionary mechanism (guided by the final cause, who is God). Thus, theistic evolution reduces the efficient cause "down" to accidental changes in matter—that is, to the material cause.

---

[26] "A perfect thing participating in any nature, makes a likeness to itself, not by absolutely producing that nature, but by applying it to something else. For an individual man cannot be the cause of human nature absolutely, because he would then be the cause of himself; but he is the cause of what human nature is in this man begotten" (S.Th. I,45,5, ad1; cf. ScG, II,21; ScG, III,65,4).

Regarding the second: According to Aquinas, when a creative act takes place, a new substantial form is produced in matter by the direct divine power that informs matter according to the clear idea in the divine intellect. In theistic evolution this cannot happen, because every being tends to become something else, and thus it is just a transition between this and something else.[27] Each being is supposed to receive ever-new form, which is never the ultimate form; therefore, a being never becomes a complete new nature. (Such an ultimate form could be the alleged ultimate end of evolution—the Teilhardian "Omega point"—but this is achieved only at the end of time.) And since it is the formal cause (not matter) which produces the substantial form,[28] theistic evolution lacks the formal cause, which is reduced "up" to the final cause alone. Thus, in theistic evolution the efficient and formal causes are missing, because the efficient cause is identified with the material cause and the formal cause is identified with the final cause.

---

[27] One of the Thomistic evolutionists expresses it quite well when saying: "There is... a fundamental and ascending current pervading the whole history of life. Whether we call that 'élan vital' as Bergson did is not the important thing; but it is important to see in this ascending current the manifestation of an immense finality. Life through its different forms is striving towards ever increasing perfection. This really is a new dimension to be added to our order of essences. In a way every form of life points to something outside itself and superior to itself; every lower organism is like a promise and an announcement of something superior, because it is the bearer of a finality that strives upward to the realization of increasing perfection..." See N. Luyten, op. cit., p. 310.

[28] *Materia est propter formam, et non e converso.* As Aquinas explains, "Matter is for the sake of the form, and not the form for the matter, and the distinction of things comes from their proper forms. Therefore the distinction of things is not on account of the matter; but rather, on the contrary, created matter is formless, in order that it may be accommodated to different forms" (S.Th. I,47,1, co).

The fifth reason why theistic evolution contradicts Aquinas's doctrine is that, according to Aquinas, God wanted different degrees of perfection in nature. This happens among different species, as well as within one organism—among its organs:

> It is part of the best agent to produce an effect which is best in its entirety; but this does not mean that He makes every part of the whole the best absolutely, but in proportion to the whole; in the case of an animal, for instance, its goodness would be taken away if every part of it had the dignity of an eye. Thus, therefore, God also made the universe to be best as a whole, according to the mode of a creature; whereas He did not make each single creature best, but one better than another (S.Th. I,47,2, co and ad1; cf. S.Th. I,65,2, co).

Hence, according to Aquinas, things less perfect and more perfect exist for the sake of the greatest perfection of the whole material world. This order is intended by God:

> We must say that the distinction and multitude of things come from the intention of the first agent, who is God. For He brought things into being in order that His goodness might be communicated to creatures, and be represented by them; and because His goodness could not be adequately represented by one creature alone, He produced many and diverse creatures (S.Th. I,47,1, co).

And this is contrary to the evolutionary view of nature, in which each part requires continual change toward greater perfection in "the struggle for life" and "the survival of the fittest."

B.1. *The historical approach*. According to Aquinas not only the creation of the world but also its formation demanded supernatural and direct divine causality (note that direct divine causality by definition is supernatural). There are three distinct moments in the history of the universe; two of these are stages, and one is a single act. This single act is the creation of heaven and earth out of nothing. And this act starts time and all beings visible and invisible at once, but without distinct forms. In order to describe this act, Thomas employs the term *opus creationis* (work of creation)[29] or *prima creatio* (first creation).[30] However, after that first creation two subsequent stages follow, that is, *opus distinctionis* (work of distinction) and *opus ornatus* (work of adornment).[31] The creation of different species of plants Aquinas attributes to the work of distinction, the creation of animals to the work of adornment (cf. S.Th. I,66–74). And after the work of

---

[29] *Per opus creationis instituta est tota creatura quantum ad esse suum informe* (Super Sent. lib.2, d.12, q.1, a.5, co, Super Sent. lib.2, d.15, q.1, pr). Sometimes, however, Thomas uses the term "work of creation" to signify both the first creation and the work of distinction and adornment: "The *work of creation* whereby the earth was *adorned* with animals and plants was accomplished in reference to the first consummation of the world" (De Pot. q. 5 a. 9 ad8.).

[30] Thomas employs the term *prima creatio* a few times in two slightly different meanings. One time he uses it when juxtaposing first creation and the new creation or re-creation of the world after the second coming of Christ. In this setting "first creation" means either first creation as we understand it here, or as the totality of divine creative work, which includes the work of all six days. (De Pot. q. 5 a. 9 ad8; In II Cor. 5, lectio 4; S.Th. I-II,103,3 ad4; De Decem Praeceptis, a. 5 co; Super Io., cap. 5 l. 2.) The explicit distinction between first creation and the formation of the universe can be found in two places: *De Potentia*, q. 3 a. 18, arg. 12 and ad11.

[31] In his commentary on Peter Lombard's *Sentences* Aquinas defends the necessity of the work of adornment that succeeds the work of creation or *opus creationis*. (Super Sent. lib.2, d.13, q.1, a.1, co). On the work of distinction see Super Sent. lib.2, d.14, q.1, a.5. Creation preceding distinction and adornment is without any preceding matter (potency): Super Sent. lib.2, d.17, q.2, a.2, ad3.

adornment was finished on the sixth day, no new species could be added to the completeness of the world.[32]

In the first creation, matter with some general form is made at once, out of nothing, whereas in the work of formation (i.e., of distinction and adornment) totally new specified forms are infused supernaturally and immediately by God into matter that had been produced in the first creation.[33] The work of formation has been finished once and for all with the creation of man. Today we live in the fourth stage, the time of God's providence and the history of salvation. Therefore, according to Aquinas, neither a natural formation of species nor the emergence of new species after creation was completed is possible, and this contradicts theistic evolution.

B.2. *The systematic approach.* Aquinas explains how new species of living beings emerge while commenting on Peter Lombard's *Sentences*. He asks if any thing besides God makes or causes anything. There were three answers to this question. According to the first, God causes everything directly, to the point that it is not fire that heats, but God, and not a hand that moves, but God. According to the second, things have their proper operations, and God does not create everything directly. However, God is the immediate cause of the first created thing and this thing is the cause of other things and so on. (And this, in fact, is the position of contemporary theistic evolutionists, who claim that God created only first being and the rest is caused by him only indirectly.) Thomas rejects this position, because by faith, we do not consider angels (let alone material beings) to be creators, but only God alone, who is the

---

[32] "Something can be added every day to the perfection of the universe, as to the number of individuals, but not as to the number of species" (S.Th. I,118,3 ad2).

[33] This is also why Thomas says that creation is not just the making of matter or form, but "the production of a thing in its entire substance." *Creatio est productio alicuius rei secundum totam suam substantiam* (S.Th. I,65,3 co; cf. S.Th. I,45,4 ad3).

Creator of all things visible and invisible.[34] The third answer is that God causes everything immediately, yet particular things have their proper operations by which they are the proper causes of things. Still, they cannot cause whatever they want, but only some things, namely those that are produced by movement or generation. According to the faith (*secundum fidem*) we need to say that only God produces things by creation. No creation can give being, neither by its own nor by someone else's power. Things that cannot be made by movement or generation must be created. There are four types of these things: (1) angels and rational souls, which cannot be generated because of their simplicity (everything that is generated must be composed of matter and form); (2) the celestial bodies; (3) the matter of the elements; and (4) those things "that require a generator (parent) similar in the species to the thing generated." Of the latter sort of things Aquinas writes:

> For this reason first hypostases were created directly by God, such as the first man, the first lion, and so on. Man cannot be born otherwise than from another man. It is different, however, with the things that do not require an agent similar in species, but only the power of heaven with active and passive qualities. This applies to those things that are born from putrefaction. But when it comes to the things that are produced by movement and generation, their cause can be a creature. This happens either when something extends causation over the entire species (as when sun is the cause of generation of a man or a lion) or when something extends causation just to one individual species (as when man generates man and fire generates fire). God is also the cause of these things and He works in them more intimately than those other causes that move them, because He alone is the giver of being to

---

[34] Super Sent. lib.2, d.1, q.1, a.4, co.

things. Other causes are something like determinants of that being.[35]

---

[35] The whole passage reads as follows: "Does anything besides God cause anything? There are three positions regarding this issue. *The first* is that God causes everything immediately to the point that nothing else is a cause of anything. The proponents of this position say that it is not fire that heats, but God, and not the hand that moves, but God causes the movement, and similarly about other things. But this position is stupid, because it destroys the order of the universe, deprives things of their proper operations, and ruins the judgment of senses. *The second* position was developed by some philosophers, who acknowledged the proper operations of things and rejected the claim that God creates everything directly. They, however, said that only the first created thing has an immediate cause, and this thing is the cause of other things and so on. This opinion is erroneous because by faith (*secundum fidem*) we do not consider angels creators, but only God alone is the Creator of all things visible and invisible. *The third* position is that God causes everything immediately and that particular things have their proper operations by which they are proximate causes of things. Not of all things, however, but some of them, because, as it has been said, according to faith (*secundum fidem*) we do not recognize any creature as bringing to being any other creature by way of creation, neither by its own nor by something else's power. Hence, all these things that come to existence through creation have God alone as their immediate cause. And these are those things that cannot come to existence neither by motion nor by generation. [There are three types of such things that cannot come about by motion or generation, each of them for a different reason:]

Firstly, owing to the simplicity of their essence in which they subsist. Everything that is generated must be composed of matter and form. Hence, neither the angels nor the rational souls can be generated, but must be created. Other forms, however, even if they were simple, do not have an absolute existence, because they are not subsistent. Hence, coming to existence does not belong to them, but rather to the composite thing that has such form. The composite by itself is called generated as if it had being by itself. But these kind of forms are not called generated, unless accidentally. For the same reason the first matter, which underlies generation, due to its simplicity is not generated but created.

Secondly, owing to the elongation from the contrary, as happens in the case of celestial bodies, because everything that is generated is generated from the contrary.

Chapter II: Aquinas and the Origin of Species

In this passage Thomas makes it clear that things are produced either by movement and generation (which stands for change of any kind) or by creation. The first type of causality allows participation of creatures, but the latter belongs to God alone and thus it is the direct divine causality. This position must be held by faith (*secundum fidem*), because the contrary, i.e., the idea that angels or any creature can create, falls into heresy.[36] Among those four types of things that are produced by creation are the first hypostases (i.e., higher

---

Thirdly, owing to the necessity of a generator (parent) similar according to species to the thing generated. And for this reason first hypostases were created directly by God. This includes the first man, the first lion, and other of this kind, because man cannot be generated otherwise but from man. It is different, however, with the things whose generation does not require an agent similar in species, but the celestial power with the active and passive qualities suffices. This applies to things generated from putrefaction. In case of other things—those that are produced through motion and generation—created being, indeed, can be the cause of them. This happens when either created being causes the whole species, as when sun is the cause in generation of a man or a lion, or when created being causes just an individual of a given species, as when a man generates a man or fire generates fire. Yet God is also the cause of these things, acting in them even more intimately than other moving causes, because He is the one who gives being to things. Other causes are something like determinants of that being. No thing assumes the total principle of its existence from any creation, because matter comes from God alone. And existence is more intimate to every thing than those [causes] by which existence is determined..." (Super. Sent., lib. 2, d.1, q.1, a.4 co).

[36] Aquinas confirms this teaching in another place: "According to faith one cannot say that something is a cause of something else after God, except by way of movement or generation. Hence all things that do not begin by generation must have God as their immediate (direct) cause. And these are the Angels, the souls, the heavenly substances, the matter of elements and the first hypostases in every species" (*Secundum fidem non potest poni aliquid esse causa alterius post Deum, nisi per viam motus et generationis; et ideo omnium eorum quae per generationem non inceperunt, oportet Deum immediatam causam ponere, ut sunt Angeli, animae, substantiae caelorum, et material elementorum, et primae hypostases in omnibus speciebus*), Super Sent. lib.2, d.18, q.2, a.2, co.

individual substances), such as man, lion, dog, cat, elephant, lizard, snake, and so on. Thomas uses here the word "hypostasis" instead of "substance" for two reasons: to avoid a confusion with the lower substances, such as the elements and compounds, and to stress that not only the form (an abstract "species") is created in this act, but the entire substance of an individual being. The two examples he gives (man and lion), combined with the metaphysical content of his utterance, leave no doubt that in his opinion first individuals of different natural species can be brought about only by creation, that is, directly by God. And this excludes any secondary causes, such as evolution.

3. REPLIES TO THE OBJECTIONS

Ad 1. Since only God can create,[37] secondary causation belongs to the order of providence (or administration) and to the order of salvation, but not to the order of creation. Thus, this popular argument stems from a confusion made between the order of creation and the order of administration of things. Specifically, the origin of species belongs to the work of the "six days" whereas their further propagation to the order of providence.[38] This confusion is more apparent when we notice

---

[37] "The Master holds that it is possible for a creature to receive the power to create not as by its own power, or authority as it were, but ministerially as an instrument. But if we look into the question carefully, it will be clear that this is impossible. The action of any thing, even though it be performed instrumentally, must proceed from that thing's power. And since the power of every creature is finite, no creature can possibly act, even as an instrument, to the effect of creating something: since creation demands infinite energy in the power whence it proceeds" (De Pot. q. 3, a.4, co; cf. Super Sent. lib.2, d.14, q.1, a.3, co).

[38] After presenting Avicenna's opinion that heavenly bodies are mediums through which God creates different things on earth, Thomas comments: "This position, however, is contrary to faith, which teaches

that authors who accept secondary causation in the formation of the universe refer only to these parts of Aquinas's teaching where he speaks about God's providence and not about the work of creation. The full answer to this objection is given by Aquinas himself:

> It happens, that something participates in the proper action of another, not by its own power, but instrumentally, inasmuch as it acts by the power of another; as air can heat and ignite by the power of fire. And so some have supposed that although creation is the proper act of the universal cause, still some inferior cause acting by the power of the first cause, can create. [And thus Avicenna and the Master say] that God can communicate to a creature the power of creating, so that the latter can create ministerially, not by its own power. But such a thing cannot be, because the secondary instrumental cause does not participate in the action of the superior cause, except inasmuch as by something proper to itself it acts dispositively to the effect of the principal agent. If therefore it effects nothing, according to what is proper to itself, it is used to no purpose; nor would there be any need of certain instruments for certain actions. Thus we see that a saw, in cutting wood, which it does by the property of its own form, produces the form of a bench, which is the proper effect of the principal agent. Now the proper effect of God creating is what is presupposed to all other

---

that the whole of nature in its first institution was created directly by God. But that one creature should be moved by another, presupposing that natural powers of each creature are given it from God's work, is not contrary to faith" (De Veritate, q. 5 a. 9 co). In another place Thomas explains: "In accordance with other writers [besides Augustine], it may be said that the first constitution of species belongs to the work of the six days, but the reproduction among them of like from like, to the government of the universe" (S.Th. I,69,2 co).

effects, and that is absolute being. Hence nothing else can act dispositively and instrumentally to this effect, since creation is not from anything presupposed, which can be disposed by the action of the instrumental agent. So therefore it is impossible for any creature to create, either by its own power or instrumentally—that is, ministerially (S.Th. I,45,5, co).[39]

Still, theistic evolutionists will argue that this reasoning is too general and should be applied only to the first creation, understood as the first act of the emanation of all being out of nothing. It would follow, then, that although no creation can create being out of nothing, it can co-create new substantial forms in the matter already created, as happens with the emergence of new animal species. To this claim Aquinas responds by putting forward his positive doctrine:

In the first production of corporeal creatures no transmutation from potentiality to act can have taken place, and accordingly, the corporeal forms that bodies had when first produced came *immediately from God*, whose bidding alone matter obeys, as its own proper cause. To signify this, Moses prefaces each work with the words, "God said, Let this thing be," or "that," to denote the formation of all things by the Word of God,

---

[39] Cf. Super Sent. lib.2, d.1, q.1, a.3, co: "The action which is creation is the one that does not rest upon an action of any precedent cause. And this kind of action belongs only to the first cause, because any action of a secondary cause rests upon the action of the first cause. Hence, as much as the first cause cannot communicate to any creature being a first cause, similarly it cannot communicate to it to create" (*Illa actio esse creatio quae non firmatur super actione alicujus causae praecedentis; et sic est actio tantum causae primae: quia omnis actio secundae causae firmatur super actione causae primae. Unde sicut non potest communicari alicui creaturae quod sit causa prima; ita non potest communicari sibi quod sit creans*).

from Whom, according to Augustine, is "all form and fitness and concord of parts (S.Th. I, 65,4, co).

Thus, Aquinas excludes secondary causation not only in the production of being as such, but also in the production of new forms in the beginning. Moreover, from this passage we learn how Thomas understands the words from Genesis 1: "Let this or other thing be"—they signify the *direct* exercising of divine power that brings about new kinds of animals and plants.[40]

Nevertheless, some will still argue that although species of living beings could have been produced only directly by God, many new species could have arisen later through natural generation. And to this claim Aquinas replies, as was already said, that the emergence of different living beings belongs to the work of formation (distinction and adornment) which finished with the creation of man. Therefore, no natural process of any kind, including the evolutionary one, can serve as an instrumental or secondary cause in the production of new species.

Ad 2. Authors who explain how God works in evolution (and by evolution they mean production of new species),

---

[40] The same idea is presented in the next question, when Aquinas replies to the objection: "Nature in its working imitates the working of God, as a secondary cause imitates a first cause. But in the working of nature formlessness precedes form in time. It does so, therefore, in the Divine working." He answers: "Nature produces effect in act from being in potentiality; and consequently in the operations of nature potentiality must precede act in time, and formlessness precede form. But God produces being in act out of nothing, and can, therefore, produce a perfect thing in an instant, according to the greatness of His power" (S.Th. I,66,1 ad2). See also "And above all it is absurd to suppose that a body can create, for no body acts except by touching or moving; and thus it requires in its action some pre-existing thing, which can be touched or moved, which is contrary to the very idea of creation" (S.Th. I,45,5 co), and "The first production of corporeal creatures is by creation" (S.Th. I,65,3 co).

assume that the proper Thomistic account of secondary causation can explain how God brings about new natures. But this approach stems from the false assumption that God works in essentially one mode over the whole of natural history. Thus, those authors end up in an entirely systematic approach that detracts from a realistic historical understanding of the origins of the universe and divine causality in it.[41] It is true that today God works through natural secondary causes (except for miracles), but this is not how God always worked in the universe. The Christian understanding of divine causality is not reducible to the systematic approach. Instead, it necessarily involves realistic historical understanding of the universe which is characterized by different modes of divine causality. After the first act of creation of the universe out of nothing, God chose to work in the universe *indirectly*, maintaining the natural operations of the created beings by

---

[41] For example, the authors of *Thomistic Evolution* present different schemes that supposedly depict the modes of divine causality and formation of the universe, but those models are detached from actual history. They present divine causality as an abstract concept, whereas Christian revelation speaks about one-time events that actually happened in history. Among them are the creative actions that started existence of different species. See Austriaco et al., *Thomistic Evolution*, pp. 65–74. Some older Thomistic evolutionists (after 1950) used to go in an opposite direction. They made an argument "from history" to save the idea of biological macroevolution. According to them, since Aquinas (following Aristotle) cannot accommodate transformation of species (because he conceives species as immutable, and rejects a possibility of lower forms generating higher forms) we need to move on from a "static" universe toward a "historical" understanding of life. In the static perspective transformation of species is impossible, but in the historical dynamic of the evolving universe this kind of increase of perfectness is justifiable. (Cf. B. Ashley, op. cit., p. 228; N. Luyten, op. cit., p. 295). Aquinas's approach is different from either of the alternatives. It consists of two principles: (1) Forms of life are static, but (2) their emergence happened in time. The first principle is metaphysical, the second comes from the Bible. The first can be known by natural reason, the second is supernaturally revealed (even if the paleontological evidence is quite compatible with it).

ordinary providence, but also *directly*, by unique creative acts that added new natures and new orders of being over the time described in the Bible as the "six days." We see the effects of these unique divine operations in the natural history of the universe in the emergence of higher physical orders among which the most distinctive are new forms of life. However, this mode of divine operation was finished with the creation of man. This is why today we do not see any novelty emerging in the biological or cosmic realm but rather debilitation and entropy. In physics, we see disintegration of matter by transition into radiation. In cosmology we see expansion of the universe, the weakening of the gravitational forces due to rarefaction of matter, and degradation of all cosmic systems. In biology, we observe convergence of races and extinction of species (devolution) instead of an emergence of biological novelty (creative evolution). Still, God maintains all being in existence and works in it by ordinary providence. In some instances, He also chooses to work beyond the natural order by miracles. Yet, even in these rare instances no new species is made; there is only restoration of some things to their natures (as in the return of life to a dead body or the return of sight to the blind), or the multiplication of individuals of existing species (as in the multiplication of bread and fish). Hence, the emergence of species in biology cannot be explained by any Thomistic concept of secondary causation, because according to Thomas species were not caused by secondary causes, but directly by God (as was shown in the response to the first objection). This is why there is no such thing as a "Thomistic concept" of "how God works in evolution" (understood as biological macroevolution). It is possible, however, to show that all the proposed concepts of God working in evolution stray from Aquinas's teaching on secondary causation. (Since the thesis is false, we can show that the arguments supporting it are also unsound).

The misunderstanding of Aquinas's doctrine on primary and secondary causation may happen in four ways: first, by attributing too little to secondary causes; second, by attributing too much to secondary causes; third, by separating natural and divine causality; and fourth, by identifying divine causality with natural causes. Aquinas points out the first mistake in the philosophical system of Avicebron, who thought that no body acts, but that the power of spiritual substance, passing through bodies, performs the actions which seem to be performed by bodies (ScG III,69,10). Aquinas provides a number of arguments to defend the real causality of things.[42] From what he says, however, it is clear that things have their proper actions and generate effects according to the type of cause they are:

> Cooling does not result from putting something near a hot object, but only heating; nor does the generation of anything except a man result from the semen of man (ScG III, 69,12). Indeed, it is part of the fullness of perfection to be able to communicate to another being the perfection which one possesses (ibid. 15). It is inductively evident in all cases that like produces like (ibid. 19). Nor, indeed, is it necessary that everything which has a form by participation should receive it immediately from that which is form essentially; rather, it may receive it immediately from another being that has a *similar form*, participated in the same way, and, of course, this being may act by the power of the separate

---

[42] "Many inappropriate conclusions follow from the foregoing theories. For, if no lower cause, and especially no bodily one, performs any operation, but, instead, God operates alone in all things, and if God is not changed by the fact that He operates in different things, then different effects would not follow from the diversity of things in which God operates" (ScG III,69,12); "If created things could in no way operate to produce their effects, and if God alone worked all operations immediately, these other things would be employed in a useless way by Him, for the production of these effects. Therefore, the preceding position is incompatible with divine wisdom" (ibid. 13); "If no creature has any active role in the production of any effect, much is detracted from the perfection of the creature" (ibid., 15, cf. 19–24).

form, if there be any such. So, it is in this way that an agent produces an effect *like itself* (ibid. 22).

We see that Aquinas, while defending the real causality of lower (bodily) things, avoids falling into the second error, which is attributing to secondary causes more than they can do. And this is the error of theistic evolution, which claims that God uses evolution as the instrumental cause of creation of species. This idea implies that the semen of a man (ape, lion, frog, lizard, etc.) can generate something different than man (ape, lion, frog, lizard, etc.), which is not possible for Aquinas. The objection says that the primary cause can act upon the secondary cause in an instrumental manner, so that the power of the instrument is exceeded by the first cause (as when a man writes with a pen). Yet, a chalk, or a pen, is designed for writing, as much as a chisel is designed for sculpting. Thus, even though a pen cannot write by itself, its nature is such that it is used for writing. In evolution, however, the very tool (a natural biological process) is not fitting for production of the effect, which would be a new species. It would be like writing with a pot of water or sculpting rock with a plastic knife. The impossibility of obtaining the effect by the primary cause while using inadequate and disproportional tools is not due to the lack of power on the part of the primary cause, but due to the lack of power and suitability on the part of the secondary cause. The same problem pertains to saying that not one or two causes (such as random mutations and natural selection), but a set or a number of causes generate the supposed evolutionary effect. In fact, it does not matter how many causes there are, but whether they are suitable to produce a particular type of effect or not. Multiplication of causes does not make them more suitable. Similarly, in designing a machine, ten uneducated people cannot make up for a counsel of one engineer, and it does not matter whether there are ten or a thousand tinkerers if none of them has the appropriate knowledge.

Theistic evolution falls into the third error when its proponents say that science has its own, and theology its own, explanation of the origin of species. This implies that divine causality works on a different (as they usually say—"deeper" or "theological") level and thus is separated from the physical causality operating among bodies. (This position boils down to NOMA, described above in Chapter I, section 2.)

Theistic evolution falls into the fourth error when its proponents claim that God works parallel to evolution in such a way that one effect (new species) is attributed to both God and nature. If two causes produce the same effect, at the same time, and in the same sense, they must be one cause: "It is impossible for two complete causes to be the causes immediately of one and the same thing" (S.Th. I,52,3, co). In this case, theistic evolution ends up in monism (either pantheistic, when nature is identified with God, or materialistic, when God is identified with nature).

Ad 3. A short reply to this objection is that Aquinas attributes to different beings those actions that correspond to their natures, according to the more general principle stating that "Every agent, in so far as it is perfect and in act, produces its like" (S.Th. I,19,2, co).[43] But the production of living beings by inanimate matter or generation of birds from reptiles is not an action appropriate to the respective beings. Thus, for instance, the fact that an amphibian cannot generate a reptile doesn't diminish the perfection of the amphibian.

---

[43] In another place Thomas explains: "Since every agent intends to introduce its likeness into its effect, in the measure that its effect can receive it, the agent does this the more perfectly as it is the more perfect itself; obviously, the hotter a thing is, the hotter its effect, and the better the craftsman, the more perfectly does he put into matter the form of his art. Now, God is the most perfect agent. It was His prerogative, therefore, to induce His likeness into created things most perfectly, to a degree consonant with the nature of created being" (ScG, II,45,2).

This objection, however, demands more explanation. The argument presupposes that secondary causation takes place in creation, which, according to Thomas, is impossible (as was said in the reply to the first objection). However, the argument also draws on a new premise, namely, that our notion of God and our understanding of dignity of creation are more sublime when God uses nature as a secondary cause for creating new species. This argument has a long history dating back to 18th century deism. It was David Hume and Erasmus Darwin who said that it is not fitting that God should create everything separately. The true God, "the highest Power," "*Ens Entium*," as they said, should rather create the causes of effects and not the effects themselves. Not only deists and early evolutionists accepted this line of thinking. William Paley, a well-known Christian apologist, fought for the recognition of divine design in the world by employing an analogy of a watch: As a watch is purposeful and we know that it is designed by man, the same is true with living beings, which work for the sake of their purpose and thus must be designed by a higher mind. But Paley didn't stop there. He developed the idea of a craftsman who produces not only watches but watches that can produce more watches. According to Paley, this kind of work, namely, the production of causes that can produce effects by their own power, reveals more of God's contrivance than a simple production of effects. This vision of God as a "Cause of causes" prevailed in academic theology and it was one of the reasons why theistic evolution enjoyed an overwhelming victory among Christian scholars a hundred years after Darwin.

Nevertheless, the vision of God that underlies this reasoning is not in accordance with the views of Thomas Aquinas. For Thomas, although more dignity is endowed with the power of being a cause, it is even greater to create directly: "It is a greater act to make something according to its entire substance, than to make something according to its substantial or accidental form" (S.Th. I,45,3, sc). Furthermore, God's infinite power is revealed by creation of things out of nothing rather than by producing finite effects. Creation is also more perfect and excellent than generation and alteration.[44] Therefore, theistic evolution does not enhance our picture of God, but rather diminishes the argument for God's omnipotence.

We should also notice that the direct creation of species does not exclude secondary causation; it only removes it from the origin of species. The whole Thomistic concept of secondary causation remains valid. Its place, however, is not in creation, but in the divine governance over creatures. It turns out that according to Thomas, God works in both ways—directly and indirectly—in the history of the universe, which by itself reveals more of divine wisdom, power, and goodness. Moreover, direct divine causality in the formation of the universe is a typically Christian idea, unknown to any non-Biblical religion or ancient philosophy.

Ad 4. In favor of this argument are also Biblical words: "He who lives forever, created all things together" (Sir 18,1a), and the wording of the Fourth Lateran Council (1215): "From the beginning of time [God] made at once (*simul*) out of nothing both orders of creatures, the spiritual and the corporeal, that is, the angelic and the earthly, and then (*deinde*) the human creature."[45]

Aquinas replies to the Biblical argument that all things were created together as far as "everything" means the creation of matter with some basic forms (because matter could not exist without a form). But this doesn't exclude some additional

---

[44] "It is an act of much greater power to make a thing from nothing, than from its contrary" (S.Th. I,45,5 ad2); "Although to create a finite effect does not show an infinite power, yet to create it from nothing does show an infinite power" (S.Th. I,45,5 ad3); "Creation is more perfect and excellent than generation and alteration, because the term "whereto" is the whole substance of the thing; whereas what is understood as the term "wherefrom" is simply not-being" (S.Th. I,45,1 ad2).

[45] *Dei Filius*, I: DS 3002; cf. Lateran Council IV (1215): DS 800.

formation of the world in the work of distinction and adornment. Thus, in this particular Biblical sentence, the word "to create" is to be understood in its proper and most significant meaning, as the first creation out of nothing.[46] And if we consider the statement of the Lateran Council, the response given by Aquinas to the Biblical argument applies as well. It is even more evident because the Council speaks in a very general way about things created at once (*simul*) by calling them "two orders"—the spiritual and the corporeal creatures. But when it comes to a human being, which is one distinct nature, the Council adds the word "then" or "next" (*deinde*), which indicates the sequence of time.[47]

Next, if we consider Thomas's statement from *De Potentia* (quoted in the objection), the word "beginning" means the beginning of "the seventh day," which is the moment when God ceased to create, but still administers beings in the history of salvation. Therefore, it doesn't follow that Thomas excluded any succession in the formation of the world or that he allowed the emergence of new natural species after the work of creation was finished.

Ad 5. The notion of *continuous creation* does not even appear in Thomas Aquinas's writings. Instead, he employs the

---

[46] "God created all things together so far as regards their substance in some measure formless. But He did not create all things together, so far as regards that formation of things which lies in distinction and adornment. Hence the word *creation* was used in one proper meaning" (S.Th. I,74,2 ad2).

[47] And that Aquinas favored succession in creation can be inferred from such or similar statements: "All things were not distinguished and adorned together, not from a want of power on God's part, as requiring time in which to work, but that due order might be observed in the instituting of the world. Hence it was fitting that different days should be assigned to the different states of the world, as each succeeding work added to the world a fresh state of perfection" (S.Th. I,74,2, ad4; cf. Super Sent. lib.2, d.12, q.1, a.2, ad1).

term "conservation (or preservation) of things" (*conservatio rerum*), which contradicts continuous creation for two reasons:

First, as it is clear from what has been argued thus far, Aquinas taught that there are three stages in the history of the visible universe—the work of creation, the work of formation, and the work of conservation. The first stage consists of the instantaneous production of being out of nothing, the second stage covers God's supernatural operation to produce new beings. At the third stage nature is completed and does not demand any further supernatural formation. Aquinas explains: "In the first works nature was instituted and for this reason it was necessary that those works were effected *directly* by the *supernatural* principle. But afterwards, when nature is established, it can achieve its proper effects through the natural operation" (Super Sent. lib.2, d.20, q.1, a.1, ad4, emphasis added). This is also why Thomas says that "in the works of nature creation does not enter, but is presupposed to the work of nature" (S.Th. I,45,8, co). Therefore continuous creation, as understood in theistic evolution, confuses creation with conservation, and thus is different from Aquinas's doctrine.

Second, conservation of things is not due to any new action of God, but only due to the continuation of that action which gave them existence.[48] Conservation is nothing else (*nihil aliud est*) but the infusion of being into a thing which is caused by God as long as the thing remains in existence.[49] Thus, although conservation is a type of operation and not just an act of providence (cf. ScG III,65), it does not lead to the

---

[48] *Conservatio rerum a Deo non est per aliquam novam actionem; sed per continuationem actionis qua dat esse, quae quidem actio est sine motu et tempore* (S.Th. I,104,1, ad4). One of the English translations unfortunately diminishes the important opposition, *nova actio—continuatio actionis*, which was deliberately introduced here by Aquinas: "The preservation of things by God is a continuation of that action whereby He gives existence, which action is without either motion or time."

[49] *Conservatio rerum in esse, nihil aliud est quam influentia esse rei [...], scilicet quod Deus, quamdiu res est, causat et efficit esse rei* (Super Sent. lib.2, d.15, q.3, a.1,5).

emergence of any new things, such as new species. Again, in the notion of continuous creation the work of creation and the work of conservation are confused.

However, it is not just the incompatibility of continuous creation with conservation of things that is problematic. There are at least two other reasons that make continuous creation impossible. First, it is Aquinas's clear teaching that after the sixth day of creation, God *ceased* to create: "God ceased on the seventh day from the creation of new creatures, yet He ever works by keeping and governing His creatures" (S.Th. III,40,4, ad1).[50] The other is his doctrine regarding the perfection of beings. According to Aquinas there are two perfections of things. The first makes a thing perfect substantially, and the second makes a thing achieve its proper end. But the perfection of species is the perfection of substance, therefore it belongs to the first perfection, which, as Thomas says, was completed within creation (Super Sent. lib.2, d.15, q.3, a.1, co; S.Th. I,73,1, co).

Ad 6. This popular argument stems from confusion between the order of God's providence and the order of creation. Authors who make this argument spend a lot of time on explaining Aquinas's teachings about secondary causation, and how chance events do not escape divine providence. And it is true that Aquinas does not exclude chance from God's providence and he maintains that God can use chance events to bring things to his intended end. However, this teaching does

---

[50] Thomas confirms the same in a few other places: "God might have made many other creatures besides those which He made in the six days, and hence, by the fact that He ceased making them on the seventh day, He is said on that day to have consummated His work" (S.Th. I,73,1 ad2; cf. S.Th. I,73,2 ad1; S.Th. I,73,3 co). A very clear explanation of this issue can be found in Super Sent., lib.2, d.15, q.3, a.1, co. In another place Thomas summarizes: *Sic dicitur ab opere cessasse die septima, quia a die septima deinceps novam creaturam non fecit quae non aliquomodo in operibus sex dierum praecesserit* (Super Sent. lib.2, d.15, q.3, a.2, co).

not apply to the emergence of new species—something which Aquinas attributed to the work of creation, not providence. Creation excludes secondary causation as well as chance.

In reply to Avicenna's claim that the distinction of things into different species is due to secondary causes, Thomas writes:

> This cannot stand... because, according to this opinion, the universality of things would not proceed from the intention of the first agent, but from the concurrence of many active causes; and such an effect we can describe only as being produced by chance. Therefore, the perfection of the universe, which consists of the diversity of things, would thus be a thing of chance, which is impossible (S.Th. I,47,1, co).

Aquinas also teaches that accidental changes between individuals cannot be the cause of new species:

> Those things whose distinction from one another is derived from their forms [and these are different natural species—M.Ch.] are not distinct by chance, although this is perhaps the case with things whose distinction stems from matter. Now, the distinction of species is derived from the form, and the distinction of singulars of the same species is from matter. Therefore, the distinction of things in terms of species cannot be the result of chance; but perhaps the distinction of certain individuals can be the result of chance" (ScG II,39,3).[51]

For Thomas, therefore, chance events can be the cause of differences between individuals (e.g., random genetic mutations

---

[51] In another place Aquinas rejects the general evolutionary idea that random events play a role in the origin of the universe: "That God acts for an end can also be evident from the fact that the universe is not the result of chance, but is ordered to a good" (ScG, II,23,6).

can make one cat deaf and another lame), but chance cannot take any part whatsoever in the formation of species.

Ad 7. The statement quoted in the objection refers to the process of generation which, according to Aquinas, is always confined to a given species. In this particular passage, Thomas speaks about development of the human embryo who, according to him, undergoes different stages of organization—from vegetative through animal to human. This, however, implies that matter will achieve nothing more and nothing else but the ultimate form of a given species. The same applies to generation of all other animals and plants: "The active qualities in nature act by virtue of substantial forms: and therefore the natural agent not only produces its like according to quality, but according to species" (S.Th. I,45,8, ad2).[52] Hence, the objection confuses a development of an individual (ontogeny) with a development of species (phylogeny).[53] The first is the

---

[52] In another place Thomas explains that the multitude of individuals of one species exists in order to preserve variety of species among composites: "And as the matter is on account of the form, material distinction exists for the sake of the formal distinction. Hence [...] in things generated and corruptible there are many individuals of one species for the preservation of the species. Whence it appears that formal distinction is of greater consequence than material" (S.Th. I,47,2 co). In contrast, in theistic evolution the multitude of individuals (populations) exist precisely for the contrary reason—to destroy existing species and bring about new ones. About achieving the proper species in animal generation see also Super Sent. lib.2, d.18, q.2, a.3, co. and ibid., ad2.

[53] It is worth noting that the same argument was first formulated outside of the Thomistic context by Herbert Spencer: "Surely if a single cell may, when subjected to certain influences, become a man in the space of twenty years, there is nothing absurd in the hypothesis that under certain other influences, a cell may, in the course of millions of years, give origin to the human race." See H. Spencer, "The Development Hypothesis," in *The Leader* of March 20, 1852, http://www.victorianweb.org/science/science_texts/spencer_dev_hypothesis.html (accessed 14 June 2016). Thomists promoting this argument are driven (consciously or not) by the same pseudoscientific "law of

object of generation, the second of biological macroevolution. According to Aquinas, matter tends to its form in ontogeny, whereas in theistic evolution, matter tends to exceed all forms in phylogeny.

There are many other instances when Thomas says that some natural being tends to its end or that matter tends to its act. Authors who refer to those passages to reconcile Thomas and macroevolution confuse creation with generation, or the first perfection of things with the second perfection,[54] or they ignore the fact that for Aquinas the potentiality of matter demands an agent to be brought to act (cf. Super Sent. lib.2, d.18, q.1, a.2, co).

Ad 8. If this argument were true there would be no need for a substantial form, because disposition of matter in the argument takes over the role of the form. According to Aristotelian-Thomistic hylemorphism, matter is disposed

---

recapitulation" (ontogeny repeats phylogeny) which inspired Spencer and early evolutionists. Jacques Maritain justifies theistic evolution by extrapolating the Thomistic idea of subsequent forms in embryonic development to emergence of higher levels of life in the whole biosphere. However, he is unable to show how this extrapolation could be found in Aquinas. Whenever he applies the Aristotelian principles of ontogenesis to phylogeny, he falls into strikingly unrealistic language similar to that of Bergson and de Chardin. See his above-cited "Toward a Thomist Idea of Evolution," esp. footnote 181.

[54] "The perfection of a thing is twofold, the first perfection and the second perfection. The 'first' perfection is that according to which a thing is substantially perfect, and this perfection is the form of the whole; which form results from the whole having its parts complete. But the 'second' perfection is the end, which is either an operation, as the end of the harpist is to play the harp; or something that is attained by an operation, as the end of the builder is the house that he makes by building. But the first perfection is the cause of the second, because the form is the principle of operation. Now the final perfection, which is the end of the whole universe, is the perfect beatitude of the Saints at the consummation of the world; and the first perfection is the completeness of the universe at its first founding, and this is what is ascribed to the seventh day" (S.Th. I,73,1 co).

only when combined with form, not such that dispositions of matter could exist apart from the form. Hence, in one sense "disposition of matter" is just a notion in the intellect which splits the substance into matter, its disposition and form. In reality (*in re*) however, disposition of matter does not exist outside of the form. For this reason it is impossible that matter would change disposition without immediately changing the form.[55] In another sense, dispositions of matter are qualities out of which the first is quantity, which is the principle of individuation of a material being.[56] Still in another sense, in a material being form is the act, matter is the potency and disposition of matter is some aptitude toward the act.[57] In none

---

[55] "Dispositions of matter remain with the substantial form" (*dispositiones materiae manent cum forma substantiali*), Super Sent. lib.1, d.1, q.4, a.2, co; "Form and matter must always be mutually proportioned and, as it were, naturally adapted, because the proper act is produced in its proper matter. That is why matter and form must always agree with one another in respect to multiplicity and unity. Consequently, if the being of the form depends on matter, its multiplication, as well as its unity, depends on matter. But if this is not the case, then the form will have to be multiplied in accordance with the multiplication of the matter, that is to say, together with the matter and in proportion to it; yet not in such a manner that the unity or multiplicity of the form itself depends upon the matter" (ScG, II,80,8); "So long as the matter's disposition to the form remains, the form itself remains, and when the disposition goes, the form also goes" (*Sentencia De Anima*, lib.1, l.9 n.13). Note that the fact that a lack of disposition of matter necessitates the departure of the form does not imply that the presence of disposition of matter necessitates the arrival of the form.

[56] Thomas places dispositions of matter below the lowest possible type of forms (forms of elements): "For we find certain lowest-grade forms whose operations are limited to the class of those proper to the qualities which are dispositions of matter; qualities such as heat, cold, moisture and dryness, rarity and density, gravity and levity, etc. And those forms are the forms of the elements: forms which therefore are altogether material and wholly embedded in matter" (ScG, II,68,8). See also Super Sent. lib.4, d.12, q.1, a.1, qc.3, co.

[57] "It is clear that something is in act according to the form, according to matter is in potency and according to the dispositions of matter is apt to the act" (*Patet etiam quod secundum formam est aliquid actu,*

of these senses disposition of matter replaces or makes up for form, unless merely an accidental one. This is why Thomas says: "The difference of form which is due only to the different disposition of matter, causes not a difference according to species but only a numerical difference: for different individuals have different forms, diversified according to the difference of matter" (S.Th. I,85,7, ad3).[58] This general principle applies specifically to creation of species:

> Forms are not consequent upon the disposition of matter as their first cause; on the contrary, the reason why matters are disposed in such and such ways is that there might be forms of such and such kinds. Now, it is by their forms that things are distinguished into species. Therefore, it is not in the diversity of matter that the first cause of the distinction of things is to be found (ScG II,40,3).

Therefore, different dispositions of matter (understood in the last sense, as accidental forms) would appear in different individuals as well as different species, but changing the disposition of matter in an individual would bring about only the accidental change in this individual, never changing it into different species, let alone generating an entirely new species. When God creates a new living nature (species) He not only creates a new form in matter; He also disposes matter to accept the form. Such disposition cannot be achieved by matter itself.[59]

---

sed secundum materiam est aliquid in potentia; et secundum materiae dispositiones est aliquid in aptitudine vel habilitate ad actum), Super Sent. lib.4, d.49, q.3, a.2, co.

[58] See also S.Th. I,115,3, ad2.

[59] "Between the operation of a creature and that of God there is this difference, that, to bring about an effect, God's activity does not need matter or any material disposition, for by His activity He produces not only the form but also the matter. However, He does not make the

Ad 9. Aquinas says that it is not necessary for the world to always exist, as its existence depends on God's will. And since God created the world not out of necessity, but by a free act of His will, it is not possible to prove by demonstration that the world is eternal (cf. S.Th. I,46,1, co). However, it doesn't follow that the *beginning* of the world is less important than its *dependence* in being. On the contrary, according to Aquinas the temporal beginning of the world can be known only by faith, but its dependence in existence can be inferred by metaphysical reasoning (as it is done, for example, in the third way in S.Th. I,2,3, co).[60] Therefore, *dependence in being* is like a preamble of faith that can be naturally recognized by the human intellect, whereas the temporal beginning of the

---

form without matter or without a disposition, but He can make matter and form together in one operation, or He can transform the matter, however unfit, to the proper disposition which is needed for the perfection which He gives. This is clear in the resuscitation of a dead man, for the dead body is altogether unfit to receive the soul. Yet by the one divine action the body receives the soul and the disposition for the soul. [And this is also clear in the creation of species when God not only creates a new form in matter but also creates disposition in matter by the same immediate act—M.Ch.] But matter and the disposition of the matter are required for the activity of a creature, for a created power cannot make whatever it wishes from anything" [In particular, created power cannot produce a new substantial form, such as the one in a new living species with properly disposed matter—M.Ch.] (*De Veritate*, q.12, a.4, co). See also "We must observe that as God who is the universal efficient cause requires neither previous matter nor previous disposition of matter in His corporeal effects, for He is able at the same instant to bring into being matter and disposition and form, so neither does He require a previous disposition in His spiritual effects, but is able to produce both the spiritual effect and at the same time the fitting disposition as requisite according to the order of nature" (S.Th. II-II,172,3, co), and "An agent of infinite power needs no matter or disposition of matter, brought about by the action of something else; and yet, looking to the condition of the thing caused, it must cause, in the thing caused, both the matter and the due disposition for the form" (S.Th. I-II,112,2, 3 and ad3; cf. S.Th. I-II,5,7, co).

[60] Cf. J. F. Wippel, "Aquinas on Creation and Preambles of Faith," *The Thomist*, Vol. 78, No. 1 (Jan. 2014), pp. 1–36.

universe is an article of faith. Now, Aquinas says that "man's final perfection must be through knowledge of something above the human intellect" (S.Th. II-II,3,6, co) and that human intellect achieves greater happiness when it contemplates a greater object (S.Th. II-II,3,7, co). Hence, the truth that the world *began* to exist is more important than the truth that the world is dependent upon God, because in the contemplation of the revealed truth human reason achieves a higher goal than in the contemplation of natural truth. And it is also more important for faith, because the truth about the temporal beginning of the universe is a proper object of the supernatural act of belief (cf. S.Th. I,46,2).

Ad 10. If these authors were right, there would be only three or four substances in the material universe. This is excluded by what was said thus far (especially in the *corpus*, part B). In fact, Thomas himself encountered philosophers who proposed similar ideas. For example, Avicebron claimed that all material beings constitute one substance. But Thomas disagrees, and says that this idea "would make an end of generation and corruption, and many other absurdities would follow." And for this reason he also says that this idea is "frivolous" and "manifestly fallacious" (De pot. q.3, a.7, co). When Thomists embrace three or four substances, instead of just one, the idea is only less "manifestly fallacious," and still many absurdities follow, such as that a dog and a cat have the same nature, or that the difference between a snake and an elephant (or any other difference of this kind) is only accidental.

Ad 11. There are two problems with this argument. First, even if science and creation are not contradictory, it does not follow that evolution and creation are not contradictory. As we have shown (in the *corpus*), Aquinas attributed the origin of species to the work of formation, which required direct acts of God. But the direct action of God is always *supernatural* and it cannot be the object of *natural* science. Thus, the origin of species is not the proper object of scientific investigation either. Explaining the origin of species belongs to theology, not to science.

The second problem is that the argument employs a false notion of creation, which is redefined as "dependence in being." But Aquinas says that no being precedes creation: "Creation, which is the emanation of all being, is from the *not-being* which is *nothing*" (S.Th. I,45,1, co). Therefore, creation initiates being from nothing and is not reducible to dependence of being on God, which, properly speaking, belongs to the conservation of things. For Thomas, based on philosophy alone, the temporal beginning of creation cannot be proven, because the universe might exist eternally and still be created (as we said in reply to the ninth argument). But even if the universe were eternally created, it would not follow that species are not created but instead can constantly emerge by natural processes explainable by science. Rather species would be also eternally created, as Aristotle (who didn't know the concept of creation out of nothing and thus believed in an eternal universe) maintained. Christian faith, however, adds something to the philosophical possibility of the eternal universe, namely, the belief in an absolute temporal beginning of creation. Of course, Thomas does not want to diminish this truth when he admits that an eternal universe would still be created. His goal is merely to distinguish what can be known by natural investigation and what must be accepted from the revelation. Truths impossible to know by philosophy and science have been supernaturally revealed in the Bible. Thomas adheres to the Biblical teaching, which adds to the natural knowledge the truth of the temporal creation and supernatural formation of the universe.

Ad 12. There are two problems in the argument. Firstly, it contains a *non-sequitur*: From the fact that the mode and order of creation is not essential to faith, it does not follow that one may believe whatever one wants regarding creation.

Similarly, from the fact that the color of the cat's fur is accidental to cat's substance, it does not follow that a cat can assume any color whatsoever (e.g., pink or turquoise). Also, from the fact that the mode and order of creation is not essential to faith it does not follow that theistic evolution is compatible with all essential elements of faith.

Secondly, the understanding of the words *mode* and *order* (*modus et ordo*, cf. Super Sent. lib.2, d.12, q.1, a.2, co) in the argument is not in accordance with Aquinas's text. Thomas says that the order of creation is not essential to faith, because it does not matter whether species were created simultaneously at the beginning—as Augustine maintained, or one after another—as Ambrose and most theologians maintained.[61] By the *mode* and *order* of creation Thomas means two things: One is the time framework, namely, whether everything was created at once (Augustine) or in a succession of time (Ambrose). The other thing is the sequence in creation, that is, what was created before and what after something else (cf. S.Th. I,74,2, co). In this sense, it is not essential for faith whether, for example, flying reptiles were created before or after crawling reptiles or dinosaurs. The dispute between Thomas and theistic evolution is not about whether species were made all at once or successively, or what the sequence of their appearance was, but whether or not the production of species required direct and supernatural action by God. Thomas does not claim that the supernatural work of God in the formation of species is accidental to the faith. On the contrary, since creation exceeds the capacity of nature, it cannot be known by any natural science, and thus it is the proper object of faith. According to Aquinas, the creation of species,

---

[61] Another passage helps to clarify how to understand the word *ordo* in the context of creation: "[T]his incorporeal agent by whom all things... are created, is God... from whom things derive not only their form but also their matter. And as to the question at issue it makes no difference whether they were all made by him immediately, or in a certain *order* as certain philosophers have maintained" (De Pot. 5,1, co).

in whatever order, belongs to the truths that we hold according to the faith (*secundum fidem*). (See our discussion earlier in this chapter, section 2, subsection B.2.) Moreover, creation, taken in its proper meaning, designates both *the fact* of temporal beginning and the *mode* or *manner* of emergence of things. The mode or manner of creation is characterized by three features: (1) instant emergence; (2) emergence out of nothing; (3) production by divine direct causality (cf. S.Th. I,45,2, ad2; S.Th. I,46,3, ad2). And because the very notion of creation includes both—*that* a thing begins to exist and *how* it begins to exist, it is redundant to discuss *how* things were created. It makes sense, though, to ask about the *mode* and the *order* of creation, according to how Aquinas understands these words.

Ad 13. Aquinas says that in Christianity there are two traditions of interpreting the Genesis account of creation. One comes from Ambrose and another from Augustine. Ambrose's tradition says that God created different species separately over the course of time. According to Augustine, different species were created simultaneously at the beginning of time, although some of them in the form of "seminal reasons" which developed only later, during the course of time. Aquinas says that Augustine's interpretation is shared by a minority and is less compatible with Scripture, but is more rational (*rationabilior*) and is more resistant to the attacks of infidels. By contrast, Ambrose's interpretation prevails among Church Fathers and holy Doctors and seems to be more compatible with Scripture, but is also more vulnerable to critics and ridicule by unbelievers. The pragmatic benefit, namely resistance to attacks of unbelievers, leads Thomas to prefer Augustine's interpretation. However, it doesn't follow that he rejects Ambrose's interpretation. On the contrary, he says that he is going to defend both traditions (Cf. Super Sent. lib. 2, d.12, q.1, a.2, co; S.Th. I,74,2, co).

Now, the Ambrosian tradition excludes theistic evolution, because it postulates the direct formation of different species immediately by God over a course of time. And the Augustinian tradition contradicts theistic evolution for the same reason, because it postulates the direct creation of different species, though at one moment, in the beginning. Theistic evolutionists claim that the idea of species being created in seminal reasons leaves room for biological macroevolution. But from the statement "species were created in seminal reasons" one cannot derive the conclusion "species were not created but evolved from one another." Whatever the hidden form of the primordial existence of species in seminal reasons means, this concept excludes (1) natural explanation for the origin of species, (2) universal common ancestry, and (3) transformation of species—all substantial elements of biological macroevolution.

Ad 14. The quote from Augustine employed in the argument appears when Thomas asks if there are waters above the firmament. This is stated in the first account of creation in the Book of Genesis. Even though Thomas does not know what those waters would be, he firmly claims that we should believe that waters are there. To support this claim he quotes another passage from Augustine: "These words of Scripture have more authority than the most exalted human intellect. Hence, whatever these waters are, and whatever their mode of existence, we cannot for a moment doubt that they are there" (S.Th. I,62,2, co). First of all, this shows the attitude of Aquinas to the Biblical account of creation—Thomas firmly holds on to the literal and historical reading, to the point that even things that seem unreasonable or counterfactual should not be dismissed or abandoned. And this is not how Genesis 1–3 is read within theistic evolution.

Next, Augustine's statement quoted in the objection refers to the existence of waters above the firmament. This state of nature belongs to the order of the universe after creation was completed. Augustine, as well as Thomas, is convinced that waters cannot stay above the firmament, because they are heavier and should naturally fall to the ground. In order to remain above the firmament, they would need to be miraculously maintained there by God. But Augustine, while commenting on Genesis, is not interested in miraculous works of God after creation was completed. Instead, he inquires about the creation and formation of the universe. This is why he says "it is our business *here* to inquire how God has constituted the natures of His creatures."[62] From this it does not follow that the formation of the universe happened through secondary causes or naturally, as theistic evolution maintains.

Moreover, we need to remark that supernatural formation of the universe is not, strictly speaking, miraculous, because in creation new natures are added to the order of the universe, whereas in miracles only the existing natures are multiplied, fixed, or elevated in the order of grace. Hence, every miracle is supernatural, but not every supernatural act is a miracle.[63] For this reason, theistic evolutionists are mistaken when they reject supernatural formation of species based on the claim that God does not supplement nature with constant miracles. That the species were instituted supernaturally we learn from Aquinas in a few places, such as the one when he explains:

---

[62] Aquinas explains it in another place, when he recounts Augustine's position with his own words: "Some say that waters (having the nature of the element which is known to us) are maintained above the heaven by the divine power. But Augustine rejects it, because in the works of the six days, in which nature was instituted, we do not ask what God could do by His power, but what the nature of things is" (Super Sent. lib.2, d.14, q.1, a.1, co).

[63] *Creatio, proprie loquendo, non est opus miraculosum, quia deficit una conditio miraculi: quamvis enim causam occultam habeat, tamen non est in re unde aliter esse deberet: immo esse rerum naturali quodam ordine a primo ente producitur, quamvis non per necessitatem naturae* (Super Sent. lib.2, d.18, q.1, a.3, ad1). When Thomas says *Sed hoc quod fit supernaturaliter, dicimus esse miraculosum. Ergo conceptio Christi ex virgine miraculosa fuit* (Super Sent. lib.3, d.3, q.2, a.2, sc1), he means the supernatural acts in the order of salvation (not in the order of creation).

The institution of the natural things may be considered in two ways: either regarding the mode of becoming or regarding the properties following the instituted things. The mode of becoming cannot be natural, because there were no natural principles existing beforehand whose actions and passions would suffice to produce the effect naturally. So it was necessary that the first principles in nature were constituted by supernatural power (*virtus supernaturalis*). This refers to the formation of the human body from earth and the body of the woman from the rib, and so on. But the properties that follow the instituted nature do not need to be attributed to miracles, like the water that would need to be miraculously kept over the heavens (Super Sent. lib.2, d.18, q.1, a.1, ad5).[64]

Ad 15. This same objection was raised in Aquinas's time, so he provides a direct answer to it:

---

[64] The same in Latin reads as follows: *Institutio rerum naturalium potest considerari dupliciter: vel quantum ad modum fiendi, vel quantum ad proprietates consequentes res institutas. Modus quidem fiendi naturalisesse non potuit, cum non praecesserint aliqua principia naturalia quorum actions et passions sufficerent ad effectus naturaliter producendos; et ideo oportuit per virtutem supernaturalem prima principia in naturis constituere, ut corpus hominis formaretur ex terra, et corpus mulieris ex costa, et sic de aliis. Sed proprietates consequentes naturas institutas non debent miraculo attribui, ut quod aquae miraculose super caelos consistant.*

In another place, Thomas speaks about the necessity of the supernatural agent to establish first forms of things: *Et quia operatio naturae non potest esse ex nihilo, et per consequens oportet quod sit ex praesuppositione, non operabatur, secundum eos, natura, nisi ex parte materiae disponendo ipsam ad formam. Formam vero, quam oportet fieri et non praesupponi, oportet esse ex agente qui non praesupponit aliquid, sed potest ex nihilo facere: et hoc est agens supernaturale, quod Plato posuit datorem formarum* (De Pot. q.3 a.8 co).

The essential perfection of the universe consists of species whereas the accidental consists of individuals. Since the multiplication of the souls does not happen according to different species, but according to the number only, it remains that the creation of the souls every day adds nothing to the essential perfection of the universe, but only to the accidental. And this is not incompatible [with the completion of creation on the seventh day] (Super Sent. lib.2, d.17, q.2, a.2, ad6).

Ad 16. Spontaneous generation was universally accepted by scholars from antiquity to the 19th century. It belonged to the body of the established knowledge about nature. Aquinas simply adopted the opinion prevailing among ancient philosophers regarding the origin of some animals. But even granting for the sake of argument the truth of spontaneous generation, there are two different problems that accompany the argument for biological macroevolution from spontaneous generation.

(1) The first problem pertains to the possibility of generating individuals belonging to species previously created in the work of formation. Even this concept is metaphysically difficult for Aquinas, because dead bodies of animals, or other substances subjected to putrefaction, do not seem to provide adequate cause to generate living beings. Aquinas finds the sufficient cause in the influence of celestial bodies.[65] We should remember that in the medieval times, celestial bodies

---

[65] "It was laid down by Avicenna that animals of all kinds can be generated by various minglings of the elements, and naturally, without any kind of seed. This, however, seems repugnant to the fact that nature produces its effects by determinate means, and consequently, those things that are naturally generated from seed cannot be generated naturally in any other way. It ought, then, rather to be said that in the natural generation of all animals that are generated from seed, the active principle lies in the formative power of the seed, but that in the case of animals generated from putrefaction, the formative power of it is the influence of the heavenly bodies" (S.Th. I,71,1 ad1; cf. ScG, III,69,4; Super Sent. lib. 2, d.18, q.2, a.3 ad5).

were considered higher causes of all works of nature on the earth. On the other hand, Aquinas knew nothing about the inner complexity of even the simplest organisms. This surely made acceptance of spontaneous generation much easier. But even then he allowed spontaneous generation only in the case of the "imperfect animals."[66] Aquinas's search for causality in spontaneous generation proves his concern about the existence of sufficient causes in any works of nature. Nevertheless, even the possibility of spontaneous generation of individuals within previously created species doesn't help to reconcile Aquinas's views with theistic evolution, for theistic evolution assumes generation of entirely new species after creation was completed, which is not the case in spontaneous generation.

(2) The second problem pertains to the origin of totally new species: Can new species appear as a result of spontaneous generation? In two places Aquinas seems to exclude this possibility by saying that animals generated from corruption were made in the first formation of things: "The material principle in the generation of either kind of animals (those born from seed and those born from putrefaction), is either some element, or something compounded of the elements. But at the first beginning of the world the active principle was the Word of God, which produced animals from material elements" (S.Th. I,71,1, ad1).[67] In the passage quoted in the objection, Thomas is not sure if new species may emerge by

---

[66] "Perfect animals, produced from seed, cannot be made by the sole power of a heavenly body, as Avicenna imagined; although the power of a heavenly body may assist by co-operation in the work of natural generation... But the power of heavenly bodies suffices for the production of some imperfect animals from properly disposed matter: for it is clear that more conditions are required to produce a perfect than an imperfect thing" (S.Th. I,91,2 ad2; cf. S.Th. I,45,8 ad3).

[67] "Since the generation of one thing is the corruption of another, it was not incompatible with the first formation of things that from the corruption of the less perfect the more perfect should be generated. Hence animals generated from the corruption of inanimate things, or of plants, may have been generated then. But those generated from

spontaneous generation from putrefaction. As a principle he adopts the completion of the universe in the work of the six days: "Nothing entirely new was afterwards made by God, but all things subsequently made had in a sense been made before in the work of the six days" (S.Th. I,73,1, ad3). Then he goes to the more specific cases and mentions the possibility of new species three times. Two of them are conditional (*si quae apparent, si novae species producantur*) and the last is unconditional. But in this last case he gives an example of a type of species he has in mind. The example is a mule, which is not a real species, but merely an infertile combination of two biological species within one family. Thomas could easily give an example of a true, fully distinct species, as he does in other places when speaking about the origin of species (human, lion). Most probably, by giving the example of a mule, Aquinas means here that if new species emerge in spontaneous generation they are nothing but variants or combinations of previously created species, which remains within the limits of microevolution. Hence, even if those species emerged in the process of spontaneous generation, they would not constitute the kind of novelty required by biological macroevolution.

Now, let's imagine, against the scientific evidence of our era, that new species actually pop up in different places of the world where some dead animal or plant rots. Would it comply with theistic evolution? Apparently not, for at least three reasons. First, it is only the lower animals that—according to Medieval science—can be spontaneously generated, which means that some new bacteria, insects, and similar creatures could spontaneously pop up into existence, but birds, fish, mammals and such would still have needed to be specially created in the work of the six days. This is quite an awkward half-evolutionary vision. Second, there would not be universal common ancestry, because the higher animals as well as the

---

corruption of animals could not have been produced then otherwise than potentially" (S.Th. I,72,1 ad5).

plants would remain separately created whereas the lower animals would spontaneously pop up without any evolutionary history, let alone any physical continuity with other beings through generation. Finally, in this scenario transformation of species does not occur. Thus, spontaneous generation does not accommodate any of the essential elements of biological macroevolution. And this is why even a very loose reading of Aquinas with regard to spontaneous generation does not make his position compatible with theistic evolution.

Ad 17. The argument begins with Aquinas's principles of Biblical exegesis, however, after presenting the Thomistic account of different Scriptural senses, it makes the point deductively. The core of the argument is that the two creation accounts are contradictory on the historical level. Aquinas, however, when speaking about historical events of creation, consistently refers to the authority of the Holy Scriptures. He adopts the order of creation from the first creation account (Cf. S.Th. I,65–74). It seems, therefore, either that Aquinas didn't see the contradiction between the historical reading of the two accounts, or (if he saw a contradiction) that he decided to adopt the historical order of events from the first account. In this latter case, the literal and historical meaning of the first account would be maintained, whereas the literal but non-historical sense of the second account would be adopted. Thus, it is not necessary that the literal historical reading of *both* accounts must be abandoned in order to avoid the supposed contradiction. In other words, if there really were a contradiction, it could be avoided by abandoning the literal historical reading of one of the accounts, but not necessarily of both.

In our opinion, however, the literal and historical reading of the first narrative does not contradict the literal and historical reading of the second narrative and thus the premise of the argument fails. To explain it, we need to go beyond the teachings of Aquinas, but in this case we are allowed to do so, because the argument itself goes beyond what Aquinas says.

The first narrative is an objective description of what happened in the history of creation. No human could have known these things unless under some special divine revelation. It tells the story of creation "from the beginning to the end," recounting events that no man witnessed. In this sense we can say it adopts a divine perspective, or a perspective of an external objective observer who watches the events from beyond time-space constraints. In contrast, the second account recounts everything as if from the inside of creation, from the human perspective. The narrator seems to be witnessing the events from the earth. He speaks about the surrounding land and how it was formed right before the creation of man. This narrative continues with the Garden of Eden, the creation of the woman, and the Fall. In our opinion, the first narrative was specially revealed to Moses, who under the influence of the Holy Spirit was privileged to know the original events in their essential historical order. Without paying too much attention to the details, he told the story of creation as it happened in the actual order in time. The second account contains knowledge of the origins as it was revealed to Adam in the Garden, when he spoke with God, and how he experienced the later events personally after he was created. Then he passed on this story to his children and those to their children and so on, up to Moses. This is why we find many elements of this original story, however distorted, in many different cultures. Then Moses decided to include this historical testimony to Genesis, as the story based on "what people say." Still, this story too is free from errors, either because it was preserved intact from the time of Adam, or because it was purified from error by the Holy Spirit when written down by Moses. In any event, it is clear that the second story has a different character and goal than the first one. The second story puts an accent on the salvific and providential events, whereas the first account stresses the creative and cosmological events. And this is the reason why, in adopting the historical time-frame of creation, we should follow the first account (as Aquinas did).

Still, this does not mean that the order of creation is different in the second account. When we read "there was no field shrub on earth and no grass of the field had sprouted…" these words (from Gen 2:5 up to 2:9) seem to refer to the particular place, the area where the garden was supernaturally planted by God, where there was no vegetation before, but only the stream. It does not follow that there were no plants in other parts of the earth, outside of the space where God chose to plant the garden. Their prior creation is implied by the opening sentence of this narration, "When the Lord God made the earth and the heavens" (Gen 2:4b). Making the earth does not need to refer to making the planet earth alone. In the Patristic and Thomistic interpretation the heavens refer to the spiritual and the earth to the material universe. This may include plants and animals. The explicit creation of animals is mentioned only in verse 19, which precedes Adam's naming of the animals and the creation of Eve. This order of narration suggests that animals were created only after there was the garden with Adam and between the creation of Adam and Eve. However, in the earlier description of the garden the river Pishon is mentioned that flows through the land of Havilah where one can find gold, bdellium, and lapis lazuli (Gen 2:11–12). All of this suggests that the earth is already very old, formed, and adorned. Moreover "bdellium" (Hebrew *bedolach*) is a product of plants, which necessitates that some plants must had existed outside of Eden. If "bdellium" is amber (as many scholars think), then it is fossilized resin that required millions of years of prior plant existence to form it. And some pieces of amber contain fossilized insects, which would indicate that at least some animals had also existed earlier and outside of Eden.

In short: It is not necessary to say that the order of creation in the second account is different from the one in the first account. However, even if it were, it does not follow that neither of the accounts have the literal historical meaning. We can still adhere to the historicity of one of them (though adhering to the historicity of the first account is better justified) and thus know from the Bible the literal historical account of creation. This is how Aquinas sees the issue, which is clear from his treatment of the topic in the *Summa* (I, 65–74). In his "sed contras" he repeatedly confirms: "The authority of Scripture suffices."

Ad 18. Science can modify our understanding of those things that belong to philosophy of nature, but not of those things that belong to faith. Ordinary operations of nature, such as planetary movements, generation of animals, and circulation of matter in the biosphere, do not require a supernatural activity on the part of God, and they constitute the proper object of scientific scrutiny. This is why science is competent to modify our views regarding the operations of nature. But supernatural events, such as the creation and formation of the universe, the miracles, the Incarnation, the Resurrection of Christ and the like, require the supernatural activity of God, which cannot be an object of natural science. In such cases, science cannot modify our views, because the subject matter exceeds the competence of science. For this reason, regardless of what scientists say about the origin of species, Aquinas would not abandon his views about the supernatural formation of the universe, including the separate creation of species.

CHAPTER III:
AQUINAS AND THE AUGUSTINIAN INTERPRETATION OF GENESIS

1. AUGUSTINE AND THE SIX DAYS OF CREATION

Previously (see Chapter II, section 1, arguments 10 and 11) we addressed two arguments of theistic evolutionists derived from Aquinas's commentary on Peter Lombard's *Sentences*. The core of the argument is that Aquinas prefers the Augustinian interpretation of Genesis over the Ambrosian one and therefore makes room for theistic evolution. This mode of argumentation is based on Augustine's theory of seminal reasons, which—according to theistic evolutionists—is compatible with, or even implies, biological macroevolution. The argument has a long history dating back to the first evolutionists of the nineteenth century. It was employed by a number of Catholic scholars, including George Mivart, Dalmace Leroy, John A. Zahm, Henri Dorlodot, and Ernst Messenger. In 1926, a Catholic philosopher, Michael McKeough, stated that Augustine's doctrine "constitutes a satisfactory philosophical basis for evolution, and merits for him the title of Father of Evolution."[1] Regrettably, the strong commitment to reading biological macroevolution into Augustine is rarely

---

[1] M. McKeough, "The Meaning of the *Rationes Seminales* in St. Augustine" (Ph.D. dissertation, Catholic University of America, 1926), pp. 109–110. However, the same author says in another place that "Augustine believed that things appeared with the same forms they had in his day and that those forms were constant" (ibid., pp. 78–79).

accompanied by the strength of evidence presented by those authors.² Because this position has increased in popularity, to the point that today it can be called a common opinion among Catholic scholars, we need to scrutinize it with special attention. In the previous chapter, we provided the answers to arguments 10 and 11 in a synthetic form. This chapter treats the topic in a more detailed and comprehensive way. Let us begin by quoting the passage in question:

> It should be said that what pertains to faith is distinguished in two ways. For some things are per se the *substance of faith*, such that God is three and one, and the like. No one may licitly have other opinion about these things... Other things, however, are only *accidental to faith* insofar as they are treated in the Scriptures, which, as we hold by faith, was promulgated at the dictation of the Holy Spirit. These latter things may be unknown without danger by those who are not obliged to know the Scriptures. And these are things such as many historical details [*multa historialia*]. On such matters also the saints disagree, explaining the Holy Scripture in different ways.³

We do not know how the two quoted statements of McKeough can be accepted without contradiction.

² For example, an ardent advocate of accommodating biological macroevolution into Catholicism by employing the Augustinian interpretation of Genesis, the late Ernan McMullin, offers many arguments (historical and theological) in favor of the Augustinian reading of Genesis, but he fails to show how Augustine's interpretation itself is compatible with biological macroevolution. See his above-cited "Darwin and Other Christian Tradition."

³ In another place Aquinas gives some background to this idea: "[O]f things to be believed, some of them belong to faith, whereas others are purely subsidiary, for, as happens in any branch of knowledge, some matters are its essential interest, while it touches on others only to make the first matters clear. Now because faith is chiefly about the things we hope to see in heaven, 'for faith is the substance of things hoped for' [Hebrews xi.1], it follows that those things which order us

Thus, with respect to the beginning of the world something pertains to the substance of faith, namely that the world began to be by creation, and all the saints agree in this. But *how* and *in what order* [*quo modo et ordine*] this happened pertains to faith only accidentally insofar as it is treated in Scripture, the truth of which the saints preserve in the different explanations they offer.

For *Augustine* holds that at the very beginning of creation some things were distinguished according to their species in their proper nature, such as the elements, celestial bodies, and spiritual substances, but others were [distinguished in their species] in seminal reasons alone, such as animals, plants, and men, all of which were produced in their proper natures in that work that God governs after it was constituted in the work of the six days… [According to Augustine] with respect to the distinction of things we should not adhere to the order of time, but to the order of nature and learning. For example, sound precedes a melody in the order of nature, but not in the order of time. Similarly [in Genesis], those things that are naturally before others were recounted first, such as the earth before animals and water before fish, and so on. Regarding the order of learning, it is like with teaching geometry: Even though the parts of a figure constitute the figure without an order of time, yet, geometry teaches that the figures are constituted by drawing line after line… In this way Moses instructed the uninformed people

---

directly to eternal life essentially belong to faith, such as the three Persons of almighty God, the mystery of Christ's incarnation, and other like truths… Some things, however, are proposed in Holy Scripture, not as being the main matters of faith, but to bring them out; for instance, that Abraham had two sons, that a dead man came to life at the touch of Elisha's bones, and other like matters narrated in Scripture to disclose God's majesty or Christ's incarnation" (S.Th. II-II,1,6 ad1).

about the creation of the universe by dividing into parts what happened in one moment.

Ambrose, however, and other saints hold that the order of time is kept in the distinction of things. This is the more common opinion and on the surface seems more consonant with the letter of the text, but the first is more reasonable [*rationabilior*] and better protects Sacred Scripture from the derision of infidels... and this opinion is more pleasing to me [*plus mihi placet*]. However—sustaining both—we should answer to all arguments (Super Sent. lib.2, d.12, q.1, a.2, co).[4]

The quoted passage constitutes the body of the article which answers the question: "Was everything created at one moment (*simul*) and divided into species?" There is another parallel text in Aquinas that raises the same problem. In the *Summa Theologiae* Thomas asks: "Whether all these days are one day?" (S.Th. I,74,2). In the quoted passage from the *Commentary*, as well as in the *Summa*, Thomas defends the six days of creation, because this is what the Bible teaches. He looks for an interpretation of the Augustinian approach that would save the division into six days even if Augustine believed that all of this happened in one day. We can see that Thomas strongly adheres to the authority of Augustine on this matter and performs hermeneutical near-acrobatics to save the idea of the six days. This is clear in the following article in the *Commentary*, when Thomas asks: "Is the distinction of days saved in Augustine's interpretation?" (Super Sent. lib.2, d.12, q.1, a.3). The answer is "yes," but how it happens is very interesting. Thomas says the nature of angels is intellectual and therefore it is light. And their

---

[4] This is a modified translation of the one found in *Thomas Aquinas: Selected Writings*, ed. and trans. with an introduction and notes by Ralph McInerny (London: Penguin, 1998), p. 91; http://dhspriory.org/thomas/Sentences2.htm#12-1-2 (accessed: 6 June 2013).

enlightenment (*illustratio*) should be called a "day." The angelic nature received the cognition of the created things in the form of intellectual light. This light of angelic cognition is like each of the six days of creation. The days are distinguished according to different categories and orders of things as they are known by angels. The same solution Aquinas adopts in the parallel passage in the *Summa*: "Augustine understands by the word *day*, the knowledge in the mind of the angels, and hence, according to him, the first day denotes their knowledge of the first of the Divine works, the second day their knowledge of the second work, and similarly with the rest" (S.Th. I,74,2, co). In this context, we can understand why Thomas says that the Ambrosian interpretation seems more consonant with the letter only superficially (*magis consona videtur litterae quantum ad superficiem*). Indeed, it takes a lot of hermeneutic effort and requires a really insightful reading to see in Genesis the Augustinian sense as presented by Aquinas.

In the passage of the *Commentary* quoted above, Thomas also saves the distinction of the six days in Augustine. This time he does it by arguing that the six days should not be understood according to the sequence of time, but according to the order of nature and the order of learning. For example, sound is prior to speech, yet not in a temporal sense but in the order of nature. Similarly, we learn the arrangement of lines and points before we learn a new geometrical figure, yet it is not that those lines are prior to the figure in time. Hence, Augustine's interpretation of Genesis (according to Thomas) is as much literal as is the one of Ambrose and other saints, although Augustine does not understand the word "day" and the sequence of days according to the temporal order. His interpretation is literal though not historical. The important conclusion for our discussion of evolution is that Augustine does not stray from the literal understanding of Genesis, while Thomas tries to highlight it and reconcile Augustine's position with that of Ambrose and the majority of saints.

Now, the problem is that scholars supporting theistic evolution do not look for the literal meaning of Genesis. For example, the authors of *Thomistic Evolution* exclude literal historical reading of the two accounts of creation because one of the accounts (in their opinion) presents an order of creation differing from the one found in the other account. But Thomas says that the order of creation is accidental to faith. Hence, the literal (non-historical) reading of the text allows us to save the fact that species were created directly and separately by God, even if the sequence of their appearance is different in both accounts. This interpretation is additionally supported by the fact that there is nothing against special creation in either of the accounts. Yet, theistic evolutionists do not even consider this option. They require a "deeper," "more spiritual," or "less physical" reading of Genesis, and by doing so they dismiss any conclusions about the actual history of creation derived from the Bible. In this approach, the Genesis account is reduced to a few very general and somewhat superficial statements, such as that "God loves all creation," that "all creation is good," that "everything is willed by God," or that "ultimately everything comes from God." As one contemporary author puts it: "The Scripture would not wish to inform us about how the different species of plant life gradually appeared or how the sun and the moon and the stars were established. Its purpose ultimately would be to say one thing: God created the world. The world is not, as people used to think then, a chaos of mutually opposed forces; nor is it the dwelling of demonic powers from which human beings must protect themselves." What this author says is definitely true, but according to Aquinas, the Church Fathers, and other holy commentators, Genesis tells us more than this.

2. AUGUSTINE AND THE *MODE* AND *ORDER* OF CREATION

As we pointed out (in objection 10 in the previous chapter), some Thomists maintain that theistic evolution is compatible with Aquinas's teaching because the *mode* (or manner) and *order* of creation is not essential to faith. But (as we responded in II,3,10) this is a *non sequitur*. Even if the way the world was formed is not essential to Christian doctrine, it doesn't follow that Christian doctrine is compatible with theistic evolution. To claim the latter, one needs to show that theistic evolution does not contain anything contradictory to the substance of faith.

An even bigger problem with this argument is that it extends the meaning of the two Latin words *modus* and *ordo* to things that Aquinas did not have in mind. In the argument it is assumed that the "mode of creation" refers to everything that can be said about the origin of species, including the alternative between creation and evolution. Since, according to those scholars, an explanation of how species came about is accidental to faith, it is just as acceptable to say that species emerged through natural evolution as to say they were formed supernaturally.

Some Biblical scholars propose a similar argument when they say that the Bible tells us only *that* the world was formed, but does not tell us anything about *how* God did it. By saying so, they exempt theories of origins from any theological scrutiny. It is the matter of science to answer the question of *how* species emerged, whereas theology tells us only *that* ultimately the whole universe depends on God as the deeper, first, or hidden cause. In effect, the Bible does not provide us with any world view, because it is entirely concerned with invisible matters.

So, how does Thomas understand the *mode* and *order* of the emergence of the universe? He himself gives an example of many historical issues (*multa historialia*) as those truths accidental to faith. Thus, it is not important for the faith, for example, how many people exactly gathered at the Mount of Beatitudes or where Israel crossed the Red Sea. In the *Summa* Thomas further explains that the difference between Augustine and other holy writers concerns their understanding of words like "light," "earth," and "firmament" (S.Th. I,74,2, co). For Augustine, the creation of earth and water means the first creation of totally formless corporeal matter (and only the subsequent creation of firmament and gathering of waters means that forms are impressed by God in corporeal matter). In contrast, other saints understood the creation of earth and water to mean the creation of different parts of the world with their proper forms, right from the beginning, and only then their further distinction in the course of the six days.

Based on these and other passages, we can conclude that for Thomas the mode and order of formation means: (1) the historical details of Genesis account; (2) the time-frame of the Genesis account (six days understood as one moment/day or six days as six natural days or some other period of time); (3) the sequence of appearance of different beings in the universe; (4) whether plants and animals were first created potentially or actually.

Applying this reasoning to the contemporary understanding of natural history, it would be accidental to faith, for instance, how long the formation of the universe lasted—whether six days, six million years, or six billion years. It would be also accidental whether flying reptiles appeared before or after crawling reptiles or dinosaurs. But when it comes to "how" creatures came about (i.e., how they began to exist), Thomas teaches that some things emerge naturally, and this is through movement or generation, and others supernaturally, and this is by creation which is the direct divine causality.[5] Then he

---

[5] Super Sent. lib.2, d.1, q.1, a.4, co; Super Sent. lib.2, d.18, q.2, a.2, co.

says that among those things that cannot emerge naturally there are the first hypostases of living beings. Since they cannot start to exist through movement or generation, they must be created. But creation belongs to God alone, and attributing creative power to any creature (such as angels) is a heresy. Therefore, their creation by God alone must be held according to faith (*secundum fidem*).

We see that Thomas does not teach in a positive way that direct creation of species is a tenet of faith, though he teaches that any other position would fall into heresy. Thus, direct creation is the only acceptable position, regardless of whether it is essential or accidental to faith. Moreover, allowing anything but creation of species (understood as direct divine causality) would destroy the principles of his metaphysics. For this reason, any other option but creation is philosophically unacceptable. Hence the argument fails for two reasons: 1. Even if the doctrine regarding the origin of species were accidental to faith, it wouldn't follow that species were formed naturally; 2. As we will see in the next section, the idea of universal common ancestry is irreconcilable with either of the Christian interpretations of Genesis.

3. THOMAS AND THE AUGUSTINIAN "SEMINAL REASONS"

Thomas says that there are two traditions in Christianity regarding the interpretation of Genesis: one coming from Ambrose, the other from Augustine. The relevant question for us concerns the origin of species. According to Ambrose, species were created over time described in Genesis as "six days." According to Augustine, species were created all at once, but in a hidden form of seminal reasons (Lat. *rationes seminales*, Gr. *logoi spermatikoi*) which developed only later, in the course of time. These two Christian traditions can be depicted in the following schemes:

Chapter III: Aquinas and the Augustinian Interpretation of Genesis

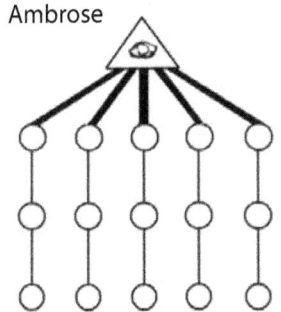
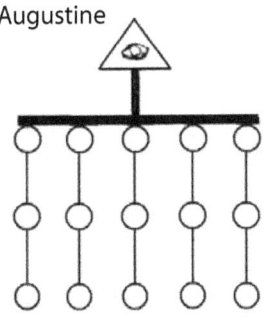

Scheme A. The Ambrosian interpretation of creation.

Scheme B. The Augustinian interpretation of creation

Two Christian interpretive traditions of Genesis 1–2. Circles represent different species (understood as natural species or distinct natures of living beings). Bold lines represent divine direct causation. Thin lines represent secondary natural causation such as generation. The schemes do not include the time line of the events or divine providence.

In the passage of the *Commentary* quoted above (Super Sent. lib.2, d.12, q.1, a.2, co), Aquinas points out advantages and disadvantages of both traditions. He says that the Ambrosian approach prevails among the saints, and is more compatible with Scripture (at least at first glance), but also more vulnerable to critics and ridicule by unbelievers. In contrast, the Augustinian approach is shared by a minority and is less compatible with the Scripture, but is more rational (*rationabilior*) and is more resistant to the attacks of infidels. That "practical aspect," namely, the resistance to attacks of unbelievers, makes Thomas say that he prefers the Augustinian interpretation. Yet, he does not draw any practical conclusions based on that preference. Instead, at the end he chooses to defend both traditions and answer all arguments against either of them. Still, if Thomas favors the Augustinian tradition, it helps theistic evolution only if Augustinian interpretation is really compatible with or supportive of theistic evolution. Therefore, we need to examine how Augustine understands the origin of species and how it relates to theistic evolution.

The main reason why theistic evolutionists use Augustine to support their views is the fact that he uses the word "evolution" in the context of Genesis. As E. Gilson observed, however, Augustine and Darwin used the word in a substantially different sense.[6] For Augustine "evolution" refers to the development or revelation of something which already exists in an "enveloped" or hidden form, whereas for Darwin evolution is a "creative" process which can produce virtually anything known to biology. This is why Darwin did not use the word "evolution" in the early editions of his main book. He introduced it in the last edition only after the meaning of the word changed in the common perception. This happened under the influence of Herbert Spencer, who promoted the concept of creative evolution—the idea that in nature there is some ongoing process that constantly shapes and invents new forms of life. Augustine is far from this kind of *vitalism*. The Doctor of Grace speaks about the creation of all living beings in the beginning in the form of seminal reasons (*rationes seminales*). The differences between the Augustinian notion of creation and a theistic understanding of evolution can be shown in the following schemes:

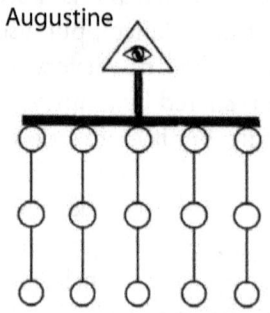
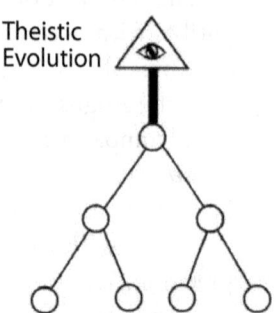

Scheme B: AugustineScheme.   C: Theistic Evolution

A comparison of the Augustinian interpretation of Genesis (B) and theistic evolution (C).

---

[6] E. Gilson, *From Aristotle to Darwin and Back Again*, trans. by J. Lyon (Notre Dame: Notre Dame Press, 1984), pp. 50–52, 87.

According to Augustine (Scheme B), God created all beings in the beginning in one act, although some of them evolved their proper natures only later, in the ordinary works of nature. In theistic evolution (Scheme C), God created only the first nature (the material universe or the first life) that gave the origin to all species via natural generation. The problem with the Augustinian interpretation is that no one, including Augustine himself, knows what those seminal reasons are. In one place Thomas understands them as active and passive principles inserted in nature by God in the work of creation:

> Nature was instituted in the work of the six days in such a way that the principles of nature, then created, subsisted in themselves and that from those principles other things could propagate by the mutual action and passion. Hence it was necessary to confer existence on them at that time, as well as on the active and passive virtues, which Augustine calls seminal reasons. By these virtues the subsequent results were produced from those principles. Regarding the beginning of those principles, they started to exist in the work of creation, by which the substance of the worldly elements was made. But among the active and passive virtues some move to the determinate species, like, for example, the virtue present in the semen of a lion or a horse. Some virtues, however, move communally to all species, like heat, cold, and others of this kind. Hence, in the work of distinction the communal active and passive virtues (those that move to all species) were attributed to things. But virtues moving to the determinate species were collected and attributed to different things in the work of adornment (Super Sent. lib.2, d.13, q.1, a.1, co).[7]

---

[7] The passage in Latin reads: *Natura in operibus sex dierum taliter instituta est ut naturae principia tunc condita in se subsisterent, et quod*

In this passage, Aquinas understands seminal reasons as active and passive virtues placed in nature at the first creation. However, during the work of distinction and adornment their powers were limited to particular species. Hence, seminal reasons are not some mysterious powers hidden behind all nature that can generate any effect, if only enough time is allowed. According to Aquinas, the actions of the communal seminal reasons (those that determine all species to one effect) were ordered in the work of distinction. This corresponds to establishing some basic forces governing the universe, such as gravity or molecular bonds. Subsequently, those seminal reasons that determine particular species were collected and attributed to things in the work of adornment. This corresponds to the creation of living beings, with their whole potentiality to adapt to different environments as well as the power to evolve numerous races and variants within their species. Thus the concept of seminal reasons makes room only for microevolution.[8] This does not comply with biological macroevolution, which assumes that the power of generating

---

ex eis alia propagari possent per mutuam actionem et passionem; et ideo oportuit eis tunc esse conferri, et virtutes activas et passivas, quas Augustinus, vocat rationes seminales, quibus ex eis effectus consequentes producerentur. Quantum ergo ad esse ipsorum principiorum, sumitur opus creationis, per quod substantia elementorum mundi in esse producta est. Sed virtutum activarum et passivarum quaedam sunt moventes ad determinatas species, ut virtus quae est in semine leonis et equi: quaedam vero sunt communes moventes ad omnem speciem, ut calidum, frigidum, et hujusmodi. Per opus ergo distinctionis attributae sunt rebus creates virtutes activae et passivae communes, moventes ad omnem speciem; sed per opus ornatus collatae sunt rebus virtutes moventes ad determinatas species. In other places Thomas mentions also other types of reason, such as, *rationes causales* or *obedientiales*, through which everything is obedient to God. See Super Sent. lib.1, d.42, q.2, a.2, ad4.

[8] In *On the Trinity* Augustine distinguishes two types of seeds: the regular ones that give rise to animals and plants as they are now (these are simply grains and sperm), and the hidden ones, that God created in the beginning. Those hidden seeds make possible spontaneous generation (animals popping up from putrefaction) and the first appearance of plants and animals according to their kinds. There is

all variety of species resides in one or a few primitive species. According to Aquinas, seminal reasons are limited to particular natures—one reason develops one nature and nothing else. This becomes clearer in another place, where Thomas argues that the work of creation and formation was accomplished on the seventh day:

> Argument: The Philosopher says that new species of animals, those that never appeared before, appear frequently. It is clear when we look at those that are borne from putrefaction. Hence, it seems that God did not cease to institute new species on the seventh day.
> Response: Those new species are produced by the power of heaven which holds the power to form the animals borne from putrefaction. Therefore, these species were produced in the work of the six days regarding their principles, that is, matter and seminal reasons. This applies also to other species which are produced by the work of nature (Super Sent. lib.2, d.15, q.3, a.1, arg.7 and ad7).

Admittedly, the entirety of this argument (and the response) is based on the false conviction that spontaneous generation is possible. Nevertheless, even assuming such a bizarre thing as new species popping up from animal corpses, Thomas defends the completion of creation in the course of the six days. After creation was completed, those species existed in their principles, i.e., matter and seminal reasons. In another place, however, Thomas says that plants were produced on the third day in their causes (*causaliter*) and only later—in the work or propagation—they were produced actually:

> Regarding the production of plants, Augustine's opinion differs from that of others. For other commentators,

---

no hint of common biological ancestry or transformation of species. See Augustine, *On the Trinity*, III,8,13 and III,9,16.

in accordance with the surface meaning of the text, consider that the plants were produced in act in their various species on this third day; whereas Augustine says that the earth is said to have then produced plants and trees in their causes, that is, it received then the power to produce them... Now the production of plants from out the earth is a work of propagation, and therefore they were not produced in act on the third day, but in their causes only. However, in accordance with other writers, it may be said that the first constitution of species belongs to the work of the six days, but the reproduction among them of like from like, to the government of the universe. And Scripture indicates this in the words, "before it sprang up in the earth," and "before it grew," that is, before like was produced from like; just as now happens in the natural course by the production of seed. Wherefore Scripture says pointedly (Gn. 1:11): "Let the earth bring forth the green herb, and such as may seed," as indicating the production of perfect plant species, from which the seed of others should arise. Nor does the question where the seminal power may reside, whether in root, stem, or fruit, affect the argument (S.Th. I,69,2, co).

Here again Thomas does not mention seminal reasons. Instead, he speaks about the power (*virtus*) that the earth received in the work of creation to produce plants. However, compared to other places, it seems that the original or causal (*originalis vel causalis*) production of things would apply to the same *matter* and *seminal reasons* that are the subject of other considerations. The ambiguity (generated by speaking sometimes of "seeds" and sometimes of "power") cannot be resolved, and only adds to the difficulties of Augustine's position even in Aquinas's interpretation. In the quoted passage there is also an interesting presentation of the other tradition, namely the one originating in Ambrose. Thomas finds

Scriptural support for this interpretation. In his view, the words "Let the earth bring forth the green herb, and such as may seed" (Gen 1:11) indicate the production of perfect plant species that give origin to the seed of others. According to this position (shared by a majority of saints) plants were created on the third day in their actual form and then they multiplied according to their species in the work of propagation.

One more place should attract our attention. When Aquinas summarizes his treatment of the six days of creation in the *Summa Theologiae*, he writes:

> Augustine differs from other expositors. His opinion is that all the days that are called seven, are one day represented in a sevenfold aspect, while others consider there were seven distinct days, not one only. Now, these two opinions, taken as explaining the literal text of Genesis, are certainly widely different. For Augustine understands by the word "day," the knowledge in the mind of the angels... In the opinion of the others, however, the days signify a succession both in time, and in the things produced.
>
> If, however, these two explanations are looked at as referring to the mode of production, they will be found not greatly to differ, if the diversity of opinion... between Augustine and other writers is taken into account. First, because Augustine takes the earth and the water as first created, to signify matter totally without form, but the making of the firmament, the gathering of the waters, and the appearing of dry land, to denote the impression of forms upon corporeal matter. But other holy writers take the earth and the water, as first created, to signify the elements of the universe themselves existing under the proper forms, and the works that follow to mean some sort of distinction in bodies previously existing... Secondly, some writers hold that plants and animals were produced actually in the work

of the six days; Augustine, that they were produced potentially. Now the opinion of Augustine, that the works of the six days were simultaneous, is consistent with either view of the mode of production. For the other writers agree with him that in the first production of things matter existed under the substantial form of the elements, and agree with him also that in the first instituting of the world animals and plants did not exist actually. There remains, however, a difference as to four points; since, according to the latter [writers], there was a time, after the production of creatures, in which light did not exist, the firmament had not been formed, and the earth was still covered by the waters, nor had the heavenly bodies been formed, which is the fourth difference; which are not consistent with Augustine's explanation. In order, therefore, to be impartial, we must meet the arguments of either side (S.Th. I,74,2, co).

Here again Thomas compares Augustine's interpretation to that of other scholars and concludes that regarding the mode of creation they are not very different (*non invenitur magna differentia*). The mode, in this case, designates the time sequence of appearance of things. In the case of plants and animals, Augustine does not differ from other writers, because he believes that there was just one act of creation which brings plants and animals in potential form. Then they develop to their actual state in the natural operation of nature. And other writers say that in the first creation plants and animals did not already exist, but that they were actually produced in the work of distinction and adornment. Hence, the final effect of creation in both cases should be the same—the actual existence of species. Now, these two interpretations would differ very much if the non-actual existence of plants and animals in the beginning was just some general potency of matter—as it is assumed in theistic evolution. Since, however, Thomas does not see a huge difference between the two interpretations, it means that for him the potential existence of species in the Augustinian approach must be somehow defined and established. The Augustinian "one-time creation" introduces order and distinction among species in such a way that nothing entirely new can appear later. Therefore, whatever those seminal reasons are, there is no hint of common descent or transformation of species.

In some places Augustine quite explicitly speaks against common ancestry or transformation of species: "[B]eans are not produced from grains of wheat or wheat from beans, nor human beings from beast or beast from human beings."[9] According to Augustine, species were created all at once, even if in merely hidden or potential forms, whereas according to the modern evolutionary story, species did not exist at the beginning and then they evolved one from another via natural generation. In sum, Augustine's idea that the animal and plant species did not exist actually in the first creation is, indeed, compatible with theistic evolution. But this is not the whole story of theistic evolution. Augustine is at odds with the rest of the story.

Reading theistic evolution into Augustine encounters one more obstacle, this time not from his interpretation of creation, but from his positive teaching on the origin of different natures. Augustine, as well as Thomas, opposed the

---

[9] Augustine, *De Genesi ad Litteram*, IX,17,32. The entire passage reads: "The whole course of nature that we are so familiar with has certain natural laws of its own, according to which both the spirit of life which is a creature has drives and urges that are somehow predetermined and which even a bad will cannot bypass, and also the elements of this material world have their distinct energies and qualities, which determine what each is or is not capable of, so to say, that whatever comes to be takes in its own particular time span, its rising and continued progress, its ends and its settings, according to the kind of thing it is. Hence the fact that beans are not produced from grains of wheat or wheat from beans, nor human beings from cattle or cattle from human beings." From St. Augustine, *On Genesis* (Volume I/13 of *The Works of St. Augustine: A Translation for the 21st Century*), ed. J. E. Rotelle, O.S.A., trans. E. Hill, O.P. (Hyde Park, NY: New City Press, 2002), p. 394.

idea that one nature can be changed into a totally new nature through accidental change. Accidental change can only lead to accidental differences. For one being to assume a totally new nature demands substantial change. Augustine explains this point in the following words:

> I attribute the creating and originating work which gave being to all natures to God... And although the various mental emotions of a pregnant woman do produce in the fruit of her womb similar qualities—as Jacob with his peeled wands caused piebald sheep to be produced—yet the mother as little creates her offspring as she created herself. Whatever bodily or seminal causes, then, may be used for the production of things, either by the cooperation of angels, men, or the lower animals, or by sexual generation; and whatever power the desires and mental emotions of the mother have to produce in the tender and plastic fœtus corresponding lineaments and colors; yet the natures themselves, which are thus variously affected, are the production of none but the most high God.[10]

We see that Augustine is aware of the different changes that may be caused in animals and humans in the process of generation. He also sees that those changes may be caused by different material and spiritual factors such as artificial selection, the influence of angels, "desires and mental emotions," and so on. Thus, Augustine has a much greater reservoir of causes than Darwin. In fact, Darwin resorts primarily to variation and selection; he does not have in mind any supernatural causes, such as angels. Even so, Darwin claims that completely new natures can be born owing to those lower causes, whereas Augustine sees no such possibility, even with angelic help. God alone is the One who "creates and originates the being

---

[10] Augustine, *De Civitate Dei*, XII, 25; cf. *On the Trinity*, III,8,15.

of all natures." In another place, Augustine, in unambiguous terms, rejects the idea that anything beside God could have created animals and man:

> We have nothing to do with those who do not believe that the divine mind made or cares for this world. As for those who believe their own Plato, that all mortal animals—among whom man holds the pre-eminent place, and is near to the gods themselves—were created not by that most high God who made the world, but by other lesser gods created by the Supreme, and exercising a delegated power under His control—if only those persons be delivered from the superstition which prompts them to seek a plausible reason for paying divine honors and sacrificing to these gods as their creators, they will easily be disentangled also from this their error. For it is blasphemy to believe or to say (even before it can be understood) that any other than God is creator of any nature, be it ever so small and mortal. And as for the angels, whom those Platonists prefer to call gods, although they do, so far as they are permitted and commissioned, aid in the production of the things around us, yet not on that account are we to call them creators, any more than we call gardeners the creators of fruits and trees.[11]

In this passage, Augustine opposes the idea that the angels served as a help to God in the work of creation of mortal natures. Since he excludes angels—the highest created causes—and confirms in a positive way that "no one but God" is the creator of natures, this implies that no other secondary causes took part in the creation of mortal natures either. In fact, if angels cannot produce mortal natures, much less is it possible for any material and accidental causes, such as

---

[11] *De Civitate Dei*, Book XII, 24; cf. *On the Trinity*, III,8,13.

random mutations and natural selection. In the last sentence Augustine hints at how the help of the angels should be understood—they help produce "things around us." Those things around us are not the first natures, but individuals generated from natures established by God alone on the day of creation. And this is why the angels cannot be creators. They are like gardeners, who do not make any new kinds of plants, but rather tend the plants that are already there.

* * *

We now know that, according to Aquinas, the two traditional approaches to the Biblical account of creation are not substantially different from each other. In Augustine, species were created all simultaneously in the beginning of time in some hidden form. In Ambrose, they were created over the course of time described in the Bible as six days. In both traditions, however, species were formed supernaturally by God who acted as the first and the only active cause in their production. This position is substantially different from the one held in the contemporary concept of theistic evolution. According to theistic evolution, species descended from one or a few ancestors by a material process working through natural generation. The differences are summarized in the following table:

	THEISTIC EVOLUTION	THE TWO CHRISTIAN TRADITIONS
CAUSATION	instrumental (secondary)	immediate (primary)
CAUSATION	natural	supernatural
DURATION	non-stop	finished on the "sixth day"
ORIGIN	universal common ancestry	distinction of species from their inception

Table 1. Theistic evolution vs. Christian traditions

We can safely conclude that, despite some superficial resemblance between the Augustinian concept of *rationes seminales* and theistic evolution, these two concepts of the origin of species are different. Hence, it is not possible to use Aquinas's argument from the commentary on Peter Lombard's *Sentences* to justify theistic evolution in the context of the Christian interpretations of Genesis.

4. AUGUSTINE IN THE CONTEMPORARY DEBATE

As Thomas mentions, Augustine's interpretation of Genesis is shared by a minority of Christians and is less compatible with the Scriptures (at least on the superficial level). Besides, Augustine's interpretation is not historical. One could therefore ask, why would Augustine stray from the majority of the saints, including his own mentor and teacher—St. Ambrose? Several reasons can be proposed. However, before we elaborate on this question, we need to observe that Augustine does not present his concept of "one-time creation" as something certain. In fact, when it comes to the interpretation of Genesis, Augustine asks questions rather than gives answers. In one place, for example, he proposes five different interpretations of the first verse of the Bible, only to conclude that one can choose whichever one wants.[12] An overall impression from reading his commentaries on Genesis is that Augustine is somewhat confused. It is also not clear how to reconcile some of his statements with others and combine them into

---

[12] Augustine, *Confessions*, Book XII, 20: "If anybody is not satisfied with the line which I have been able in my small measure to explore or to trace, but requires another theory about the numbering of those days, by which they may be better understood, not as prophetic types and figures, but as a strict and proper account of the way the foundations of this creation were laid, then by all means let him look for one and with God's help find one" (Augustine, *De Genesi ad Litteram*, Book IV, 28,45; see also Book I, 20,40).

a coherent worldview. For example, he puts out the idea of the seminal reasons, but when it comes to the origin of man, he asks:

> In what manner did God make him [Adam] from the mud of the earth? Was it straightaway as an adult, that is, as a young man in the prime of life? Or was it as he forms human beings from then until now in their mothers' wombs? [And he immediately answers:] The only thing proper to Adam was that he was not born of parents but made from ear... Adam was not made otherwise when he was formed from mud already in adult manhood (*perfectae virilitatis*).[13]

Thus, Augustine teaches the direct formation of Adam in the adult form. Following all tradition, he also teaches the formation of Eve from Adam's rib as a true, historical, and literal manner of the first woman's creation. It is not clear how these teachings would be compatible with his own idea that separate living natures (and human nature is one of them) develop from seeds over the course of time. Aquinas resolves this apparent contradiction by explaining that the potential creation of man in the first creation means only a passive existence in matter.[14] This means that God created matter in

---

[13] Augustine, *De Genesi ad Litteram*, Book VI, 13,23 and VI, 18,29.

[14] In S.Th. I,91,2, 4 Thomas formulates the objection: "Augustine says (Gen. ad lit. vii, 24) that man's body was made during the work of the six days, according to the causal virtues which God inserted in corporeal creatures; and that afterwards it was actually produced. But what pre-exists in the corporeal creature by reason of causal virtues can be produced by some corporeal body. Therefore the human body was produced by some created power, and not immediately by God." Thomas responds: "An effect may be said to pre-exist in the causal virtues of creatures, in two ways. First, both in active and in passive potentiality, so that not only can it be produced out of pre-existing matter, but also that some pre-existing creature can produce it. Secondly, in passive potentiality only; that is, that out of pre-existing matter it can be produced by God. In this sense, according to Augus-

the first creation which—at the moment of the formation of Adam—was immediately transformed into his flesh. By giving this interpretation to Augustine, Thomas makes Augustine's teaching on the origin of man entirely compatible, indeed, identical with the Ambrosian tradition (as we will see in the next chapter). But this means that the Augustinian idea of seminal reasons was practically abandoned by Thomas. When it comes to the origin of the human body, he defends the Ambrosian tradition.

We come back now to the question of why Augustine developed such a peculiar interpretation of Genesis. One reason is his personal experience and long-lasting liaison with Stoic philosophy. When he, after his conversion, read the account of creation, it seemed somewhat strange to him that God would create the universe in stages, over time, as if subsequently amending His own works. For him this vision conflicts with the stronger Biblical principle that all works of God are perfect. Augustine was therefore looking for a *metaphysical model* that could combine the two things—the Biblical account of creation and the perfectness of divine actions. He found it in the notion of the *rationes seminales* that he had known from the Stoics and other pagan philosophers. Thus, he ended up saying that all creation happened at once, but because the crude recipients of the Biblical message would have problems with understanding it, Moses divided it into six days. The six days refer to the six kinds of knowledge that the angels received from God regarding the creation of the material universe.

Of course, this does not mean that Augustine simply squeezed Genesis into his philosophical presuppositions. He also found a Scriptural argument supporting his interpretation. The problem is that he relied on the Old Latin (*Vetus Latina*) translation of the statement from Sirach 1:18 that

---

tine, the human body pre-existed in the previous work in their causal virtues" (S.Th. I,91,2, 4 and ad4). See also Augustine, *De Genesi ad Litteram*, Book VI, 5,8.

reads: *Qui vivit in aeternum creavit omnia simul* ("Who lives eternally, created everything simultaneously"). The Latin word *simul* means "at one time" (as in the English word "simultaneously"). This word was used in the Latin translation to signify the Greek word *koinē* that we find in the Septuagint. However, the better translation for *koinē* would be "commonly" or "altogether." For example, the New Revised Standard Version (NRS, 1989) reads: "He who lives forever created the whole universe." The Greek word refers to inclusion of space rather than time. Hence, the message is that God created each and all being, without exception, but it does not require that He did it in one moment. We see therefore that it was an inadequate translation of the Bible that reinforced Augustine's peculiar reading of the "six days."

We are far from embracing here the charge (originating in the writings of Adolf von Harnack) that the influence of Greek philosophy distorted early Christianity and that today our task is to regain the original, "pre-philosophical" understanding of the faith by stripping off layers of Western philosophy. Yet, however false this charge is in general, it may turn out to apply in particular cases—for instance, in the case of the Genesis account of creation as interpreted by Augustine. Augustine represents an isolated approach, shared by a minority of saints; still, his approach is a good example of how a Greek rather than Hebrew mentality can deform, or at least negatively influence, the correct understanding of the Biblical text. That Augustine's understanding of creation is deformed we know from the natural history of the universe as presented by science. Today we know that the universe did not appear all at once, with all the planets and stars as they are. Neither do we find any traces of the seminal reasons whose creation in the beginning of time Augustine imagined. We know that species appeared in perfectly developed forms, subsequently over time, as if popping up here and there out of nowhere. Indeed, we can speak of waves of emergence of species, or of "explosions" of species in different moments of geological history. We also see that many species lasted essentially unchanged over millions of years (i.e., exhibited *stasis*). Thus, the Augustinian interpretation has been ruined not by any philosophical or theological arguments, but by the progress of natural knowledge alone. At the same time, we see how the alternative interpretation, the one that was common among the saints, is supported by the facts discovered by modern science. Paleontology and geology have not discovered a single fact that would contradict the Ambrosian tradition in what it holds as essential. And the time-scale, as we said, is not an essential element of any Christian interpretation. In other words, it doesn't matter for faith whether the time axis of the creative events is scaled at six natural days or billions of years. What matters though, is the fact that species were created separately, by direct divine causation, and this happened over time rather than in one moment. This position in the contemporary debate is called "progressive creation."[15]

Proponents of theistic evolution often complain that scholars on both sides of the creation-evolution debate do not see any position between young earth creationism and purely materialistic or atheistic evolution.[16] They claim to cover that "middle ground" which supposedly reconciles the two—as they say—"extreme positions." But that is to ignore the concept of progressive creation, which also avoids these "extremes." And from what we said until now, it is clear that not theistic evolution, but progressive creation, is the position which is compatible with the Ambrosian tradition and with all scientific *facts*. Progressive creation is not compatible with some scientific *theories*, supposedly supported by facts, such as the theory of biological macroevolution. But Biblical interpretations should be judged in the light of *facts*, not *theories*, even

---

[15] Progressive creation is one of the four major positions in contemporary debate regarding the origin of species. Regarding the details of the four positions see our book *Catholicism and Evolution: From Darwin to Pope Francis* (Angelico Press 2015), pp. 58–63.

[16] See, for example, *Thomistic Evolution*, pp. 1–2.

if some theories have gained an overwhelming popularity in science and the general culture.

Interestingly enough, Thomistic theistic evolutionists want to reconcile Christianity and evolution by resorting to two concepts present in Aquinas and Augustine—spontaneous generation and the concept of the seminal reasons. But spontaneous generation is an exploded scientific theory that no reasonable person would take seriously today. In turn, the Augustinian interpretation of creation as a one-time event is excluded by scientific evidence from astronomy, geology, and paleontology. Moreover, it is less congruent with the text of Genesis, was influenced by pagan philosophies, and—if all of this is not enough—was inspired by a mistaken translation of the Bible. Thus, theistic evolution ends up in a paradox: In order to reconcile Christianity with "modern science," it resorts to the two ancient concepts that have been disproven by modern science.

* * *

One last remark regarding Augustine and his understanding of the relation between science and the Bible is warranted. Christian scholars—those who support evolution—sometimes express concern about jeopardizing the credibility of Christianity by countering evolution using the text of Genesis. Beside their established set of arguments—that Genesis is not a biology textbook, that one cannot understand it literally, that it is poetry that conveys only one important message (that everything comes from God), and so on—they also refer to the famous passage from Augustine:

> There is knowledge... about the earth, about the sky, about the other elements of this world, about the movements and revolutions... of the constellations, about the predictable eclipses of moon and sun, about the

cycles of years and seasons, about the nature of animals, fruits, stones, and everything else of this kind. And it frequently happens that even non-Christians will have knowledge of this sort in a way that they can substantiate with scientific arguments and experiments. Now it is quite disgraceful and disastrous, something to be on one's guard against at all costs, that they should ever hear Christians spouting what they claim our Christian literature has to say on these topics, and talking such nonsense that they can scarcely contain their laughter.[17]

The proponents of theistic evolution usually take it for granted that Augustine speaks here about those Christians who counter biological macroevolution. Surely, those are ridiculed by the unbelievers, and even accused of speaking nonsense. But if we read the passage carefully, we should notice two things. First, Augustine speaks about the theories of nature that describe the universe as it is now in operation. There are enough examples in the text to be sure that he means the current state of the universe. Biological macroevolution, however, is a theory of origins. It does not answer the question of *how* one or another element of the universe works, but *where* all the species *came from*. These are two different questions. If a theory addresses the origins of the universe, it entertains a significantly lower level of scientific certainty. Macroevolution, even if it were actually happening, could not be observed, measured, or put under the test in the laboratory. All of the experiments in biology demonstrate only microevolution. The theories Augustine refers to are those "substantiated with scientific arguments and experiments," but there is no way to do it with biological macroevolution. Second, Augustine does not say that a Christian cannot use the Bible to disprove theories of nature, even if those theories are supported by the authority

---

[17] Augustine, *De Genesi ad Litteram*, Book I, 19,39. Cf. Aquinas, S.Th. I,32,1 co.

of the "scientific community" and "scientific consensus." The origin and the destination of the universe should be primarily explained by theology rather than natural science. Hence, if a theory of origins contradicts what the Bible teaches, a Christian should follow the Bible and do everything to disprove the theory, not the Bible. Augustine is clear that we should believe in the Bible even against a scientific theory if the theory contradicts the Bible. Augustine continues:

> But more dangerous is the error of certain weak brethren who faint away when they hear these irreligious critics learnedly and eloquently discoursing on the theories of astronomy or on any of the questions relating to the elements of the universe... I have learnt that a man is not in any difficulty in making a reply according to his faith which he ought to make to those who try to defame our Holy Scripture... When they produce from any of their books a theory contrary to Scripture, and therefore contrary to the Catholic faith, either we shall have some ability to demonstrate that it is absolutely false, or at least we ourselves will hold it so without any shadow of doubt.[18]

---

[18] *De Genesi ad Litteram*, 20,40 and 21,41.

CHAPTER IV:
AQUINAS AND THE ORIGIN OF MAN

1. THE CONTEXT OF THE CONTEMPORARY DEBATE

In order to properly formulate the question about Aquinas's teaching on human origins and evolution, first we need to make a few historical remarks. The origin of humans has been considered in two aspects—the origin of the human body and the origin of the soul. All Christianity, from the very beginning, maintained that the first human body was created out of dust of the earth by the immediate divine power. This truth was never challenged, unless by some authors recognized as heretics (e.g., Gnostics, Manicheans). The argument from the Fathers of the Church, holy Doctors, and the teaching authority of the Church testifying to immediate creation is overwhelming.[1] However, over centuries there was a lot of controversy regarding the human soul. For example, Augustine believed that the first human soul (that of Adam) was created at the beginning of time, at the moment of the creation of the angels, whereas his body was created later. In the fifth century St. Jerome says that traducianism—the idea that the human parents generate the souls of their offspring—is a common idea in the East.[2] Over time, however, the concept of the immediate creation of each human soul prevailed in the Church.

---

[1] For support for this claim, see the previously cited *Catholicism and Evolution*, pp. 310–335.

[2] St. Jerome: "The majority of Oriental writers think that, as the body is born of the body, so the soul is born of the soul." See L. Saltet, "St. Jerome," in *Catholic Encyclopedia*, Vol. 8 (New York: The

Thus, for nearly two thousand years Christianity unanimously supported immediate creation of the human body and, after some controversies, the Church established the immediate creation of the first and all subsequent human souls.

After Darwin challenged the traditional understanding of origins, Catholic theologians reacted unanimously by rejecting his ideas regarding the human body. The common opinion for another fifty years or so after Darwin was that Catholics could not accept the descent of the human body from a beast. The evolutionary origin of the soul was out of question.[3] However, within a few decades this teaching was slowly abandoned. First, theologians generally agreed that species could have evolved, but not the human species. Then, they agreed that the human

---

Encyclopedia Press, 1909), pp. 341–343; online 1910 edition at http://www.newadvent.org/cathen/08341a.htm (accessed 19 June 2016).

[3] A good example of the Catholic position can be found in the work of the famous and influential theologian, Joseph Matthias Scheeben. His theology textbook *Dogmatik* underwent a number of editions and shaped the theological views of hundreds of seminarians and priests of the late nineteenth century. Scheeben writes about the origin of the human body: "As to the body of man, the Church, basing her doctrine on its revealed origin, teaches that it is composed of earthy or material elements; that its organization as a human body is not the result of either chance or the combined action of physical forces, but is formed after a clearly defined Divine Idea, either directly by Divine action, as in the case of the first man, or indirectly through the plastic force of generation. Hence we cannot admit the descent of man from ape-like ancestors by a process of gradual organic modification, even supposing that God directly created the soul when the organism had acquired a sufficient degree of perfection. Even apart from Revelation, sound philosophy will never admit that such a transformation of the types of organic beings is possible as would be required to arrive at the human organism. The astonishing unity in the immense variety of organisms is conclusive evidence of the Divine Wisdom of the Creator, but it is no evidence whatsoever of a successive transformation of the lower into higher organisms." Based on the English translation of Scheeben's work: J. Wilhelm and T. B. Scannell, *Manual of Catholic Theology based on Scheeben's Dogmatik*, Vol. 1, 4th ed. (London: Kegan Paul, Trench, Trübner, 1909), p. 397. For more about early debates regarding theistic evolution in Catholicism, see *Catholicism and Evolution*, chapters 3–5.

body could have evolved but not the human soul. This was a popular opinion around the time of Pius XII's encyclical *Humani Generis* (1950). In 1941 Pius had stated that "only from man could there come another man."[4] This logically excluded the evolutionary origin of man, even regarding his body. But in *Humani Generis* the same Pope modified his view. Pius XII came up with two theses:

> 1. [T]he Teaching Authority of the Church does not forbid... research and discussions... with regard to the doctrine of evolution, in as far as it inquires into the origin of the human body... for the Catholic faith obliges us to hold that souls are immediately created by God.
>
> 2. When, however, there is question of another conjectural opinion, namely polygenism, the children of the Church by no means enjoy such liberty. For the faithful cannot embrace that opinion... [because] it is in no way apparent how such an opinion can be reconciled with that which the sources of revealed truth and the documents of the Teaching Authority of the Church propose with regard to original sin...[5]

Even though the Papal words were entrenched with multiple reservations, they opened the door to the overwhelming abandonment of the previous teaching on humanity's origin. The first statement allows Catholic scholars to enquire into the

---

[4] "Address of Pius XII to the Pontifical Academy of Sciences of November 30, 1941," *AAS* 33 (1941), p. 506. English translation after: *Papal Addresses to the Pontifical Academy of Sciences 1917–2002* (Vatican: The Pontifical Academy of Sciences, 2003), p. 92.

[5] Pius XII, *Humani Generis*, in *AAS* 42 (1950), 575, 576 (Latin text), at http://www.vatican.va/archive/aas/documents/AAS-42-1950-ocr.pdf. For the full English translation of these passages and of the whole relevant section of the encyclical, see Paragraphs 35–37 of the document, at http://w2.vatican.va/content/pius-xii/en/encyclicals/documents/hf_p-xii_enc_12081950_humani-generis.html.

evolutionary origin of the human body. Yet, if this is permissible, it follows that the Church does not any longer hold special creation as certain, but only as possible. Otherwise, this kind of inquiry would be vain and could not bring anything but rejection of the evolutionary hypothesis. Moreover, if paleontology can give any positive knowledge about how the human body came about, its origin is not a matter of faith. And this is the greatest shift in Pius XII's teaching—the truth belonging to faith was passed over to the judgment of natural science. This is the main reason why, after *Humani Generis*, Catholic theologians ceased to defend the immediate creation of the first human body.

In the second statement, the Pope forbids theologians from inquiring into the hypothesis of polygenism, but he does it conditionally—because this idea seems irreconcilable with the doctrine of original sin. Theologians read this statement not as a ban on polygenism, but rather as an incentive to look for a theological theory that would combine multiplicity of the first parents with the propagation of original sin through generation. This is why, within a decade after the papal document, Catholic theology abounded in new interpretations of original sin. Those ideas were discussed and propagated in theology departments, in academic journals, and at university conferences, with hardly any opposition from the Magisterium.

But evolutionism did not stop there. Many Catholic authors, more or less explicitly, favored the idea that the human psyche emerged as a result of the evolutionary development of the brain. Also these authors did not encounter any direct or official condemnation. It seems therefore that Pius XII's permission to discuss the evolutionary origin of the human body (with the exclusion of the soul) was stretched beyond what the Pope intended. The problem is that once the special creation of the body is abandoned, there is no way to defend the immediate creation of the soul, monogenism, the historicity of Adam and Eve, etc. The reason is that by accepting the evolutionary origin of the human body, we accept much more than just one "scientific hypothesis." We accept all its implications, as well, which include:

> (a) The abandonment of the historical interpretation of Genesis. (If the account of the creation of Adam's body is figurative, why wouldn't the account of the creation of Adam's soul be the same? Why should Adam and Eve be treated as historical persons? Why, for that matter, does anything in Genesis need to be taken historically?)
> (b) The gratuitous acceptance of scientific theories as criteria by which we must judge theological doctrines. (At the end of the day any atheist can tell a Christian what he can believe and what he cannot because "science excludes it.")
> (c) The removal of divine direct causality from the visible into the invisible realm. (The visible realm is reserved for science, because "God does not intervene." Theology speaks only about the invisible events, such as the creation of the soul.)
> (d) The rejection of the uninterrupted theological and philosophical tradition regarding the origin of man.

All these principles can be collectively called "the principles of naturalism." If any of them are allowed into theology (implicitly or explicitly), there is no way to defend the traditional truths regarding human origins. The truths of faith constitute a kind of net (*nexus mysteriorum*) and the removal of one of them, such as the creation of the human body, must lead to the collapse of others, such as the creation of the human soul.

In our opinion, therefore, the problem of human origin concerns not the soul, but the body. If we give up on the special creation of the human body, we cannot solidly justify anything else regarding human origins. And this is true also the other way round: if we successfully defend the special creation of the human body, then the rest of the truth follows.

This is why we will not address here the problem of polygenism or the evolutionary emergence of the human soul. Our goal is to show that Aquinas is incompatible—indeed, flatly excludes—anything like the evolutionary origin of the human body. If we manage to show this, the historicity of Adam and Eve as the first human couple should be taken for granted.

Thus, we are going to challenge even the most moderate version of theistic evolution, the version currently defended only by the most "conservative" theistic evolutionists. Their story goes something like this: "Some animals evolved towards greater biological complexity. At some point, owing to yet unknown processes, some of the brutes evolved features like bipedalism and larger brains. At some later point, God chose one of them and transformed him by infusing a new substantial form, i.e., the rational and immortal soul. This animal became the first man."

This story is something like a "common opinion" among contemporary theologians. It seems to save at least three Catholic truths (some or all of which are challenged in other evolutionary stories): (1) the special creation of the human soul; (2) monogenism; (3) the transformation of the body at the infusion of the soul. The third point requires more explanation.

If we consistently adopt the assumptions of biological macroevolution, each species, including man, should appear in the continual process of transformation, without any empirically detectable break. This assumption is crucial for evolution because evolution must be a natural process, whereas any process that would include "physical leaps" would not be natural and explainable by science. This is why evolutionists make a distinction between the "physical leap" and the "ontological leap." According to them, in the hominization of an animal only the ontological leap takes place, but the physical continuity is preserved.[6] This position, however, cannot

---

[6] The defense of this position can be found even in the John Paul II's 1996 Address to the Pontifical Academy of Science: "With man, we find ourselves facing a different ontological order—an ontological

be true, as long as we understand the human soul according to the solemn teaching of the Council of Vienne, later confirmed by the Fifth Lateran Council.[7] The Council defines the rational soul as the substantial form of the human body. Any other position the Council deems heretical. Now, if the substantial form of a living being is replaced with another form, it is clear that this is a substantial change that affects not just the form but also matter. Yet, if at some moment of physical development, matter is instantaneously transformed by the divine power, there cannot be physical continuity in the process. Therefore, the *physical continuity* and the *ontological leap* can be claimed simultaneously only if we deny the Catholic understanding of the soul, which would be heresy.

---

leap, we could say. But in posing such a great ontological discontinuity, are we not breaking up the physical continuity which seems to be the main line of research about evolution in the fields of physics and chemistry? An appreciation for the different methods used in different fields of scholarship allows us to bring together two points of view which at first might seem irreconcilable." Text at https://www.ewtn.com/library/papaldoc/jp961022.htm (accessed 23 June 2016).

[7] The Council of Vienne (1311–1312) stated against the errors of Pietro Olivi: "We reject as erroneous and contrary to the truth of the catholic faith every doctrine or proposition rashly asserting that the substance of the rational or intellectual soul is not of itself and essentially the form of the human body... We define that anyone who presumes henceforth to assert, defend, or hold stubbornly that the rational or intellectual soul is not the form of the human body of itself and essentially, is to be considered a heretic." Text at www.ewtn.com/library/COUNCILS/VIENNE.HTM#09 (accessed 31 January 2015). The confirmation of this teaching came two centuries later at the Fifth Lateran Council: "We condemn and reject all those who insist that the intellectual soul is mortal, or that it is only one among all human beings, and those who suggest doubts on this topic. For the soul not only truly exists of itself and essentially as the form of the human body, as is said in the canon of our predecessor... promulgated in the general council of Vienne, but it is also immortal; and further, for the enormous number of bodies into which it is infused individually, it can and ought to be and is multiplied." The Fifth Lateran Council, Session 8, 19 December 1513. Text at: http://www.papalencyclicals.net/Councils/ecum18.htm (accessed 23 June 2016).

This is why those "conservative" scholars who believe in evolution embrace the solution called "special transformism" (in contrast to the traditional Christian position, which is special creation). According to this view, hominization, which entails infusion of a new substantial form, is like a total transformation of a hominid into a human. This process lacks both ontological and physical continuity. Furthermore, since the body of the last hominid is specially transformed, some of the proponents of this view claim that the human body is created immediately by God, simply by adding the entire new form to the matter of the hominid. So, in this view, not only is the Catholic doctrine of the origin of the soul preserved; one may even say that the body is directly formed by God by means of transformation.

We need to notice that this story is already unacceptable for scientific naturalism, because it makes the origin of the human body inexplicable in natural biological terms. This is why it is rejected by hard-headed theistic evolutionists. It is accepted, however, by those who have already abandoned the authentic belief in creation, but are still hesitant to accept fully-fledged naturalism, mainly for philosophical reasons. Special transformism accepts the formation of the human body from an animal, whereas special creation speaks about the human body being formed immediately from the dust of the earth. Special transformism is the closest position to the original Christian faith among all of the evolutionary stories. Even so, our goal is to show that Aquinas's teaching excludes special transformism. If we show this, there is no need to show anything else, because the rest of the truth is protected by this one.

2. AQUINAS AND THE ORIGIN OF THE HUMAN BODY

Aquinas provides a detailed account of human origins in his *Summa Theologiae* in Questions 90 through 92. Question 90 treats the origin of the human soul. We won't comment on this, because, as we said, questioning the direct creation of the soul is only a consequence of denying the special creation of the body. Once creation of the body is secured, no one claims an evolutionary origin of the soul (at least not in today's debate). The special creation of the human body constitutes the most evident discrepancy between Aquinas's teaching and theistic evolution. The Angelic Doctor explains the origin of the human body in Question 91.

In the *first article*, Thomas asks whether the body of the first man was made of the slime of the earth. There are four objections against this truth. The first objection is based on the different degrees of perfection of divine actions. Since man is the most honorable among material beings it seems that he deserves the most honorable way of being created. And being created out of nothing is greater than being created with a use of some material. Therefore, man should be created out of nothing rather than from slime. Thomas responds that God's power of creating out of nothing was demonstrated at the creation of matter out of nothing in the first creation. Man, however, being a creature dwelling on the earth and somehow connected to it, should have the bond with the physical creation established in his very origin. We could add that if man was created out of nothing it would suggest that he is not the part of this universe, but some alien being accidentally stepping onto this planet. The fact that man was created from the substance of this earth makes him familiar to the rest of material creation.

The second objection comes from the degrees of nobility among physical beings. Heavenly bodies are nobler than earthly bodies, and the human body has the noblest form, because of the spiritual and rational soul. It would be more fitting, therefore, to make the human body out of a heavenly body rather than the earthly one. Thomas's response is based on the ancient and medieval conviction that heavenly bodies are made of the fifth element—something substantially different from the four earthly elements (water, air, earth, and fire). The fifth element is impassible, which means it cannot change, deteriorate or decay, as things made of the earthly elements do. But precisely because things made of the fifth element are unchangeable, it cannot become the matter for the human body. The human body must be passible, because the rational soul acquires information through senses (from the material universe). The heavenly element, if it were constitutive of the human body, could not be affected or moved by sensations. Thus, a human body made out of the fifth element would not be suitable to receive a human soul that performs sensory functions.

The third objection is based on the hierarchy found among the four earthly elements. Fire and air are subtler than earth and water. Since the human body is the noblest among earthly bodies it should be made out of the noblest elements. Yet, it is made of earth. To this Thomas responds that if there were predominance of fire and air in the human body, there would not be an appropriate balance of the elements, because fire and air (as more active than other elements) would draw into themselves the other two. The operation of the senses, however, requires a proper balance of the elements, and this is especially true for the sense of touch, which is the foundation of other senses. Now, all senses must be neutral to their object in order to perceive the object. For example, the pupil of the eye is transparent (devoid of a color) in order to perceive all colors. In the sense of touch, however, this kind of transparency is not possible, because this sense is made of what it perceives (it is constituted of the elements and by this sense we recognize the qualities of the elements by direct contact with them). Therefore, sensing through touch requires some other type of neutrality of the organ. This is achieved by the neutral composition of the elements of which the sense is built, so that the sense may react for heat (fire) or wet (water) and so on. Hence, earth (which is the least active element) must dominate in the human body in order for the sense of touch to work.

The fourth objection is that there is a mixture of the four elements in the human body, therefore, it must have been produced out of four elements, not just one. In response,

Thomas says that the slime of the earth already contains water and earth. The other two elements are not mentioned, because there are less of them in the human body and they are not perceivable to the uncultured men who were the first recipients of the Biblical description.

In the *sed contra* section of the article, Aquinas quotes Gen 2:7, "God made man of the slime of the earth," which means that he understands this phrase literally, as the actual mode of the emergence of the human body. In the body (*corpus*) of the article, Aquinas presents man as a composition of different substances that relate to different elements of creation. With angels man has in common the spiritual soul. With the heavenly bodies man has in common the lack of contraries due to man's utmost equality of complexion (internal organic harmony). When it comes to the elements, man is built of their very substance. This, however, is in such a way, that the higher and more active elements (fire and air) are present mainly through their power, whereas the lower elements (water and earth) predominate in their substance. And this is why it is said that the body of man was formed out of slime, which contains water and earth.

Thomas is explicit enough to settle the question of whether man was made of a beast or of the inanimate matter of elements. If he argues for earth against air and fire, it is evident that he understands earth literally as the material of which human body was formed. The only way that evolutionists could challenge this teaching is by claiming that Aquinas speaks of elements in a philosophical rather than physical sense. The four elements are more like "philosophical concepts" that were designed to explain the internal composition of different bodies (dead and living) before the modern understanding of matter came about. So Aquinas could have in mind something else than the physical dust, clay, or slime of the earth, and we do not know what he means here by earth. After all, the predominating element in the body of a beast is also earth, so maybe Thomas means here the body of a beast?

But this argument reveals misunderstanding of what the medieval people understood by the elements. Today we know of over a hundred elements categorized in Mendeleev's table. Water is not an element but a compound of two elements (hydrogen and oxygen). Earth might consist of just one element (silicon), but it usually contains some other elements, such as iron or calcium. For the medieval people everything heavy and solid would have a predominance of earth. Thus, their understanding of the elements was phenomenal: it was built on perceptions, rather than understanding of the internal structure of those things. But this is precisely why we cannot deny the literal understanding of earth in Aquinas. His concept of the four elements is philosophical not because it is some speculative concept detached from reality, but because this is all that the medieval (and ancient) people could have known about the nature of material beings, based just on the pre-scientific, phenomenal approach to nature. Those concepts were created precisely to explain material reality as it appears to the senses. The elements were invented "post factum"—after having experienced the material being, not a priori. Reading into the idea of four elements anything besides the physical being, considered at its basic material level, is an anachronism and a deformation of Aquinas's thought. "Earth" means for him the element of a body that makes it heavy, dark, and "passive." Earth, in the context of the formation of the human body, by no means refers to a living being, but to some kind of sand combined with water that constitutes slime. This material was used by God to produce the human body. And this teaching of Aquinas excludes special transformism.

The *second article* addresses the question: "Whether the human body was immediately produced by God?" The first objection is based on Augustine's statement that God disposes the corporeal things using angels. In his reply, Thomas says that some things God does using the angels and some He does immediately, without using the angels. Among the latter there are things like bringing the dead to life, restoring sight to the blind, and forming the body of the first man out of slime. However, angels could have had some role in the creation of Adam's body, namely, gathering the dust at one place. In the same way, they will gather the ashes of the saints on the day of resurrection. This response excludes the active cooperation of angels (as secondary causes) in the formation of the first human body. Moreover, by employing the analogy between the first creation of the human body and the future restoration of the bodies, Aquinas again confirms that he understands literally the creation of the first man out of slime. Otherwise resurrection would be just a figure of speech, not a physical reality awaiting human bodies.

The second objection is based on the outdated and later disproven theory of spontaneous generation: If some animals are born from putrefaction under the influence of the heavenly bodies, then the human body also could have been produced by the influence of the sky. Thomas responds that only some of the lower animals can be produced in this way, not the higher animals. And man is not a lower animal. Thomas accepts the premise of the objection, because he does not know exactly how animals (whether lower or higher) are naturally generated. Still, he excludes (against Avicenna) the higher animals from this process, and thus neither the first nor any subsequent man could have been spontaneously generated.

The third objection is based on the medieval understanding of nature, in which all material change is caused (directly or indirectly) by the movement of heaven. If this is the case, then there must have been some influence of the heavenly bodies in the production of the first human body. To this Aquinas responds: "The movement of the heavens causes natural changes; but not changes that surpass the order of nature, and are caused by the Divine Power alone, as for the dead to be raised to life, or the blind to see: like to which also is the making of man from the slime of the earth."

The fourth objection is derived from Augustine's teaching that the human body was created first in the form of a causal virtue (or seminal reason). But things existing in causal virtues can be produced by some corporeal bodies. Hence, the human body was made by a corporeal creature and not immediately by God. To this Aquinas says that the human body existed in the causal virtue only in passive potentiality that required the work of God to be brought to act. Here Aquinas again accepts Augustine's interpretation which today we should deem untenable, because (as we explained in the previous chapter) it contradicts the natural history of the universe. But this only makes Aquinas's case stronger: There is no need to tinker with active and passive potencies represented by the causal virtues (whatever they are). The human body was potentially created in the first creation only in this sense, that God created matter with some primitive form. In this way everything else was created in the first creation. Moreover, Thomas, by excluding the operation of a corporeal creature in the production of the human body, excludes anything like genetic mutations, natural selection, and any other evolutionary factors. He places all those "material changes" on the one side and the direct divine causation on the other, and then he favors the latter at the cost of the first.[8]

In the *sed contra*, Thomas simply quotes another Scriptural passage referring to the creation of man: "God created man out of the earth" (Sirach 17:1). This completely contradicts the position of some Thomistic evolutionists, who claim that reading Genesis in the context of other Biblical passages diminishes the historical meaning of the creation account and makes it more compatible with evolution.[9] In fact we see in Aquinas the opposite: He understands Gen. 2:7

---

[8] A good example of an evolutionary misrepresentation of this teaching of Aquinas may be found in E. McMullin's previously cited paper, "Darwin and the Other Christian Tradition," p. 300.

[9] See, for example, *Thomistic Evolution*, p. 126. When speaking about the origin of Eve, Aquinas also understands Genesis's message in the light of another Biblical text, again quoting Sirach (17:5): "He *created of him*, that is, out of man, *a helpmate like to himself*, that is, woman" (S.Th. I,92,2 sc).

literally, and other Biblical passages only confirm his literal and historical reading of that verse. In the *corpus* of the article Thomas explains:

> The first formation of the human body could not be by the instrumentality of any created power, but was immediately from God. Some, indeed, supposed that the forms which are in corporeal matter are derived from some immaterial forms; but the Philosopher refutes this opinion (Metaph. vii)... So a form which is in matter should be the cause of another form that is in matter, because composite is made by composite. Now God, though He is absolutely immaterial, can alone by His own power produce matter by creation: wherefore He alone can produce a form in matter, without the aid of any preceding material form. For this reason the angels cannot transform a body except by making use of something in the nature of a seed, as Augustine says (De Trin. III,19). Therefore, as no pre-existing body has been formed whereby another body of the same species could be generated, the first human body was of necessity made immediately by God.[10]

In this explanation, we see that the human body must have been produced immediately (i.e., directly) by God. This logically excludes theistic evolution, because theistic evolution claims that evolution is a secondary cause of creation. Direct formation excludes any secondary causes. Moreover, we see that for Aquinas the immediate creation of the first human body is not just a matter of faith derived from the literal understanding of Genesis. In fact, it is a metaphysical necessity stemming from the basic principles of realistic philosophy. If man is a separate species whose substance exists in each individual, this substance cannot start to exist otherwise than

---

[10] S.Th. I,91,2 co.

by direct creation by God. Neither angels nor material beings can produce form in matter, i.e., a composite of a new kind. And for the same reason theistic evolution undermines not just Thomas's reading of the Bible, but the very foundations of his metaphysical enterprise.

The *third article* concerns the problem of the physical constitution of the human body. Aquinas asks whether it was given an apt disposition. In his response, he clarifies that different creatures receive different forms according to the measure of perfection which God designed for them. The human soul is the most perfect among those informing material beings, so this soul requires a different type of disposition of the body. The human body is designed in such a way that it can perform the functions of the rational soul.

Now, the most common opinion among theistic evolutionists is that an animal body received the human soul and this is how man started to exist. But this is impossible for the reasons mentioned in the third article—the human soul can animate only the human body, whereas the animal body can be animated only by the animal soul. Thus, Aquinas's teaching excludes anything besides special transformism (which, as we have shown, is excluded in the first article explicitly and in the second article implicitly). To avoid this problem, most theistic evolutionists see the emergence of man as a long-lasting process in which a beast acquires different human features and behaviors one by one and little by little. For example, some theistic evolutionists believe that there were some brutes that evolution transformed into hominids. Hominids (like *homo erectus*) were bipedal. Later they might have used tools, hunted, built shelters, even displayed elements of art, yet they were not human.[11] Only at the final stage of their evolution

---

[11] John S. Wilkins, though not Catholic, understands the problem quite well when he admits: "Catholic teaching on evolution insists that God created souls in one hominid species and that before then they had none. This is quite acceptable if the having of souls is empirically indemonstrable, but the available evidence suggests that morality,

did they become "truly human" by, for example, acquiring the ability of moral choice, or recognizing God as their Master. It is said that they received a "spark of an intellect" that made them cross the "Rubicon of anthropogenesis."[12] But if we accept this story, it means that the human being was started not by a substantial change that produced man in its entirety (body and soul), but instead by the addition of a new faculty to a pre-existent non-human creature. This idea is contrary to Aquinas's teaching for two reasons (both already mentioned):

reason, and tool use, for example, are traits that existed well before there was a human species, and so from our perspective, it would be unacceptable to employ souls as explanations for these capacities. If this is not how the notion of soul is employed, then there is no reason to reject either the Catholic view of humanity or to modify science to subserve it; but if it were, then so much the worse for the doctrine." Idem, "Could God Create Darwinian Accidents?," *Zygon*, Vol. 47, No. 1, March 2012, pp. 30–41, 39. In Wilkins's thinking the human soul does not make man think or have moral choice. If Catholics claimed that the human soul is in charge of any capabilities expressed visibly, then their doctrine would be impossible for "scientific" reasons.

[12] One contemporary theologian presents this position characteristically: "The clay became man at that moment in which a being for the first time was capable of forming, however dimly, the thought *God*. The first Thou that—however stammeringly—was said by human lips to God marks the moment in which spirit arose in the world. Here the Rubicon of anthropogenesis was crossed. For it is not the use of weapons or fire, not new methods of cruelty or of useful activity, that constitute man, but rather his ability to be immediately in relation to God. This holds fast to the doctrine of the special creation of man; herein lies the center of belief in creation in the first place. Herein also lies the reason why the moment of anthropogenesis cannot possibly be determined by paleontology: anthropogenesis is the rise of the spirit, which cannot be excavated with a shovel." See J. Ratzinger, *Creation and Evolution: A Conference with Pope Benedict XVI in Castel Gandolfo*, ed. S. O. Horn and S. Wiedenhofer (San Francisco: Ignatius Press, 2008), pp. 15–16. François Euvé, S.I., even claims that "the abundance of the [fossil] material excludes the possibility of a sudden appearance of the human species." According to Euvé, we do not really know when man emerged and a full definition of humanity is impossible. See F. Euvé, *Darwin et le christianisme*, and the Polish edition, *Darwin i chrzescijanstwo* (Krakow: WAM, 2010), p. 34.

First, the human soul may animate only the human body. But the human soul is a rational soul, and only this kind of soul can perform rational functions, such as the production of tools or art. Therefore, wherever we find the products of rational activity, we can infer truly human authors, regarding both their bodies and their souls.

Second, Aquinas teaches that the human soul is the only form of the human body that is "in charge" of its physical composition as much as the mental skills (see S.Th. I,76). But this would not be the case if the human being were constituted by an addition of a new faculty. The evolutionary story implies either that the rational soul (the one that makes humans capable of knowing and loving God) is added to the animal soul that animates the hominid, or that reason is just an added faculty to an animal that makes the animal human. In the first case there are two forms (two souls) in the human body. In the second case, the animal soul animating the hominid is only amended or perfected by God, and thus there is no human soul at all. Both solutions go against Aquinas's explicit teaching. Hence, the third article excludes those stories of theistic evolution which see the emergence of a human being as an addition of a new faculty to a hominid.

In the *fourth article* Aquinas asks: "Whether the production of the human body is fittingly described in Scripture?" This article does not even contain the usual "body" (*corpus*) section, because for Aquinas the authority of Scripture, affirmed in the "on the contrary" (*sed contra*) section, is enough. Either one accepts it, and then one agrees that Genesis fittingly describes the origin of man, or one rejects it; and for a Christian, Scripture is the source of knowledge about how man was made regarding his body and soul. Still, Thomas provides answers to five objections, of which the third is of interest for us. It reads: "[T]he form of the human body is the soul itself, which is the breath of life. Therefore, having said, *God made man of the slime of the earth,* he should not have added: *And He breathed into him the breath of life*" (S.Th. I,91,4, 3).

The objection is built on the true premise that the formation of the human body means nothing else but bestowing on it the human form, which is the rational soul. But if this is the case, the addition stating that God breathed into the body the breath of life would seem to be redundant, or to suggest that the spiritual soul is something else than the bodily form of man. Responding to this argument, Thomas says:

> Some have thought that man's body was formed first in priority of time, and that afterwards the soul was infused into the formed body. But it is inconsistent with the perfection of the production of things, that God should have made either the body without the soul, or the soul without the body, since each is a part of human nature. This is especially unfitting as regards the body, for the body depends on the soul, and not the soul on the body (S.Th. I,91,4, ad3).

This statement excludes the concept of theistic evolution in which it is claimed that God prepared the human body by the evolutionary process, and only after the bodily element of a beast achieved the human level God infused the human soul. This is not the case in Aquinas. According to Thomas, the human body was not made before the infusion of the soul. Moreover, the idea of adding the soul only after the body was formed denies the perfection of divine work in creation. And the same problem applies to the whole evolutionary paradigm—it deprives God's creatures of their completeness in their first production and requires them to be amended and brought to their substantial (or natural) perfection by the work of evolution. This vision contradicts what the Angelic Doctor teaches.[13] Aquinas continues his response:

---

[13] Aquinas explains the perfection of creation as follows: "The perfection of a thing is twofold, the first perfection and the second perfection. The 'first' perfection is that according to which a thing is substantially perfect, and this perfection is the form of the whole;

> To remove the difficulty some have said that the words, *God made man*, must be understood of the production of the body with the soul; and that the subsequent words, *and He breathed into his face the breath of life*, should be understood of the Holy Ghost… But this explanation… is excluded by the very words of Scripture. For we read farther on, *And man was made a living soul*; which words the Apostle (1 Corinthians 15:45) refers not to spiritual life, but to animal life. Therefore, by breath of life we must understand the soul, so that the words, *He breathed into his face the breath of life*, are a sort of exposition of what goes before; for the soul is the form of the body (ibidem).

We see that according to Aquinas, the breath of life that God breathed into the body refers to the animal life (sensory life). This excludes hominization of an animal, because animal life cannot be infused into a beast that already possesses the animal life. Again, the only way to overcome this difficulty is to say that at the hominization God replaced the totality of the animal form with the human soul (special transformism). But this option was excluded in the first article, as we explained before. So, how to understand the addition "God breathed… the breath of life"? Aquinas rejects the time sequence, in the sense that "formation" and "breathing" would not happen in one moment. He also rejects the idea that formation refers to animal life, but then "breathing" refers

---

which form results from the whole having its parts complete. But the 'second' perfection is the end, which is either an operation, as the end of the harpist is to play the harp; or something that is attained by an operation, as the end of the builder is the house that he makes by building. But the first perfection is the cause of the second, because the form is the principle of operation. Now the final perfection, which is the end of the whole universe, is the perfect beatitude of the Saints at the consummation of the world; and the first perfection is the completeness of the universe at its first founding, and this is what is ascribed to the seventh day" (S.Th. I,73,1 co).

to the gift of the Holy Spirit, or any supernatural life that differentiates men from beasts. Thomas's solution is that the second part of the sentence is more like an explanation of the first—at the moment of the formation of man there happened so much that the Scripture uses two phrases to explain it; yet, this is all about one event. There is no human body without the human soul. A similar problem is observed when the soul abandons the body. Dead body—body without the soul, is not the human body. It becomes a corpse, meat, or flesh, but not the human body. The message relevant for our topic is that this article excludes all versions of theistic evolution except for special transformism.

3. AQUINAS AND THE ORIGIN OF WOMAN

When it comes to the origin of the first man, the proponents of theistic evolution have produced a few stories, out of which some (e.g., special transformism) even bear some superficial similarity to the Christian faith. As we have shown in the previous section, none of them is compatible with Aquinas's teachings or Catholic tradition before 1950.[14] But when it comes to the origin of the first woman, the problems of the evolutionary scenario dramatically increase. It is easy to say that the production of the first woman out of the first man is just a metaphor, a figure of speech. But if woman was not created of Adam's rib, how did she begin to exist? Apparently there are two possibilities: One is that the first woman was a female hominid who was endowed with the human soul right after the male hominid. This story, however, encounters the problem of disconnection between two sexes. To avoid it, some theistic evolutionists proposed that Eve was a uniovular twin of Adam, and both received the human soul at

---

[14] Regarding Catholic teaching before 1950, see *Catholicism and Evolution*, pp. 72–84.

the moment of conception. Someone could raise a biological objection that the uniovular twins are of the same sex, but this surely is not a problem for those who believe that an animal can give birth to a human. Still, this concept does not satisfy the Biblical message about the derivation of the woman from man, because we do not say that one twin is derived from the other, but rather that both come from one egg.

Theistic evolutionists encourage the believers to read Genesis metaphorically in order to find the "true" or "deeper" meaning of the text. What would be the "true" and "deeper" meaning of Eve's being formed from Adam's rib? This would probably include: the unity of human race (because Eve was derived from Adam); the equal dignity of sexes (because both were created immediately by God); the call to constitute human community in marriage and family (because they have a natural inclination to each other and because woman was created as a help for man). These are the exemplary "deeper" messages of the Biblical text. Yet, none of the stories proposed within theistic evolution actually saves all these truths.

For example, if the first woman was another hominid endowed with the soul as an adult, there is no unity of the human race or mutual dependence between the two sexes. Rather they are independent species who tend to compete. If their bodies were shaped by more or less accidental processes of the struggle for life and the survival of the fittest, there is no justification for the dignity of the human body. If humans come from animals via natural generation they are their cousins in a literal way (not just metaphorically, as a part of creation). If a man is a cousin of an ape, he is a cousin of a spider in exactly the same way as he is a cousin of another man (the difference is only in the distance of familiar kinship). If living nature is perceived as a continuum there is no room for substantial differences and ultimately no universal definition of human nature is possible. Equalizing human and animal rights (in fact, some radicals advocate more rights for animals than for man, in order to protect our "weaker cousins") is a logical consequence of accepting the evolutionary origin of species, and especially the animal origin of man. The proponents of theistic evolution believe that adding the human soul to an animal (more often they speak about a "spark of an intellect" that God dropped on a hominid) explains the substantial difference between man and the rest of animal kingdom and secures human dignity. This, however, implies that what constitutes humanity is just a soul, or an intellect added to an animal. In contrast, according to Christian tradition, a human is an entirely different substance with its rational soul and its human (not animal) body which is designed from scratch and produced directly by God to be capable of the union with the human soul. This is why only the literal and historical understanding of the origin of man, as described in Genesis and defended by Aquinas, secures those "deeper" theological truths pertaining to the human nature, dignity, and destination.

In Question 92, Aquinas explains how the first woman was created. In the *first article* he clarifies why there was the need to create the woman. In the *second article*, Thomas justifies the creation of the woman from man. The second objection in this article is of the greatest interest for us. It reads: "Therefore, as man was made of the slime of the earth, so woman should have been made of the same, and not from man" (S.Th. I,92,2, 2). In the reply, Thomas does not remove the premise of the objection, but explains it thoroughly. Matter is something of which things are made. And it is true that created nature has a determined principle according to which it has also a determined mode of proceeding (as in animal generation individuals of a given species are generated in the same way and normally achieve their own nature). For this reason, each nature produces a determined species from determined matter. But, as Thomas explains, divine power is unlimited and can produce things of the same species from different matter, such as man from the slime of the earth and woman from man. It is clear that Thomas does not understand creation of Eve from Adam as a metaphor, because he speaks about determined matter and the ability of God to transcend the ordinary works of nature. By the way, we see here a good example of Thomistic essentialism, which excludes production of one nature from another nature, because every nature acts and propagates according to the determined principle (inherent to that nature). And this idea is irreconcilable with transformation of species, because if species can mutate into other species there is neither a determined principle of their action nor determined effect of generation.

In the *third article* Thomas asks, "Whether the woman was fittingly made from the rib of man?" The first objection is based on *reductio ad absurdum*: If Eve was made of Adam's rib, there was either addition of new matter to the rib, or the rib was rarefied in order to achieve the dimension of Eve's body. If the first happened, we should not say that Eve was made of the rib, because there was more matter added than already present in the rib. The second is not possible either, because then the body of the woman would be much rarer than the body of man, and we do not see that. In his response Thomas clarifies that it is not possible to multiply matter without any addition or rarefaction. But he agrees that rarefaction is not possible in the case of Eve, so he opts for adding new matter. And this might have happened either by creation of new matter, or by conversion of other matter taken from somewhere else. Thomas says that the latter solution is more probable. Still, we say that Eve was made of the rib, because the original matter that was used was the rib. Similarly we say that Jesus fed the crowd with bread even though there was more matter added than there was in the five loaves he used. In the same way today, we say that we make pudding or instant soup from powder even though we add more matter in the form of milk or water than we have in the original powder.

In the second and the third objections Thomas deals with apparent problems arising from removing Adam's rib. The second objection says that since God's creation is perfect there was nothing superfluous in Adam's body. Hence if God removed his rib, He left him imperfect. We should not think that this is what God would have done. However, according to Thomas, Adam was created with one additional rib, and this is why removing it did not make him imperfect. The third objection is that there was no pain before sin, but removing the rib would cause pain. Thus, God did not remove Adam's rib. Thomas responds that "the rib belonged to the integral perfection of Adam, not as an individual, but as the principle of the human race; just as the semen belongs to the perfection of the begetter, and is released by a natural and pleasurable operation. Much more, therefore, was it possible that by the Divine power the body of the woman should be produced from the man's rib" (S.Th. I,92,3, ad2).

In the *fourth article* Aquinas asks "Whether the woman was formed immediately by God?" The first and the second objection against the immediate creation of woman entail the mediation of the angels and the mediation of the Augustinian "causal virtues." These were the objections that Thomas brought up when speaking about the creation of man. And here Thomas again responds that there was no active help of any creatures or any middle causes in the production of woman. The third objection is metaphysical in nature: Individuals of a given species are not made immediately by God, but rather generated from other individuals of that species. But Eve was an individual of the human species that began to exist with the creation of Adam, so she should not be created immediately by God. Aquinas responds that this is true only in natural generation. Eve, however, was not made in a natural way. Thomas explains it in the Body of the article:

> [T]he natural generation of every species is from some determinate matter. Now the matter whence man is naturally begotten is the human semen of man or woman. Wherefore from any other matter an individual of the human species cannot naturally be

generated. Now God alone, the Author of nature, can produce an effect into existence outside the ordinary course of nature. Therefore God alone could produce either a man from the slime of the earth, or a woman from the rib of man (S.Th. I,92,4, co).

There are three things stemming from this passage that contradict theistic evolution. First, generation within each species is determined regarding both the matter that takes part in generation and the effect of generation, which is an individual of the same species. Second, the formation of woman did not happen naturally. Third, there were no secondary causes in the production of woman, because only God could have made her body outside of the order of nature.

* * *

Having presented Aquinas's teaching on the origin of man, we can safely conclude that it is not possible to find in it anything else but the direct creation of the first parents regarding both their bodies and souls—man from nothing else but slime of the earth and woman from nothing else but Adam's rib. This excludes any alternative stories, including special transformism. Moreover, we have shown that Aquinas derives his teaching from Scripture. This means that he adopts literal and historical readings of the passages that speak about the origin of man. He also finds confirmation of this teaching in other parts of Scripture (e.g., the Book of Sirach). We have also established that for Aquinas special creation is the only way that the human species could have begun even in the light of philosophy alone, without revelation. Aquinas's metaphysics excludes other options because new species (new distinct natures) cannot start otherwise than by supernatural and direct divine causality. So, philosophy excludes any natural mode of human emergence as well as any active help of secondary causes, and theology (the Bible) teaches in a positive way *how* it happened. This positive historical explanation of the human origin cannot be known naturally—it must be adopted by faith. We also see that Aquinas is more certain and explicit when it comes to the origin of man than when he speaks about the origin of species in general. Still, the same metaphysical principles apply to all distinct natures. This leaves us with a vision of the origin of species quite different from that presented by Darwin and contemporary theistic evolutionists.

EXCURSUS 1: HUMAN ORIGIN IN THE 1992 CATECHISM

As we noticed above (in I,6), Thomists supporting theistic evolution oftentimes refer to modern theologians or some low-ranking statements of the recent popes. It is clear that these references do nothing to support their main thesis, because even if the current position of the Church were compatible with evolution it would not follow that Aquinas's teaching is compatible too. Given the fact of the great confusion regarding human origins, we need to add here a digression on the latest Catechism of the Catholic Church. The reason is that many scholars, including some Thomists, see in it an unambiguous support for their pro-evolutionary approach.[15] This requires a few explanations that will show that the argument "from the new Catechism" should not play any significant role in the debate.

First of all, we need to observe that the Catechism is not the same as the teaching office of the Church. The teaching bodies of the Church are the popes and the bishops. So the Church's Magisterium is represented and expressed by the bishops, who are the successors of the Apostles gathered and united under the Pope. Their teachings may be expressed through various channels (such as councils, synods,

---

[15] See, for example, *Thomistic Evolution*, pp. 165–169.

documents of the Roman congregations, and different commissions—if they are endowed with the proper authority). In order to evaluate a given piece of magisterial teaching, one needs to consider the rank of the document and its wording. It is clear that papal homilies or addresses (let alone *ad hoc* interviews) do not have the same authority as encyclicals, and these in turn, do not have the same authority as, for example, conciliar constitutions. The Church publishes Catechisms in order to summarize the magisterial teaching and present it in a concise and approachable form. They have a pastoral character. Yet catechisms do not establish or regulate any truths; they only present them. For this reason, catechisms are infallible only by the authority of the Church Magisterium, not by themselves. So, if a catechism does not represent Church teaching accurately, it contains an error, while the Church teaching remains infallible. In this case, the Catechism must be corrected, even though the Church teaching does not change. This partially explains why there is need for new catechisms over time and why corrections are added in the subsequent editions of catechisms.

Regarding the origin of man, the 1992 Catechism teaches the immediate creation of each human soul (Nos. 366 and 382). However, when it comes to the origin of the human body, it does not clearly present the case. Number 362 reads as follows:

> The human person, created in the image of God, is a being at once corporeal and spiritual. The Biblical account expresses this reality in symbolic language when it affirms that *then the Lord God formed man of dust from the ground, and breathed into his nostrils the breath of life; and man became a living being.* Man, whole and entire, is therefore willed by God.

Then, we read about the creation of the woman (No. 371):

God created man and woman together and willed each for the other. The Word of God gives us to understand this through various features of the sacred text... The woman God *fashions* from the man's rib and brings to him elicits on the man's part a cry of wonder, an exclamation of love and communion: *This at last is bone of my bones and flesh of my flesh.*

In the first passage, the Catechism says that the Biblical account (Gen 2:7) uses *symbolic language* when it says that God fashioned man from the ground. How should we understand this interpretation? We know already that neither Thomas Aquinas nor Augustine understood the Biblical account in a symbolic way. Indeed, none of the Church Fathers or Doctors of the Church understood it only symbolically.[16] Still, saying that the Biblical text confers something in a symbolic way does not exclude the literal and historical understanding. Such exclusion is implied by the Catechism, but not stated explicitly. This text may still have the literal meaning which is supplemented by the symbolic sense, according to different senses contained in the Bible. Moreover, even if the 1992 Catechism (against the whole tradition) excluded the literal and historical reading of Gen 2:7, this would only mean that one cannot make the theological argument for the special creation of the human body using Gen 2:7. It would not follow that the human body was not specially created. After all, there are many other places in the Bible that confirm special creation.[17] In our opinion, therefore, one can maintain the

---

[16] For further evidence, see *Catholicism and Evolution*, pp. 310–335.

[17] Job 10:8–9: "Your hands have made me, and fashioned me wholly round about, and do you thus cast me down headlong on a sudden? Remember, I beseech you, that you have made me out of the clay, and you will bring me into dust." (It is clear that Job himself was not produced directly by God from clay. But this does not mean that the utterance is symbolic. It is literal; however, it refers to Job only in a species-specific sense, inasmuch as he represents the human

special creation of the human body even if the Catechism (no. 362) excludes the literal reading of Gen 2:7.

In the case of the first woman, the Catechism does not quote Genesis. Instead, it only refers to its message. The word "fashion" in the context of making the woman from the rib is in the quotation marks, which again implies that this is a symbolic language, meaning that God did not literally fashion Eve from Adam's rib. The exclamation of Adam, "This at last is bone of my bones and flesh of my flesh," according to the Catechism, expresses "wonder, love and communion," which again implies that it has no realistic and historical, but only moral, psychological, or spiritual, meaning. In another place, when speaking about the gift of the Holy Spirit, the Catechism quotes St. Irenaeus: "God fashioned man with his own hands [that is, the Son and the Holy Spirit] and impressed his own form on the flesh he had fashioned, in such a way that even what was visible might bear the divine form" (No. 704). Irenaeus, of course, understands the "fashioning of the flesh" absolutely literally, as the actual means by which the first man started to exist. The Catechism, however, is not clear, because this quotation appears outside of the context of human origin. Here the closer context is the work of the Holy Spirit in creation. The quote from Irenaeus is too general to make the argument for the special creation of man and, by itself, may be interpreted symbolically. Irenaeus speaks about the special

---

species.) See also Job 33:4: "The Spirit of God has made me, and the breath of the Almighty gives me life"; Job 33:6: "Behold, I belong to God like you; I too have been formed out of the clay"; Sir 17:1: "God created man of the earth, and made him after his own image"; Wis 7:1: "I myself am a mortal man, like all others, and of the race of him, that was first made of the earth"; Ps 119:73: "Your hands have made me and formed me"; 2 Macc 7:28: "I beseech you, my son, look upon heaven and earth, and all that is in them, and consider that God made them out of nothing, and mankind also." Particularly in the last passage, the Bible emphasizes that when God creates, He does not use secondary causes. Neither does the genealogy of Jesus (Lk 3:38) introduce any intermediate creation between Adam and God.

creation of the human body very explicitly in a couple of other places,[18] but none of them is quoted by the Catechism. When teaching about the sacrament of matrimony, the Catechism again mentions that man and woman "came from the hand of the Creator" (No. 1603), but this passage, too, is quite general and leaves a lot of room for the evolutionary interpretation. For example, we do not know whether this divine work was direct or mediated. It is clear, therefore, that the Catechism is not clear. It does not say anything positive about the origin of the human body. Instead, it only suggests that Gen 2:7 is merely symbolical, not a realistic description of how man was made.

Someone can say that it is not the role of the Catechism to bring up the convictions of the Fathers of the Church or holy Doctors. The Catechism should, as we said, refer to magisterial teachings, not convictions of particular theologians, even theologians of such great stature as Aquinas or Augustine. But even this is not properly fulfilled in the 1992 Catechism when it comes to the origin of man. Unfortunately, the Catechism fails to mention at least four doctrinal documents that speak explicitly about the origin of man in a way that rules out evolution from animals. This includes the solemn confession of faith proclaimed by Pope Pelagius I in 557:

> Adam himself and his wife, were not born of other parents, but were created: one from the earth and the other from the side of the man.[19]

It is quite clear that when the Pope juxtaposes creation and generation, and then opts for creation, he does not speak in a figurative way, but rather wants to explain how the human race began to exist. Some critics could claim that this

---

[18] Irenaeus, *Adversus Haereses*, Book III, ch. 21, n. 10 (PG, Vol. 7/1, c. 954–955); Book V, ch. 3, n. 2 (PG, Vol. 7/2, c. 1129).

[19] DS 443. Cf. Denzinger-Schönmetzer, *Enchiridion Symbolorum Definitionum et Declarationum*, ed. 34 (Freiburg: Herder, 1967), p. 155, no 228a.

pronouncement dates from long before the scientific era and should not be used in contemporary debates involving advanced science. The claim is not correct, because if something is a matter of faith it cannot be disproved by scientific theories—the truths of faith, by definition, are outside of the competence of science. Geocentrism, spontaneous generation, only six thousand years of history, and similar things were never taught as matters of faith. This is why, even after Darwin, the Church kept defending the special creation of the human body. Probably the most explicit is the teaching of the synod in Cologne (1860), which declared the following:

> Our first parents were created immediately by God. Therefore we declare that the opinion of those who do not fear to assert that this human being, man as regards his body, emerged finally from the spontaneous continuous change of imperfect nature to the more perfect, is clearly opposed to Sacred Scripture and to the Faith.[20]

The decrees of the synod in Cologne were independently recognized by Pope Pius IX. Twenty years later, Pope Leo XIII confirmed the same teaching on human origins in his encyclical *Arcanum Divinae Sapientiae* (1880):

> We record what is to all known, and cannot be doubted by any, that God, on the sixth day of creation, having made man from the slime of the earth, and having breathed into his face the breath of life, gave him a companion, whom He miraculously took from the side of Adam when he was locked in sleep.[21]

---

[20] *Acta et decreta Concilii Provinciae Coloniensis* (Coloniae: 1862), p. 30.
[21] Leo XIII, *Arcanum divinae sapientiae* in *AAS*, 12 (1879; reprint 1968), p. 386.

Another few decades later (1909), the Pontifical Biblical Commission (PBC) established that the special creation of man (*peculiaris creatio hominis*) and the formation of the first woman out of the first man (*formatio primae mulieris ex primo homine*) cannot be doubted as *historical* and *literal* truths contained in Genesis. It is important to note that at that time the PBC enjoyed a higher authority than today—it was a teaching organ of the Church, answering Biblical questions on behalf of the Pope. Thus, those early pronouncements of the PBC constitute a valid and never-revoked voice of the Magisterium.[22] It is also worth noting that the Synod of Cologne and the 1909 Decree of PBC teach explicitly the opposite of what is implied by No. 362 of the 1992 Catechism. Along the lines of the PBC 1909 decree, there is a statement of Pope Pius XII. In his Address to the Pontifical Academy of Sciences (1941), the Pope says that "only from man could there come another man who would then call him father and ancestor." By this the Pope excludes the possibility of man descending from a nonhuman ancestor.

Not surprisingly, the same teaching about the origin of the human body is found in the first Catechism of the Catholic Church (published in 1566) as well as all other catechisms before 1950 (if they addressed the problem of the origin of man).[23]

---

[22] For further justification of this claim, see *Catholicism and Evolution*, pp. 162–167.

[23] The first Catechism (of Pius V) states: "God not only clothed and adorned the earth with trees and every variety of plant and flower, but filled it, as He had already filled the air and water, with innumerable kinds of living creatures. Lastly, He formed man from the slime of the earth, so created and constituted in body as to be immortal and impassible... Man's soul He created to His own image and likeness." One of the local Catechisms—The Baltimore Catechism, No. 4—is probably the most explicit of all: "On the sixth day God created man and called him Adam... God could have made Eve as He made Adam, by forming her body out of the clay of the earth and breathing into it a soul, but He made Eve out of Adam's rib to show that they were to be husband and wife."

None of these magisterial teachings is mentioned—not even in the footnotes—of the 1992 Catechism. In our opinion, therefore, the new Catechism does not correctly represent the Catholic faith regarding the origin of the human body as it has been expressed in ecclesiastical documents throughout the ages.

When it comes to the origin of the human soul, the Catechism speaks about its immediate creation by God. However, it does not say that the human soul is created at the moment of conception. The authors of the Catechism probably did not want to overstate the case. In fact, there was a lot of controversy around the origin of the human soul throughout the centuries—not over the *direct creation* of the human soul, but over the time *when that direct creation happens*.[24] Most theologians, including Aquinas (who followed Aristotle) believed that the rational soul starts organizing the human body only when the body reaches a certain level of the organic development, allowing the soul to actualize all her functions. For Aquinas and the scholastics it was not the moment of conception, but a few weeks later, during embryonic development.[25] Over a period

---

[24] For the sake of accuracy it is necessary to clarify here that there are two aspects of the origin of the human soul. The first refers to the creation of the first human soul as a new substance. The second is the creation of each individual soul at the origin of each individual man. Regarding the first aspect—it is true that no Christian author questioned the direct creation of the human soul. But the moment when it happens was understood differently. For example, Augustine supported the "pre-existence of the souls," that is, their creation at the first act of creation by God. According to this view, souls created at the beginning later on join the subsequent human bodies conceived in human procreation. This view was shared by a minority and ultimately was abandoned in ecclesiastical thought. When it comes to the second aspect (the origin of each individual soul), for a few centuries there was a popular view called "traducianism": the idea (supported even by Tertullian) that the human soul is produced by the parents in the same way they produce the body, that is, as a consequence of their physical unification. This view was rejected by the majority of Tradition and the Church.

[25] M. L. Condic and K. L. Flannery, S.J. successfully (in our opinion) explain that the contemporary understanding of ensoulment as

of centuries, Catholic theologians became more and more inclined to recognize the creation of each rational soul at the moment of conception.²⁶ Regardless of the current state of the discussion, there is definitely more willingness among scholars

---

taking place at conception does not conflict with Aristotelian metaphysical principles, especially the principle that there cannot be a function of the soul without an organic element in the body corresponding to that function. According to these authors, the Aristotelian theory of three subsequent souls in the human embryonic development resulted from a lack of knowledge about the human embryo. The authors claim that contemporary biology yields evidence that the embryo, from the very beginning, possesses the material element necessary for the ultimate development and, by implication, for the rational soul. See M. L. Condic and K. L. Flannery, "A Contemporary Aristotelian Embryology," *Nova et Vetera*, Vol. 12, No. 2 (2014), pp. 495–508. This, however, does not diminish the fact that Aristotle's specific teaching on ensoulment negatively influenced Christianity for many centuries and hindered the proper understanding of human generation with respect to the rational soul.

[26] In the encyclical *Evangelium Vitae* (1995), Pope John Paul II does not state explicitly that the human soul is created immediately by God at the moment of conception. In one place the Pope seems to imply it when he writes: "In procreation therefore, through the communication of life from parents to child, God's own image and likeness is transmitted, thanks to the creation of the immortal soul" (No. 43). The Pope uses the phrase "immortal soul," but this must refer to the rational soul, because only the rational soul is an immortal soul. No. 60 reads: "Over and above all scientific debates and those philosophical affirmations to which the Magisterium has not expressly committed itself, the Church has always taught and continues to teach that the result of human procreation, from the first moment of its existence, must be guaranteed that unconditional respect which is morally due to the human being in his or her totality and unity as body and spirit: The human being is to be respected and treated as a person from the moment of conception; and therefore from that same moment his rights as a person must be recognized, among which in the first place is the inviolable right of every innocent human being to life." Again the Pope does not speak about the creation of the rational soul at the moment of conception but rather about the necessity of treating the result of human procreation as a human being from the very beginning.

to present the creation of each human soul at the moment of conception as the Catholic position. This development could not be included in the Catechism due to the fact that it has not been officially confirmed by the Magisterium.

Nevertheless, the 1992 Catechism nearly misrepresents the teaching on the origin of the human body. As we showed (in IV,1), the special creation of the human body was implicitly abandoned by Pius XII in his 1950 encyclical *Humani Generis*. It is doubtful, however, that *Humani Generis* could overturn the explicit teaching of all previous more authoritative documents. Even so, the 1992 Catechism does not make any reference to *Humani Generis* when speaking about human origins. This leaves us with an impression that the editors of the Catechism really did not know how to present the problem. On the one hand, they had the overwhelming tradition and the authority of Church documents favoring the special creation of the human body; on the other, they faced the alleged "scientific evidence" and the strong *conviction* of scientific and theological communities defending the evolutionary paradigm. In this context, they decided to present the teaching that would satisfy all parties, or at least that would not provoke a controversy by challenging the "scientific consensus." In our opinion, however, the Catechism should at least make it clear that there is a controversy, mention the older teaching, and perhaps explain that the Church is currently confounded (if this is the case).[27] Otherwise, the Catechism is vague and leaves room for abuse by any party. And this is what is being done by those Thomists who appeal to the Catechism in order to defend their evolutionary interpretation of Aquinas.

---

[27] For example, J. A. Hardon, S.J., in a private catechism published in 1981, makes an attempt to show the evolution of Catholic teaching on the origin of man. Although Hardon also fails to mention the relevant documents, his approach at least points out the fact of the existing controversy. See J. A. Hardon, *The Catholic Catechism: A Contemporary Catechism of the Teachings of the Catholic Church* (New York: Image Books, 1981), pp. 91–96.

CHAPTER V:
AQUINAS AND INTELLIGENT DESIGN

Before we start our inquiry into the theory of intelligent design (ID) we need to ensure we understand the term correctly. Intelligent design may be considered, in a general way, as any conclusion about the presence of an intentional order in the universe derived from the features of the universe alone. This type of reasoning constitutes a premise in arguments for the existence of God and specifically the minor premise in Aquinas's Fifth Way (see the *corpus* of this chapter). In this sense, intelligent design refers to *any argument that concludes the necessity of the existence of a designer* derived from an observation of the universe. But this is not how we understand intelligent design in this chapter. Our understanding is more specific. It does not reach the conclusion about the existence of God; nor does it refer to natural bodies (*corpora naturalia*) in general, but only to some highly specified and information-rich organic structures. Our definition of ID reads:

> The theory of intelligent design holds that certain features of the universe and of living things are best explained by an intelligent cause, not undirected processes (such as natural selection) or the laws of nature alone.[1]

The question we are addressing in this chapter is not whether Aquinas believed in intelligent design in this scientific

---

[1] This is a slightly modified version of the definition found on the intelligentdesign.org website associated with the Discovery Institute. See https://intelligentdesign.org/whatisid/ (accessed 13 January 2019).

sense, but rather whether or not his teaching and his own arguments for God's existence exclude the theory of intelligent design. Surely, Aquinas could not have known ID in the contemporary scientific sense, because he did not know modern science. However, the "Thomistic" critics of ID do not say that ID is just different from Aquinas. They claim that ID is excluded by Thomism, or that ID distorts design arguments as presented by Aquinas. Hence, our first goal is to prove that ID is not contradictory to Aquinas's teachings. It does not follow that ID is reducible to Aquinas's design argument—lack of contradiction does not entail identity, and lack of identity does not entail incompatibility. Hence, our second goal is to show the *supplementary* character of both arguments. In order to do so, we will need to go beyond the teachings of Aquinas wherever the answer to the objection requires it.

1. IT SEEMS THAT AQUINAS'S TEACHING EXCLUDES ID (OBJECTIONS)

1. ID is the "god of the gaps" type of argument

ID proponents say something like this: "Here is something science hasn't yet explained; probably God is the explanation." But this argument will be disproven when science discovers the cause of the thing. Hence, ID inserts intelligent causation into the current gaps in scientific knowledge. With the progress of science, ID explanations will disappear, with a detriment to religion and belief in God.[2]

---

[2] M. W. Tkacz, "Aquinas vs. Intelligent Design," https://www.catholic.com/magazine/print-edition/aquinas-vs-intelligent-design (accessed 13 March 2019); E. Feser, *The Last Superstition* (South Bend, Indiana: Saint Augustine's Press, 2008), pp. 81, 113; M. Shea, "Intelligent Design vs. the Argument from Design," http://www.ncregister.com/blog/mark-shea/intelligent-design-vs.-the-argument-from-design/#ixzz4DE85uK6v (accessed 6 June 2016); G. M. Verschuuren, op. cit., pp. 169–170.

2. ID is an argument from ignorance

"[T]he biologists' current ignorance of how certain biological features have arisen does not establish that these features arose through non-natural processes."[3] In other words, a lack of natural explanation cannot be an argument for ID.

3. ID can be disproven in the future

Since the argument for intelligent design rests on irreducible and specified complexity, if it were shown that the emergence of structures bearing these two characteristics can be explained by some natural process or law then intelligent design would be disproven. Hence, ID should not be pursued, because it may be disproven in the future by the progress of science. In contrast, the Thomistic arguments for design do not rest upon those notions, and therefore cannot be disproven by future scientific discovery. Moreover, in the Thomistic perspective, one expects to find laws of nature that would explain the emergence of new organs, including those that are irreducibly complex. Further, for Thomists the newly discovered laws would be nothing but another evidence for design.[4]

---

[3] This common argument against ID is reported and discussed by M. George, in "Thomistic Rebuttal of Some Common Objections to Paley's Argument from Design," *New Blackfriars*, Vol. 97, No. 1069, May 2016, p. 285, doi:10.1111/nbfr.12187. See also W. Newton's previously cited "A Case of Mistaken Identity: Aquinas's Fifth Way and Arguments of Intelligent Design," p. 571.

[4] F. J. Beckwith, "Intelligent Design, Thomas Aquinas, and The Ubiquity of Final Causes," p. 6, https://biologos.org/uploads/projects/beckwith_scholarly_essay.pdf (accessed 7 July 2016); Feser, *The Last Superstition*, p. 113. M. George claims that the weak point of Dembski's argument for ID is that it has a theoretical character (in a scientific sense) and thus can be disproven in the future as any other theory. See her previously cited "What Would Thomas Aquinas Say about Intelligent Design?," p. 679.

4. ID is mechanistic

Some of the intelligent design arguments use the analogy between human machines and biological structures. For example, Michael Behe explains irreducible complexity using the example of a mouse trap, and he compares the bacterial flagellum to the boat engine with its propeller. But this reduces organisms to machines and implies that they can be fully explained in terms of physics and chemistry. "ID advocates assume the very mechanistic philosophy of nature that drove both Paley and his atheist critics."[5] This is not how Aquinas sees living beings. For him every living organism constitutes a unity organized by a substantial form. Hence, according to Aquinas, a living being is not reducible to its parts and cannot be explained without reference to the immaterial form.[6]

5. ID diminishes the Thomistic argument for design

If design is discernible through specified complexity and irreducible complexity, it is not discernible where these two do not exist. "For Behe and Dembski no design inference about nature is warranted short of achieving that threshold of

---

[5] Beckwith, "Intelligent Design, Thomas Aquinas, and the Ubiquity of Final Causes," p. 6.

[6] Cf. M. Ryland, op. cit., p. 55. Similarly, Edward Feser writes: "Both Paleyan *design arguments* and ID theory take for granted an essentially mechanistic conception of the natural world. What this means is that they deny the existence of the sort of immanent teleology or final causality affirmed by the Aristotelian-Thomistic-Scholastic tradition, and instead regard all teleology as imposed, *artificially* as it were, from outside." (E. Feser, "The Trouble with William Paley," November 4, 2009, http://edwardfeser.blogspot.com/2009/11/trouble-with-william-paley.html, accessed 9 July 2016). W. Newton presents a variant of this argument: Comparing complex organisms to machines (such as watches and mousetraps) is unacceptable because "watches are artifacts whereas an eye is a natural substance." According to Newton, "Aquinas would balk at comparing eyes to watches" (W. Newton, op. cit., p. 575). Yet, this is exactly what Aquinas does in S.Th. I-II,13,2, ad3 and other places (see the "*Sed contras*" in this section).

irreducible or specified complexity."⁷ Thomists, however, recognize design in cosmic fine-tuning (CFT), in laws of nature, as well as in any teleological arrangements of the elements. Hence, ID excludes the Thomistic argument for design.

6. ID, unlike Aquinas, denies the role of chance

"Intelligent design arguments, like those mounted by Behe and Dembski, concede a premise that should never be conceded and that Aquinas would certainly not concede. The whole logic of the argument is built upon the premise—shared by materialists—that if chance is a significant element in the evolution of species then God's involvement in directing the development of species must be discounted... God might just as easily cause events (like the development of species) by chance as by regular predicable sequences of causes."⁸

7. "Design is everywhere"

Thomas speaks about "things which lack intelligence, such as natural bodies," and he concludes: "[S]ome intelligent being exists by whom all natural things are directed to their end; and this being we call God." Therefore, everything in nature is designed by God (for that matter, everything that exists). Hence, there is no reason to detect design.⁹

---

⁷ F. J. Beckwith, op. cit., pp. 4, 6; G. M. Verschuuren, op. cit., p. 169.

⁸ W. Newton, op. cit., pp. 574–575.

⁹ S. Barr, "The End of Intelligent Design?," *First Things*, 2 October 2010, http://www.firstthings.com/web-exclusives/2010/02/the-end-of-intelligent-design (accessed 5 July 2016); Verschuuren, op. cit., p. 171. E. Feser declares: "There is absolutely nothing in this argument [the Fifth Way] that has to do with the allegedly *irreducible complexity* of eyeballs... Even if the universe consisted of nothing but an electron orbiting a nucleus, that would suffice for the Fifth Way." (E. Feser, *The Last Superstition*, p. 116.) F. Beckwith makes a similar point: "For St. Thomas, the design or purpose of nature refers to the interrelationship of *all things* in the universe, including scientific laws and all inanimate and animate things and their powers..." See Beckwith, "Intelligent Design and Me, Part 2: Confessions

8. ID is not science

Science is defined according to three aspects: the object (subject matter), the method, and the goal. (1) The object of science is nothing but physical reality. (2) The method of science is observation and experiment, which deals with particular physical structures and/or events. (3) The goal of science is to find the natural—material and efficient—causes of physical structures and events. This is called the principle of methodological naturalism. Now, all of this is denied in the theory of intelligent design. (1) The object is not scientific, because intelligence is not a physical reality and thus transcends the object of science. (2) The method is not that of science, because intelligence is immaterial and eludes observation and experiment. (3) The goal of ID is also non-scientific, and this for a few reasons. First, since intelligence is immaterial, it cannot be the material cause of anything. Thus ID is non-scientific, because its goal is to detect an immaterial cause. And if intelligence is the efficient cause then—also owing to it being immaterial—it is unaccountable for in terms of mechanism or any physical process. Moreover, intelligence implies final causes, because every mind works for the sake of a goal, whereas science is not concerned with final causes. Additionally, if intelligence were the cause of things in nature, it would be a universal cause, whereas science looks for particular and immediate causes. Moreover, ID violates the principle of methodological naturalism by proposing a supernatural cause of physical objects. Therefore, ID theory is not scientific.

9. ID is anti-scientific

Intelligent design excludes scientific explanations of natural phenomena and replaces them with the evidence for God's existence. "Science must fail for ID to succeed. In the famous

---

of a Doting Thomist," BioLogos, 20 March 2010, http://biologos. org/blogs/archive/intelligent-design-and-me-part-2-confessions-of-a-doting-thomist#sthash.1g2YeG6H.dpuf (accessed 9 July 2016).

explanatory filter of William A. Dembski, one detects *design* by eliminating *law* and *chance* as explanations. This, in effect, makes it a zero-sum game between God and nature. What nature does and science can explain is crossed off the list, and what remains is the evidence for God. This conception of design plays right into the hands of atheists, whose caricature of religion has always been that it is a substitute for the scientific understanding of nature."[10]

10. ID is anti-metaphysical

Intelligent design does not appeal to classical metaphysical notions, such as final cause or the nature of a thing. Yet the universe cannot be fully explained without employing these notions. Therefore, ID adopts the approach which is characteristic of materialistic and atheistic scientists, rejects classical metaphysics and, by doing so, implements reductionism in biology.[11]

11. ID implies interventionism

Intelligent design implies that God needs to occasionally work in a direct way in nature in order to fill in the discontinuities in the physical processes. This is an interventionist view of

---

[10] S. Barr, "The End of Intelligent Design?," previously cited.

[11] E. Feser, "The Trouble with William Paley," cited above. M. Ryland even claims that ID falls into the same errors as neo-Darwinism: "In some respects, standard reductionist neo-Darwinism and IDT [intelligent design theory] are mirror images of each other and suffer some of the same defects. Both arise in an intellectual culture plagued by scientism and thus reject any serious role in the design debate for philosophy. Both reject (or ignore) substantial form and final causality, thus accepting a mechanistic conception of nature. Both share a commitment to an understanding of nature that opposes law and design, that excludes intrinsic teleology of finality, and thus both draw an absolute distinction between the concept of nature and that of intelligence." (M. Ryland, op. cit., p. 55.)

nature, which denies the "functional integrity of creation."[12] "Thomism provides a corrective to the ID theorists who claim that the lack of certain kinds of explanation in natural science shows the necessity of divine intervention into nature as a substitute for natural cause."[13]

12. ID implies direct divine causation

ID proponents resort to direct divine causation in explaining biodiversity, whereas Paley and the Thomists can accommodate mediated causation. "Unlike ID thinkers, Paley [like the Thomists[14]] sees that the causes immediately responsible for the production of something whose parts are ordered to achieve a goal need not also be responsible for this very ordering… ID thinkers fail to make this distinction, as their reasoning is based on the false dichotomy that either blind natural causes produce a result or intelligent ones do so… Paley would not be fazed if he were to become acquainted

---

[12] The idea of creation's functional integrity was developed by Howard Van Till. He defines it as follows: "The creation was gifted from the outset with functional integrity—a wholeness of being that eliminated the need for gap-bridging interventions to compensate for formational capabilities that the Creator may have initially withheld from it." H. Van Till, quoted at: http://www.asa3.org/ASA/education/origins/methods-hvt.htm (accessed 9 July 2016). Idem, "Basil, Augustine, and the Doctrine of Creation's Functional Integrity," *Science & Christian Belief* 8, No. 1 (1996), pp. 21–38, http://www.asa3.org/ASA/topics/Evolution/S&CB4-96VanTill.html#1 (accessed 9 July 2016). Van Till believes that according to ID: "Some non-natural action (called acts of "intelligent design") must, it is claimed, supplement natural processes in order to accomplish certain formational feats that natural action alone presumably could not." Idem, "Is the Creation a 'Right Stuff' Universe?," *Perspectives on Science and Christian Faith*, Volume 54, No 4, December 2002, pp. 232–239, 236 n.

[13] M. W. Tkacz, "Aquinas vs. Intelligent Design," http://www.catholic.com/magazine/articles/aquinas-vs-intelligent-design (accessed 9 July 2016). Cf. G.M. Verschuuren, op. cit., p. 166–169.

[14] Even though the author defends Paley, her paper is entitled "Thomistic rebuttal" which implies that Thomists would concur with her defense. For reference see the next footnote.

with evolutionary explanations of how organic features arose, for he maintains that while blind causes can explain the production of an effect which is ordered, they cannot explain the order in the effect."[15]

13. ID implies that design is externally imposed on nature
According to the theory of intelligent design, design is externally imposed on nature by an external mind. In the Thomistic tradition, however, design is immanent in nature.[16]

14. ID does not prove the existence of the Christian God
ID may prove the existence of some god, but it is not the God of Christianity.[17]

---

[15] M. George, "Thomistic Rebuttal of Some Common Objections to Paley's Argument From Design," pp. 284–285.

[16] E. Feser, "'Intelligent Design' Theory and Mechanism" (10 April 2010), http://edwardfeser.blogspot.com/2010/04/intelligent-design-theory-and-mechanism.html (accessed 9 July 2016). In another place Feser files the same argument against W. Paley. Feser does not seem to see a difference between Paley's arguments and that of ID. See E. Feser, "Between Aristotle and William Paley: Aquinas's Fifth Way," *Nova et Vetera*, Summer 2013, Vol. 11, No. 3, pp. 740–749, esp. p. 742. See also E. Feser, "The Trouble with William Paley." F. Beckwith explains it in this way: "According to Dembski, we discover design in nature after we have eliminated chance and law. And we do so by a conceptual device he calls the explanatory filter. If something in nature exhibits a high level of specified complexity for which chance and law cannot account, Dembski concludes that it is highly probable that the gap is the result of an intelligent agent. Design, therefore, is not immanent in nature. It is something that is imposed on nature by someone or something outside it." We do not know, however, how Beckwith draws this conclusion from the premises he provides. (See F. Beckwith, "Intelligent Design and Me, Part 2: Confessions of a Doting Thomist," cited above.)

[17] E. Feser, "Between Aristotle and William Paley: Aquinas's Fifth Way," p. 746; idem, "The Trouble with William Paley."

15. ID reduces God to merely one among the natural causes

Since intelligent design is a theory of nature, it should speak about natural causes in the universe. But if this is the case, the intelligence to which ID appeals is merely one of the causes operating in the universe. Christianity, however, identifies the Author of design in biology with God, who is no part of nature. Therefore, ID reduces God to one among many natural causes. As one Thomistic critic of ID puts it: "According to Thomism [and in contrast to ID], God is indeed the Author of nature, but as its transcendent ultimate cause, not as another natural cause alongside the other natural causes."[18]

16. ID is creationism, therefore it is neither Catholic nor scientific.

Science speaks about natural causes of the natural phenomena. Creationism, however, is a religious doctrine that speaks about supernatural causes of the natural phenomena. Since ID is creationism it cannot be science.[19] And for the same reason it cannot be a Catholic position, because the Church accepts theistic evolution, which contradicts creationism.

Sed contra:

1. Aquinas teaches: "[T]hat which results from the action of an agent, but apart from the intention of the agent, is said to happen by chance or by luck. But we observe that what happens in the workings of nature is either always, or mostly, for the better. Thus, in the plant world leaves are arranged so as to protect the fruit, and among animals the bodily organs

---

[18] W. Tkacz, "Aquinas vs. Intelligent Design," http://www.catholic.com/magazine/articles/aquinas-vs-intelligent-design (accessed 9 July 2016).

[19] ID is commonly misrepresented by both popular media (such as Wikipedia) and academic sources as creationism. B. Forrest even uses the name "intelligent design creationism." See B. Forrest, "The Non-Epistemology of Intelligent Design: Its Implications for Public Policy," *Synthese* 178 (2011), pp. 331–379, esp. p. 332.

are disposed in such a way that the animal can be protected. So, if this came about apart from the intention of the natural agent, it would be by chance or by luck. But this is impossible, for things which occur always, or for the most part, are neither chance nor fortuitous events, but only those which occur in few instances" (ScG III,3,9). It follows that the arrangement of parts in animals and plants is not caused by chance, but instead comes from the intention of an agent. This is not contradictory to saying that some organic structures are not explainable by chance, but need to be explained by intelligent causality.

2. In another place Aquinas teaches: "[Empedocles] asserted that it was by accident and as if through friendship that the parts of animals came together in such a way that the animal could live. This was his explanation of a frequent occurrence. This explanation, however, cannot be true, because those things that happen by chance, happen only rarely. But we see harmony and usefulness in nature either at all times or at least for the most part. This cannot be the result of chance; it must be because an end is intended. What lacks intellect or knowledge, however, cannot tend directly toward an end. It can do this only if someone else's knowledge has established an end for it, and directs it to that end. Consequently, since natural things have no knowledge, there must be some previously existing intelligence directing them to an end, like an archer who gives a definite motion to an arrow so that it will wing its way to a determined end. Now, the hit made by the arrow is said to be the work not of the arrow alone but also of the person who shot it. Similarly, philosophers call every work of nature the work of intelligence" (*De Veritate*, q. 5 a. 2 co). It follows that the parts of a plant or an animal cannot achieve their goal, which is to constitute one organism, by chance; they require an intelligent agent. And it does not matter for the argument whether the design is immanent or externally imposed, neither does it matter (for the argument) whether

the intelligent agent acts directly or indirectly. This is compatible with intelligent design, to say that some features of living beings must be attributed to intelligent causality regardless of what the intelligence is and how it works.

3. Aquinas teaches: "[I]n all things moved by reason, the order of reason which moves them is evident, although the things themselves are without reason; for an arrow through the motion of the archer goes straight towards the target, as though it were endowed with reason to direct its course. The same may be seen in the movements of clocks and all devices put together by the art of man. *Now as artificial things are in comparison to human art, so are all natural things in comparison to the Divine art.* And accordingly order is to be seen in things moved by nature, just as in things moved by reason" (S.Th. I-II,13,2, ad3). And in another place: "A wise artificer, arranging the parts [of his work], takes into consideration not only the good of the individual parts, but the good of the whole even more. For this reason a builder does not make all parts of a house equally valuable, but gives them greater or lesser importance inasmuch as this is required for the good disposition of the house. Likewise, in an animal's body, not all parts have the transparency of the eye… In the same way, God, in His wisdom, did not make all things in the universe of equal worth, because if He had, the universe, lacking many grades of being, would be imperfect" (*Quaestiones Disputatae de Anima*, art. 7, co). From both passages it follows that it is possible to build the analogy between a human designer and the divine designer. It is also possible to compare natural designs (such as animals) to human designs (artifacts). This confirms the method of ID, where the conclusion about intelligent causation in organic structures is derived from the comparison to human-designed machines.

2. AQUINAS AND INTELLIGENT DESIGN (*CORPUS*)

I answer that,
Since Aquinas did not know modern science he could not have had the notion of intelligent design in its currently proposed form. Therefore, it is impossible to show Aquinas teaching ID. Still, it is possible to demonstrate at least two things: one, the compatibility between Aquinas's philosophical principles and the scientific theory of intelligent design, and the other, the complementary nature of intelligent design and Thomas's argument for God's existence as he presents it in the Fifth Way. In order to demonstrate these two points we will go through four steps, out of which the first three address the first point and the fourth step addresses the second point.

The first step needed to understand Aquinas and ID is to acknowledge that there are three independent (not isolated) levels of knowledge—natural science, philosophy, and theology. Those who do not recognize the autonomy of science from philosophy will never understand the theory of intelligent design. The three levels of knowledge differ according to their object (subject matter), method, and goal. The primary object of theology is God (Aquinas uses the term "subject" [*subiectum*] in this context, since God can hardly be an object of anything). The secondary object of theology is the material universe considered with respect to God. Theology derives its premises from revealed sources. Hence, its main "data" or "input premises" are unattainable by human reason—they are known thanks to the supernatural knowledge revealed to humans by God. In contrast, philosophy deals with God and the universe (material and immaterial), but it derives its conclusions from natural experience (e.g., the experience of nature) and natural reason operating on the first principles of cognition (*prima principia cognitionis*). Philosophy deals with being as such, comprehended on the most abstract level without employing supernatural premises. Science, in turn, deals only with the material universe, looking for regularities and laws.

Thus, science deals with particular beings, whereas philosophy deals with being as such; science looks for particular causes of material phenomena, whereas philosophy looks for ultimate causes of all phenomena. Science, like philosophy, does not employ any supernaturally revealed premises, but, in contrast to philosophy, it does not look for the *Archē* (the Principle) of all reality, but only for explanations of given regularities and effects in the material realm. Hence, it is not the goal of science to explain the whole of reality, but only to discover the proper (or secondary) causes of different physical objects and events.

Now, owing to the fact that intelligent design remains within the level of science, it is not its goal to explain the whole of reality by finding one principle of everything. Neither is it possible for ID to reach beyond the physical universe in order to establish the ultimate source of all being or the existence of God. Intelligent design explains the causes of some natural phenomena. The ID theory adds a third explanatory factor to the two commonly recognized in science, that is, chance and necessity. This third factor is intelligence. Yet, answering the questions regarding the nature of intelligence—such as whether it is supernatural or natural, eternal or temporal, one or many, personal or impersonal, omnipotent or limited—does not fall in the domain of intelligent design because it is not proper to science. For science it is enough to recognize whether a given physical structure or event is best explained by chance, necessity or intelligence. To explain the nature of chance, necessity, or intelligence is a task of another level of knowledge, such as philosophy. Hence, ID does not speak about a designer, but only about the ability of science to discover intelligent causation in some physical structures and events.

Having explained the distinctions among the three levels of human knowledge (science, philosophy, and theology) and having placed ID at the level of science, we can now move on to *the second step*, which is the distinction between the *articles* of faith and the *preambles* of faith. According to Aquinas, some things about God and the universe that are otherwise supernaturally revealed, can be discovered by natural reason (i.e., without the help of supernatural revelation).[20] The classic example is the existence of God. Man can know that God exists based on the observation of nature, by drawing more general conclusions about the ultimate cause of everything. This is an example of the philosophical reasoning (preamble of faith) that enables humans to discover the article of faith saying that there is God. Similarly, man can know naturally divine attributes, such as that God is one, that He is eternal, omnipotent, etc. All of these are the preambles of faith. In contrast, man cannot discover by natural reasoning that God is the Trinity of Persons. This truth must be revealed to humans supernaturally by God. There is also another set of preambles of faith, namely those regarding the universe. For example, man can know by natural reason that the universe is not a self-sufficient entity. Rather it requires some self-sufficient and unchanging being to keep it in existence. Hence, the fact that the universe is dependent on God can be known without revelation, but the fact that the universe was created out of nothing at the beginning of time cannot be deduced from observing the universe. This latter truth, even though it concerns not God but the physical universe, must be revealed to humans by God. Since philosophy uses only natural reason, the preambles of faith are at the level of philosophy, whereas the articles of faith belong to theology. Still, Aquinas maintains that the preambles of faith can also be learned from divine revelation, especially by

---

[20] "In sacred doctrine we are able to make a threefold use of philosophy: First, to demonstrate those truths that are preambles of faith and that have a necessary place in the science of faith. Such are the truths about God that can be proved by natural reason—that God exists, that God is one; such truths about God or about His creatures, subject to philosophical proof, faith presupposes. Secondly..." (*Super De Trinitate*, Pars 1, q.2, a.3, co.3).

those people who are unable to deduce them from observing nature (S.Th. I,2,2, ad1).

Now, intelligent design may be considered in a broad (general) or in a strict sense. Considered in a general sense, intelligent design may be seen as falling in with the second type of preambles of faith, that is, the truths concerning not God, but the universe. Reason alone tells us that the universe is not chaotic. Instead, it is intelligently designed. The evidence for this is that the universe consists of many parts working toward their goals even though they do not have cognition. This means that they must have been ordered by some higher mind that organized all parts in such a way that they fulfill their tasks. This is the premise operating in Aquinas's argument for God's existence known as the Fifth Way. The theory of intelligent design considered in a strict sense is more specific—it does not speak about the universe as a whole, but rather about particular structures or events in biology. Hence ID, taken strictly, is not among the preambles of faith even in the second sense (truths regarding the universe). This fact is coherent with the scientific character of ID: Since ID is not philosophy, it cannot be a preamble of faith, because the preambles of faith are at the level of philosophy. Nevertheless, intelligent design may be seen as the *preamble to the preambles* of faith. ID relates to the preambles of faith in the same way as the preambles of faith relate to the articles of faith. Similarly, science relates to philosophy in the same way as philosophy relates to theology. Thus the conclusion about intelligent design in science opens science to philosophy as much as the conclusion about God's existence in philosophy opens the natural mind to the supernatural truths of faith conveyed by theology. The philosophical arguments for God's existence and the scientific claims about intelligence as the best explanation for some natural structures and/or events constitute two independent arguments (they remain on different levels of knowledge), but at the same time they are entirely compatible and—at least in the Christian perspective—they are complementary.

The third step is the distinction between two types of arguments—the *design argument* and *design inference*.[21] The first is the domain of classical philosophy, whereas the second belongs to science. The design argument may be presented in the form of the following syllogism:

(1) Everything that is designed must have a designer.
(2) The universe is designed.
(3) Therefore, the designer of the universe exists.

Design inference takes the form of a different syllogism that may be phrased like this:

(1) Everything that has certain characteristics indicating design is actually designed.
(2) Some elements in the natural world bear these characteristics.
(3) Therefore, some elements of the universe are designed.

The logic of all classical arguments for God's existence derived from the order in the universe is expressed by the first syllogism. Intelligent design, however, follows the logic of the second syllogism. It neither concludes with the existence of God nor provides any characteristics of the designer. The "metaphysical" claim of the ID theory is quite modest; it takes us to the conclusion that some structures/events belonging to physical reality cannot be attributed to either chance or necessity. They are explainable only by reference to intelligence, or intelligent causality. The nature of that intelligence would be an interesting subject for further philosophical and theological investigations, but this does not belong to ID theory itself.

The following table (Table 2) summarizes the first three steps by showing how intelligent design supplements and differs from classical philosophy and theology:

---

[21] The author of this distinction is W. Dembski. See his book *The Design Revolution* (IVP Press, 2010), pp. 75–77.

LEVELS OF KNOWLEDGE	PARTICULAR DISCIPLINES (examples)		PARTICULAR CONCEPTS WITHIN THE DISCIPLINES (examples)	THE ORDER OF DEPENDENCE
THEOLOGY	REFERRING TO GOD	-Treatise on God	-God is one and omnipotent -God is the Trinity of Persons	The articles of faith
	REFERRING TO THE UNIVERSE	-Treatise on creation	-creation out of nothing -the work of distinction and adornment -special creation of the human body	
PHILOSOPHY	REFERRING TO GOD	-Natural theology	-God is one and omnipotent -God is unchangeable	The preambles of faith
	REFERRING TO THE UNIVERSE	-Philosophy of nature	-the universe is not self-sufficient, but dependent on a self-sufficient being -natural bodies are ordered toward their goals	
SCIENCE	REFERRING TO GOD	X	X	The preambles to the preambles of faith
	REFERRING TO THE UNIVERSE	-The theory of intelligent design	-irreducible complexity -specified complexity -design inference	

Table 2. The place of intelligent design theory with respect to the three levels of the human knowledge, disciplines within each level, and different concepts within each discipline. On the level of science the field including disciplines whose subject is God is empty, because God (as well as any invisible reality) transcends the scope of science. No natural science addresses the supernatural realm.

The fourth step needed to understand the relation between ID and Aquinas's teaching is to comprehend the relation between the argument for design as presented in ID and Aquinas's argument for God's existence in the Fifth Way (*ex gubernatione rerum*). Aquinas's argument in the Fifth Way may be phrased as follows:

(1) Everything that acts toward a goal must be directed by a mind.
(2) Natural bodies have no cognition; therefore they cannot direct themselves to a goal.
(3) Natural bodies always (or almost always) achieve their goals.
(4) Therefore, they do not act accidentally and there must be a mind that directs all natural things to their goals, a mind who we call God.

The difference between the Fifth Way (FW) and design inference (DI) is found in both (A) the premises and (B) the conclusions.

(A) The FW derives its premises from observation of the natural bodies (*corpora naturalia*), which are those things that do not have rational cognition. The premises highlight the disproportion between the goal which natural things regularly achieve and their own inability to achieve that goal. In contrast, the human being has cognition and thus does not work out of necessity, but out of intelligence and free will that enable him to take proportionate means toward desired ends. In fact, since natural things have no cognition, they cannot achieve anything beyond what is embedded in their nature. In this sense, they act out of necessity. Necessity, therefore, is the closer (or immediate) explanation of the action of natural bodies. Thomas, however, firmly claims that necessity cannot constitute the ultimate explanation of the way that natural bodies act. Their ordering toward their ends must be given to them by an external mind. He explains this thoroughly in *De Potentia*.[22]

---

[22] "Every agent acts for an end, since all things seek the good. Now for the agent's action to be suited to the end, it must be adapted and proportionate to it, and this cannot be done save by an intellect that is cognizant both of the end and of its nature as end, and again of the proportion between the end and the means; otherwise the suitability of the action to the end would be fortuitous. But this intellect

Now, the premise of the design inference is that in nature we see structures/events that bear characteristics of being caused either by chance or necessity, or by intelligence. The chance factor requires more explanation. For example, we call a throw of a die random only because it is hard to account for all forces involved. Yet, we know that the outcome is not random, but determined by the direction given to the die and forces such as gravity, impetus, and friction. If we could precisely measure all of them we could predict the outcome. Hence, the throw of a die, as well as any lottery of this type, is not random, but necessary—it follows laws of nature.

Apparently, the only example of randomness in the physical world is found on the quantum level. But even there we do not really know whether the events are truly random, or just unaccountable for us. The difference with the lottery is that in the lottery it is difficult to account for all the forces and thus it is hard to predict the outcome, whereas at the quantum level the outcome is unpredictable in principle (the uncertainty

---

ordering the means to the end is sometimes united to the agent or mover; such is man in his actions: sometimes it is separate, as in the case of the arrow whose flight in a definite direction is effected by an intellect united not to it but to the archer. Now that which acts of natural necessity cannot determine its end: because in the latter case the agent acts of itself, and when a thing acts or is in motion of itself, there is in it to act or not to act, to be in motion or not to be in motion, which cannot apply to that which is moved of necessity, since it is confined to one effect. Hence everything that acts of natural necessity must have its end determined by an intelligent agent. For this reason philosophers say that the work of nature is the work of an intelligence. Therefore whenever a natural body is united to an intellect, as in man, as regards those actions whereby that intellect determines the end, nature obeys the will, as when a man walks; whereas as regards those actions by which the intellect does not fix the end, nature does not obey, as in the process of nourishment and growth. Accordingly we conclude that a thing which acts from natural necessity cannot be a principle of action, since its end is determined by another" (De Pot. q.1, a.5 co).

principle).[23] Nevertheless, whenever we deal with unaccountable phenomena, such as those at the quantum level, the particular unpredictable result is irrelevant for scientific research. For example, we cannot predict where an electron orbiting the nucleus is positioned in a given moment, or when a given atom will decay. But this is irrelevant for us, because what counts is not a particular position of an electron, but the fact that it travels in the region outside the nucleus, thus preserving the important qualities of matter. And this applies to every other case of unpredictability in nature—whenever random events enter the scene, whether they only look random or are truly random, what we need is not the events themselves, but the order that they produce in the larger scale (such as nuclei and electrons accounting for the structure and properties of matter). Therefore, we conclude that chance events, if they are relevant for our understanding of nature, boil down to necessity. Chance, strictly speaking, is either a hidden necessity, or is irrelevant, or is rare and exceptional, and thus it does not constitute any law or part of nature. And this is why Aquinas does not speak about chance in his argument. His premise in the Fifth Way rests on the *necessity* of natural bodies to act in a certain way.

Speaking in modern terms, necessity is expressed in the form of laws of nature, because all natural things obey laws of nature. For the design inference, however, to recognize necessity is not enough. The claim goes further. In nature there are structures/events (or using Aquinas's term—*corpora naturalia*, natural bodies) that cannot be explained otherwise but by reference to intelligent causality. And here rests the difference in the premises: For Aquinas, natural things are attributable to the laws of nature which, in turn, must be explained by the intelligent cause, the mind. For intelligent design, similarly, some natural things are attributable to the laws of nature, and

---

[23] Cf. D. Bohm, *Causality and Chance in Modern Physics* (Philadelphia: University of Pennsylvania Press, 1971), pp. 87–88.

because the laws of nature are finely tuned, they need to be explained by intelligent causality; however, the core of the *design inference* is that some other natural things are not attributable to laws of nature. Instead, they must be attributed to intelligent causality, which is the only known cause capable of generating this kind of effect. Hence, the *differentia specifica* of design inference is that it begins with recognizing some natural things whose properties cannot be explained otherwise than by intelligence.

Does it mean that these structures/events (for Aquinas, natural bodies) must be produced each time directly by the mind? No. Design can be passed on by the laws of nature, but it cannot be generated by these laws in the first place. Still, it differs from the Fifth Way: In the Fifth Way necessity (laws of nature) explains the actions of the natural bodies, but then the laws themselves require explanation by the mind. So the logical dependence in the Fifth Way is as follows:

FW: Mind → Laws of nature → The actions of natural bodies

In the design inference the logical dependence is different:

DI: Mind → Designed structures/events → Transmission by laws of nature

To see this difference clearly we need to refer to a few examples. According to Aquinas, the actions of natural bodies must be ordered to an end by a mind. But, as we said, the immediate explanation of the actions typical for natural bodies is not mind, but the laws of nature that make things work in this or some other way. The conclusion of intelligent governance is derived from the fact that the laws direct the bodies in a way unattainable for them by their nature. The same is true about the modern theory of fine-tuning. It is in fact a more specific version of the Fifth Way, supplemented by the contemporary understanding of the laws of nature. Similarly to FW, the fine-tuning argument is based on a perception of the laws of nature and the way they match each other and thus enable nature to operate. This happens thanks to their mutual perfect pairing (hence the name "fine-tuning"). To discover the mind in the argument from fine-tuning we need to make an additional step—from fine-tuning of the laws to the mind.

In contrast, design inference begins with those structures/events which cannot be attributed to any laws. For example, there is no law of nature—no chemical, physical, or structural necessity—that would require a specific arrangement of the base pairs in the double helix of the DNA molecule. Indeed the phosphate-deoxyribose backbone (constituting the "skeleton" of the DNA double helix) can accept any of the four nucleobases (A, G, C, T) at any attachment location. Yet, it is precisely the arrangement (the sequence of the base pairs) that decides what kind of information (and therefore function) the gene contains. The function of the gene is not attributable to any law of nature and takes us directly to a mind, or intelligent causation. Hence, only intelligence could have produced the specific arrangement of the base pairs in the gene.[24] As we said, it does not follow that each gene must be produced directly by intelligence. Once the specified information (in the form of arrangement of the base pairs) is present, it can be passed on by the laws governing nature, such as the power of generation that passes the genetic information on from parents to posterity over and over again, over millions of years.[25]

---

[24] It is not our task here to elaborate in detail upon this claim. For evidence see William Dembski, *The Design Revolution*, and Stephen Meyer, *Darwin's Doubt*.

[25] Apparently, most of M. George's criticism of intelligent design is based on a faulty understanding of this distinction. See, for example, her previously mentioned paper, "What Would Thomas Aquinas Say about Intelligent Design?," pp. 676–700, 682–683.

Another example is derived from irreducible complexity. There are organic structures in living beings, such as bacterial flagella, that lose function if they do not have all parts at once properly combined. Such irreducibly complex structures cannot be attributed to the process (law) of natural selection working on random variation because this kind of process can work only step by step, by slow, minute modifications of the previous organic states. In this process each step can lead to another step only if the previous step provides competitive (survival) advantage. Otherwise natural selection will not support the change. But what gives survival advantage are new organs and new functions. Hence, irreducibly complex organic structures cannot be built by natural selection, because a new function comes only after the organ is completed. It does not follow that random variation and natural selection do not exist as laws (regularities) operating in nature. It only means that these laws cannot account for the emergence of irreducibly complex organs such as the bacterial flagellum (even if they produce many other effects in nature, like perhaps bacterial resistance to antibiotics). In consequence, there is no law of nature that could produce irreducibly complex organic structures, and they must be attributed directly to intelligent causality. Again, it does not mean that every such structure must be produced by an intelligent cause. In fact we see that bacteria, which lack intelligence, produce them in every generation. But the first flagellum could not have been produced in the same way.

So the difference between FW and DI (regarding their premises) is that FW, in contrast to DI, does not rest upon the distinction between the things that come ultimately from intelligence and those that cannot be explained otherwise than by intelligence. In DI the way from the universe to intelligence is direct, whereas in FW it is mediated through laws of nature (natural tendencies). And it is obvious that the certainty of the conclusion is stronger when fewer steps are required to obtain it. In this sense, the design inference is a stronger argument for intelligent causality than the Fifth Way. This should not be surprising to a Thomist, because if all our knowledge about God which is not supernaturally revealed must come from creatures (and this is what Aquinas holds as true in S.Th. I,2,2, co), then a better understanding of creatures enables to build a stronger argument from design.

The premise of the Fifth Way virtually includes the premise of DI, but Thomas cannot make it explicit, because he lacks a good understanding of what happens in nature. He does not know of natural bodies that cannot be explained by their "natural tendencies." This is why he appeals to the fact that natural bodies work beyond their natures—they act according to the order that they themselves cannot generate. Some of his examples include the movements of heavenly bodies, the actions of animals, or simple properties of the elements, such as the fact that air tends upwards, whereas earth tends downwards, and thus everything tends to its proper place.[26] The premise of DI provides clear distinction between those things that are explicable by laws from those that must be attributed to the mind.

For medieval people it was quite appealing to see the movements of celestial spheres as very sophisticated and divinely ordered, since as a consequence so many interesting things happen on earth. The heavenly bodies had almost magical powers. However, over time, with the progress of science, the "spell" was broken. It turned out that there is nothing particularly exceptional about the celestial bodies: They are not perfect, they are corruptible, they do not have some of the causal powers once attributed to them, and they are not made of any special material—*quinta essentia*—but of the same elements as the things on earth. Moreover, it turned out that they are not moved by angels but rotate thanks to the same law of gravity that makes an apple fall from the

---

[26] See, for example, Aquinas's *Commentary on the Physics*, Book II, chapters 12–13.

tree. Consequently, the progress of science made the premise of the Fifth Way less appealing to the pragmatic and anti-metaphysical mind of modern people. The premise of design inference may overcome this weakness because it is based on the modern and more accurate understanding of nature.

(B) When it comes to the conclusions of both arguments, we need to again appeal to the difference between science and philosophy. Aquinas's argument speaks about nature as such, in an abstract way, which is the domain of philosophy. This is why it employs abstract terms such as "natural bodies" and "goals" of natural things, i.e., final causes. Design inference—in contrast—is a scientific argument; therefore, it is built on observing particular phenomena, such as DNA and bacterial flagella. It does not look for the final cause, but merely the efficient cause of a given fact. Also, the conclusions of both arguments follow the requirements of the different levels of knowledge: The Fifth Way ends up with discovering God (this is possible in philosophy), whereas design inference ends up with merely identifying the efficient cause of some organic structures as intelligence (this is possible in science). It is important, however, to observe two things:

The first is that these two conclusions are not exclusive but complementary. The scientific conclusion about intelligent cause refers to the philosophical conclusion about God's existence in the same way as the philosophical conclusion about the existence of God refers to the theological article of faith stating that there is a God. And as much as Catholic tradition values the philosophical arguments supporting faith, it also values the scientific claims about intelligent causation found in nature. The reason is that even though the scientific arguments prove less, they prove it experimentally, i.e., in a way more appealing for modern people.

The second thing to notice is that the design inference could be remade into a philosophical argument simply by extending its conclusion to the invisible realm. By adopting principles of classical metaphysics and proofs developed in natural theology, it is possible to philosophically demonstrate that the intelligently designed structures/events disclose internal teleology. It is also possible to demonstrate that the intelligence which is needed as a cause of these structures is one, immaterial, eternal, omnipotent, and so on, and is thus properly called God.

3. REPLIES TO THE OBJECTIONS

Ad 1 and 2. There are two problems with the "god of the gaps" charge against ID. One is that the logic of the argument is defective; the other is that the premise of the argument does not apply to intelligent design.

The first problem is that the same charge of "god of the gaps" can be filed against any explanation that appeals to any supernatural power. For example, Christians believe that the universe was created directly by God out of nothing. But atheists believe that the universe is eternal. Therefore, according to the logic assumed in the objection, the belief in *creatio ex nihilo* is "the god of the gaps argument": We do not know how the universe started, so we appeal to God. Another example is miracles, such as the Resurrection. Christians believe that Christ came back to life by his own power, not through any natural process. But atheists have suggested that perhaps he was only in a coma, or that the Resurrection was made up by the Apostles, who stole the body of Jesus. So there are at least two natural explanations for the empty tomb. According to the logic of the objection, the belief in the Resurrection is based on a "god of the gaps" argument, because it replaces possible natural explanations with the supernatural one. The same is evident with any other miracle. We do not know how Jesus multiplied bread, so—according to the logic of the objection—we insert the supernatural explanation, which is the divine power of Jesus capable of working beyond any physical limits. But how do we know that science will not show in the future that bread can be multiplied naturally? So, again, our explanation by the appeal to the divine supernatural causation falls under the charge of being the "god of the gaps" argument, which is clearly not the case. The only type of explanation that is not vulnerable to this accusation is one that does not appeal to God at all. But this leaves us with a tautology: The "god of the gaps" explanations are those that appeal to God, and the explanations that appeal to God rely on the "god of the gaps."[27] Hence, if we follow the logic of the objection, we end up saying that only natural explanations for miracles are acceptable or possible. This comports with the principle of methodological naturalism, but it does not accord with

---

[27] It is worth noting that the authors of the document *Communion and Stewardship* issued by the International Theological Commission make an awkward attempt to resolve this problem. They propose a distinction between "genuinely causal" and "merely explanatory" gaps in our knowledge. Thus, when it comes to the origin of the human soul we can appeal to direct divine causality because this is the *genuinely causal* gap, whereas in the origin of irreducibly complex systems we cannot appeal to intelligent causality, because this would employ a *merely explanatory* gap. As the document concludes: "The appeal to divine causality to account for genuinely *causal* as distinct from merely *explanatory* gaps does not insert divine agency to fill in the "gaps" in human scientific understanding (thus giving rise to the so-called *God of the gaps*)." So, we learn here about two types of gap, one of which leads to "god of the gaps" thinking, while another does not. However, the theologians from ITC do not explain why one gap is only *explanatory* and another is *causal*. They do not provide any criterion to distinguish between the two types of gaps. Hence, they do not resolve the problem of the tautological character of the objection. A critic of their solution could easily claim that appealing to the divine direct causation in the origin of species is as much "genuinely causal" as it is in the case of the creation of the human soul. See International Theological Commission, *Communion and Stewardship: Human Persons Created in the Image of God*, no. 70, at http://www.vatican.va/roman_curia/congregations/cfaith/cti_documents/rc_con_cfaith_doc_20040723_communion-stewardship_en.html (accessed: 12 July 2016).

Christianity's claim that God worked supernaturally in both the history of creation and the history of salvation.

In order to break the circular reasoning of the "god of the gaps" accusation, we need to acknowledge that there are sources of knowledge different from science that allow us to establish which events require supernatural divine causality. One of those "non-scientific" sources is the Bible, which teaches that bread was multiplied by Jesus, and calls it a miracle (Jn 6:14). Similarly, the Bible teaches that species were created according to their kinds by the Word of God, which means that they were not generated from a single ancestor, and did not appear little by little, but many at once, which is contrary to the natural explanation. And this is why appealing to the supernatural divine causality to explain the origin of species is not "god of the gaps" but faithfulness to the word of God, which we accept not by empirical evidence but by believing in the truthfulness of divine revelation.[28]

The second problem is that the objection rests on the false premise that intelligent design theory appeals to ignorance. The reason why ID concludes that intelligent causation must have been at work is not that "we do not know how the bacterial flagellum came about," but that we do know that it *could not* have been produced otherwise than by intelligence.

There are three types of causality detectable by science. These are chance, necessity, and intelligence. Establishing the nature of each of them is beyond the scope of science. Yet, attributing the proper type of causality to the given physical structure/event is not beyond science. Indeed, the task of science is finding the proper causes of physical phenomena. In the case of bacterial flagella, the conclusion about intelligent causality is derived from the fact that it is irreducibly complex. But to know that the biological system is irreducibly complex,

---

[28] For more about the fallacious logic and other problems with the "god of the gaps" charge, see B. Larmer, "Is There Anything Wrong With 'God of the Gaps' Reasoning?," *International Journal for Philosophy of Religion*, Vol. 52, 2002, pp. 129–142.

we need to know what its function is, what its parts are, and whether or not all of the parts are necessary for the system to perform its basic function. So, it is an insightful understanding of the biological system that leads to the conclusion about intelligent design, rather than a gap in our knowledge. Therefore, ID neither inserts a god into the gaps of our knowledge, nor argues from ignorance.

Ad 3. To respond to this objection we need to establish two things: first, what kind of explanations are available for science (A), and then, how scientific progress may influence those explanations (B).

(A) According to Aquinas, every cause produces an effect similar to itself. This is also true in the physical universe, where different types of cause produce different types of effect. If the effect (in the form of a physical structure or event) does not exhibit any pattern or regularity, it should be attributed to chance. If the structure or event follows a pattern or regularity it should be attributed to a law. It cannot be attributed to chance, because chance is unable to produce regularities. Laws, however, are recognized precisely because of the regularities they create. Irreducible complexity and specified complexity exhibit some regularities, but they also transcend regularities and thus cannot be explained by laws or simple formulas. For example, the bacterial flagellum, which is an irreducibly complex system, contains regularities such as perfectly round bushings. Yet, this is not what makes it irreducibly complex. The bacterial flagellum requires many parts put together to perform one function. A cause producing this kind of effect must operate from foresight, that is, from a previous knowledge of the effect even before the effect is obtained. Foresight does not belong to either chance or necessity. The only power known to have foresight is intelligence.

Similarly, specified complexity contains some regularities (for example every language follows rules), but also requires an independent pattern (specification) that can be abstracted and implemented only by the work of an intellect (which alone is capable of conceiving universal concepts). Therefore, intelligence is the only available explanation of specified and irreducible complexity. And just as explanation by laws is not reducible to explanation by chance, so explanation by intelligence cannot be reduced to explanation by laws.

(B) The progress of science may happen in two ways. The first way involves finding another explanation within the same category of explanations. For example, a structure/event attributed to the random collisions of particles perhaps may be explained by some other random event, yet the explanation remains in the category of randomness. Similarly, something attributed to one law may turn out to be explicable by another law; e.g., the law of gravity is explicable in terms of general relativity. And similarly, something attributed to one intelligence may turn out to be caused by another intelligence.

The other way in which scientific progress occurs is through finding a higher (or more sophisticated) explanation which replaces a more basic one. In this way laws may be discovered where until now no explanation had been known (something was thought to just happen, apparently by chance), and intelligent causation may be found where until now only laws or chance had been recognized. For example, random collisions of particles in gases may be explained by laws of thermodynamics (on a large scale). Similarly, the multiplicity and perfect match of cosmic constants and laws have brought many scientists to the conclusion that laws are not just "by necessity" but rather are purposefully designed (the theory of cosmic fine-tuning). And similarly, the neo-Darwinian theory, which allegedly explained the origin of biological systems by chance and necessity, was found to be inadequate, and the progress of science discovered intelligent design.

Now, this movement cannot happen in the opposite direction (from intelligence to laws to chance), because we need more knowledge to conclude that something is caused by intelligence than we need to conclude that something is caused by a law. Similarly, we need more knowledge about an event to establish that it follows a law than we need to simply attribute it to chance. (For example, we need to discover the mutual dependence between different events to establish a law.) In fact, we need to exclude chance to attribute something to a law, and to exclude law to attribute something to intelligence. Hence, if science moved in the opposite direction, this would not be a progress, but a decline and reduction of scientific knowledge. For this reason, once science discovers that something is caused by law, it will not attribute it back to chance, and if an intelligent cause is found, science will not attribute it back to a law or chance.

When it comes to Aquinas—his argument from design (The Fifth Way) cannot be disproven by the progress of science, not because it is irrelevant for the argument whether something is attributable to intelligence or to law, but because Thomas assumes that laws of nature by themselves are the evidence of intelligent causation. Therefore, no matter what new laws science may discover, it does not affect Aquinas's Fifth Way. His argument would be disproven only if it was demonstrated that nothing in nature is governed by any laws and that everything happens by chance instead. If this were the case, however, science would not be possible.

Ad 4. Three things should be observed when responding to this objection. The first is that Aquinas himself employs the analogy between humans designing machines and God designing natural things. This is clear from the quotations provided in the *sed contras* (*De Veritate*, q.5, a.2, co; S.Th. I-II,13,2, ad3; *Quaestiones Disputatae de Anima*, art. 7, co), as well as from the following:

> All creatures are compared to God as artificial things (*artificiata*) to an artificer... Whence, the whole of nature is like an artifact (*artificiatum*) of divine art (ScG III,100,6).

Natural things depend on the divine intellect, as artificial things depend on the human intellect (S.Th. I,17,1, co).

> Art imitates nature. The reason for it is that principles relate to each other in the same way as the operations and the effect relate proportionally to each other. The principle of the things happening by art is the human intellect, which is derived from the divine intellect according to some similarity. And the divine intellect is the principle of natural things. Hence, it is necessary that the operations of art imitate the operations of nature. And those things that are produced by art imitate those found in nature (*Sent. Politic.* pr.1).

Hence, there is nothing reductionist in comparing the works of human minds found in nature, such as machines, to the works of divine mind, unless Aquinas himself is a reductionist, which is probably not what Thomistic evolutionists want to say.

The second thing to notice is that science and philosophy today are much better distinguished from each other than they were in Aquinas's times. The fact that some scientists speak of living beings as biological systems does not mean that they reduce them to machines. There are at least two reasons why it is not so. One is that science typically deals with just a part of an animal, like a cellular organelle or a protein, which is far from being a complete substance (it is not a complete living being). Some of these parts clearly act like human mechanisms and then the analogy is obvious. A second reason is that science does not employ typically philosophical terms and notions. It is not the task of science to define a substance, or look for the teleology in a being. As we said before (*corpus*), science looks for the material and efficient cause of particular structures and events. This is how it differs from philosophy, which additionally seeks for final and formal cause. When a scientist discovers the material or the efficient cause while not finding any other, it does not follow that no other causes exist. It simply means that the scientific explanation does not include those other causes.

This is not reductionism, because drawing more abstract and general conclusions about living beings as separate substances (or nature as a whole) is outside of science. Reductionism begins not when scientists speak about material and efficient causes alone, but when they (or anyone else) claim that scientific knowledge is the *only possible* type of knowledge, or that science explains everything, including the mystery of life. And this is not what the proponents of intelligent design do. Reductionism occurs not in pursuing science according to the limits of its subject matter, method, and goal, but only in extending science beyond its limits.

It may also happen that one attempts to reduce science to philosophy. This takes place when a philosopher replaces the concrete and highly specific explanations typical of science with the abstract and general notions borrowed from metaphysics. Neither of the reductionisms (all knowledge to science, or all knowledge to philosophy) is fruitful for either of the disciplines. And this is why, in order to understand the methodology of intelligent design, it is crucial to understand and acknowledge the distinction between science and philosophy.

The third thing to notice is that the Thomistic critics of ID reject ID for "philosophical reasons" and adopt the Darwinian explanations for the "scientific reasons." But this means that they fight the alleged mechanistic reductionism of intelligent design and, at the same time, they accept the real and quite blatant reductionism of the Darwinian theory.[29]

---

[29] For example, F. Beckwith accuses ID of mechanicism, but at the same time he doesn't see any problem with the Darwinian's claim that "natural processes, including scientific laws, are sufficient to account for the variety of life forms that now populate the world." See Beckwith's previously cited "Intelligent Design, Thomas Aquinas, and the Ubiquity of Final Causes," p. 6. Similarly, E. Feser claims that

Indeed, there is no greater misunderstanding of life and no greater reductionism in biology than saying that all species came about by the mechanism of blind mutations and natural selection. Yet, this is the main tenet of neo-Darwinism. The reason why some Thomists make this fatal mistake is that they do not adhere to the distinction between science and philosophy. When they think about intelligent design they judge it by philosophical categories, whereas when they think of neo-Darwinism they adopt the "scientific" point of view. Both theories, however, are on the same level of science and should be judged according to the requirements of science, not philosophy.

Yet even if we apply the same scientific measure to both theories, neo-Darwinism, unlike ID, will still fall into the category of reductionism (scientific reductionism). The reason is that on the very level of biological investigation we can discover intelligent causation, which is the only type of cause able to produce the type of structures we find in the living beings. Neo-Darwinism *a priori* and by definition excludes this type of causality. Neo-Darwinism is an attempt to explain a higher effect (things intelligently designed) by an appeal to a lower cause (chance and laws), and this is what reductionism consists of. In contrast, ID by definition allows all types of causes available in science and appeals to intelligence only after rigorous investigation. As the ID proponents say: "Scientists should go wherever the evidence leads."[30] Thus, the way to overcome reductionism in science (a dream of many

---

"many biological phenomena might be explained in terms of purely physical processes like natural selection." Then he adds that others, like our capacity to form general concepts, cannot be (*The Last Superstition*, p. 114). It follows that for Feser everything below mental skills, including the emergence of species, is actually explicable by physical processes.

[30] See, for example, the *Seattle Times* interview with Stephen Meyer from April 26, 2006, available at http://www.discovery.org/a/3505 (accessed 9 September 2016).

Thomists) is not by adopting neo-Darwinism and trying to show how it is compatible with classical philosophy, but rather by embracing intelligent design as the alternative scientific explanation, and then showing how ID is compatible with classical metaphysics.

Ad 5. From the fact that irreducible complexity (IC) and specified complexity (SC) prove design it does not follow that laws of nature and cosmic fine-tuning (CFT) do not prove it. Indeed, any regularities in physical reality, inherent tendencies, laws of nature and CFT testify to design, because none of those can be produced by chance. However, each of these supports design in a different way and with a different level of certitude. If no laws or regularities were found in nature we could only believe and hold it by faith that the universe is designed. The conclusion about the universe being designed would be derived from revelation, not from studying nature. But we do find an order in the universe. Aquinas perceives it in a general way in all natural beings. As he says, everything tends to its goal, works for something else, and hence everything is somehow ordered by the supreme mind. Aquinas's argument is therefore philosophical, because in philosophy the universe is perceived in a general and abstract way.

When it comes to science such as physics (and derivative disciplines), the regularities observed in nature are called laws of nature. Strictly speaking, laws do not constitute a scientific argument for design, because in physics they are the ultimate explanation—to explain a natural phenomenon in physical terms means to find a law that governs it. This is why intelligent design does not say that gravity or electromagnetism is evidence for design. However, physics observes that laws of nature together with cosmic constants are finely-tuned. Hence, science recognizes that there is more than just the laws—there is also their mutual, extremely improbable relations. Since extremely improbable things do not happen often, whereas fine-tuning is a rule rather than an exception, it is apparent that constants and laws must have been somehow ordered by a mind. Still, the argument for design from CFT is mainly probabilistic (it relies on extremely low probability of physical constants and laws coming together into one ensemble by chance). This also explains why those who reject design argument from fine-tuning do it by proposing the multiverse. By doing so, they enlarge "probabilistic resources" and claim that the fine-tuning not only might have happened, but must have happened, in one of the universes. This, however, is not a scientific argument, because science cannot speak about anything outside the universe.

We can conclude, therefore, that chance is not an argument for design at all (even if chance events were actually designed). Laws are more like constituents of science; therefore their existence cannot serve as a scientific argument for design, and CFT is a merely probabilistic argument, unless it could be demonstrated that it entails specification. On the other hand, the irreducible and specified complexity found in living things cannot be explained otherwise than by intelligent causation. Therefore, it is the strongest type of argument for intelligent design available in science, and the only one that cannot be overturned by enlarging probabilistic resources or proposing the eternity or self-sufficiency of the laws of nature. This should not be surprising, given that biology deals with the most perfect natural things, i.e., living organisms. The organization of matter in living beings is not just quantitatively but qualitatively different from that in any non-living physical structures. Hence, the argument for design derived from biology must differ not only in degree, in the sense that it is stronger, but also according to its nature, namely, that it cannot be overturned by an appeal to chance or necessity. Still, all of the arguments for design are complementary rather than exclusive.[31]

---

[31] A good example of a misunderstanding of the qualitative difference between different levels of organization of matter by a Thomist is Benedict Ashley's famous paper "Causality and Evolution." At the time when the paper was published little was known about epigenetic

Philosophical conclusions are permanent, because they are derived and separated from changeable particulars by abstraction. This makes philosophical arguments more certain and permanent than scientific ones. Scientific arguments, however, are more concrete and easier to grasp for those who do not have much ability for metaphysical thinking. This is the reason why the persuasive power of the scientific arguments for ID often turns out to be greater than that of the philosophical arguments for the existence of God. It is also the reason why ID creates more resistance among unbelievers than any of the five ways proposed by Aquinas.

Ad 6. This objection is built upon false understanding of both ID and Aquinas. First, since ID is a scientific theory, it is silent about the role of God in evolution, including whether God works through random events or not. Second, ID does not exclude chance events from biology altogether, but only from creating some structures or events, namely those exhibiting specified and irreducible complexity. Such structures or events cannot be brought about by chance, because if chance events produced planned effects they would not be truly chance. This is sheer logic—one event cannot be chance and designed at the same time. So, when Aquinas says that God uses chance events to realize His plans, Aquinas means

---

information and the inadequacy of the neo-Darwinian mechanism to produce new forms of life. Still, it was already evident that genetic material contains information which is not reducible to patterns. Even so, Ashley builds his argument on the assumption that the difference between physical, chemical, and biological orders has a quantitative rather than qualitative character. For example, he claims that "The decrease of noise (random, disordered, unpatterned) sound in a radio signal means an increase in patterned sound, and it is this pattern which carries *information*." But a simple removal of chaos does not produce patterns and patterns do not carry the type of information present in genetic material. Genetic information is not reducible to patterns—it requires specification, and thus the explanation of the emergence of patterns on physical or chemical level does not contribute to explaining the origin of genetic information. See B. Ashley, op. cit., p. 203.

that some events look chance for us, but absolutely speaking they are designed by God to bring about His intended effects. But atheists and materialists do not say that God uses chance events; instead, they say that there is no God, and that chance produces the appearance of design by itself. And this is not what the proponents of ID postulate. Therefore—contrary to what is stated in the objection—they do not embrace the premise of materialists. Third, it is not true that Aquinas allows chance in the formation of species, as we have shown above (Chapter II, section 3, ad 6). Instead, Aquinas advocates direct formation of species by God, which is more than ID postulates. Still, ID and Aquinas agree that chance events cannot form entirely new species, whereas the author of the objection, along with atheists, believes it can happen.

Ad 7. Everything in nature is designed, but not every design in nature is equally manifest. The reason is that some things God designed in such a way that they happen by chance, some in such a way that they happen by necessity, and some other things in such a way that their design may be detected by science. And those who deny design in nature are not those who see it everywhere, but rather those who see it nowhere. Thus, the design inference in science is needed for two reasons. One is to convince those who think that everything spontaneously emerged from chaos of the true cause of natural things; another is to better understand the material things themselves, especially living beings. There is also a need for the design argument in philosophy, but the reasons to develop the philosophical arguments are different—one is to convince unbelievers to faith, another to rationally justify the faith. Thus, even though design is everywhere, detecting design separately by science and philosophy is both possible and necessary.

Ad 8. ID does not transcend the object (i.e., subject matter) of science, because the object studied by ID is not intelligence, but physical structures/events. Neither does ID violate the method of science, because it resorts to experiments, induction, statistics, and inference to the best explanation (abductive method). All of these are methods commonly accepted in different scientific disciplines. But to show that ID does not transcend the goal of science requires more explanation.

Science may be understood in a narrower or in a broader sense. If we define science narrowly, only the strictly experimental and observational disciplines will be included, such as physics, chemistry, and astronomy. In a broader sense, science includes also historical disciplines, such as archeology, paleontology, and cosmology. For historical sciences their object is the past, which cannot be directly observed. This is why historical disciplines use an indirect method; they draw conclusions about the past by extrapolating facts and laws currently observed in nature.

There are two types of question that can be asked about physical reality. One type concerns the operation of nature—how a given thing is built, how it functions, what are the conditions of its operation, etc. The other type concerns the origin of a thing—how it began to exist, where it comes from, who made it. It is important to realize that all natural science addresses only the first type of question, whereas the second is outside of science. This is very clear when we think of extreme cases. For example, natural science cannot explain the origin of matter and laws, because natural science can exist only when its objects, i.e., matter and laws, are already present. And the same applies to every particular discipline—none explains the origin of its object. In this sense, physics cannot explain the origin of physical reality, even if it explains some changes, like the transformation of matter into radiation or one element into another. Similarly, chemistry cannot explain the origin of elements, astronomy the origin of laws governing the cosmos, and biology the origin of the entire biodiversity. In each case, a given science may explain changes, but not the very origin of its object. It is important to realize that even the historical sciences do not explain the origin of their objects, but rather just the changes in the object over time (*evolution* in the original meaning of the word). Thus, cosmology may explain the evolution of the cosmos, but not where the cosmos came from, geology may explain the formation of mountains, but not where the very geological processes came from, paleontology may explain what forms of life lived on earth, and when and where they lived, but not how the forms came about, etc. (For further development of this argument see Chapter VI, section 1 below.)

When it comes to intelligent design in biology, this theory does not explain the origin of species, but only why a given biological structure is such and such today. For example, ID claims that the bacterial flagellum shows characteristics of being designed, because it is designed. But to say how these structures came about in the first place is beyond intelligent design, inasmuch as it is beyond science. Intelligent design does not offer any mechanism, or physical explanation of origins, and this is precisely what makes it scientific—by not providing an answer to the question of origins ID remains within the limits of science. The claim that some creative or divine intelligence must exist does not belong to the ID theory itself. In fact, it is a metaphysical conclusion that may be derived from the ID theory. But metaphysical conclusions are implied by many other theories in science, and this fact does not make the theories less scientific. For example, the Big Bang theory in cosmology may have strong metaphysical implications, but this does not render the theory philosophical. In contrast, Darwin addressed the question of origins. The very title of his book reads: *On the Origin of Species*. His grand claims, such as universal common ancestry or transformation of species, are metaphysical; they are meant to explain the origin of the entire biodiversity, and for this reason they cannot belong to the science of biology.

The next question is whether or not ID violates methodological naturalism. The answer to this question depends on whether or not ID requires a supernatural cause to explain natural objects. The distinction between supernatural and natural cause should not be confused with two other distinctions, namely, material vs. immaterial, and immanent vs. transcendent. For example, human intelligence is immaterial, but we do not call human rational activity supernatural. Human intelligence is not absolutely transcendent, because it is attached to the human body and naturally limited to cognition through the senses. Angelic intelligence is not absolutely transcendent either, because it is created and does not transcend the limits of creation. Aquinas, as well as all classical philosophy, firmly claims that intelligence cannot be material and thus cannot be a material cause. However, many scholars of our times would disagree. And many Darwinists claim that human intelligence is an effect of the evolution of the brain, which renders it a mere derivative of a highly organized matter. According to Christianity, the intelligence that created the universe is God, who is immaterial, supernatural, and absolutely transcendent. Yet to establish these attributes of the creative intelligence does not belong to the theory of ID. Intelligent design appeals to an intelligent cause not because it is supernatural, immaterial, or transcendent, but because it is intelligent. Hence, ID does not require a supernatural cause, but only an intelligent cause, and thus it does not violate methodological naturalism and remains within science.

Now, assuming that intelligence by definition must be immaterial, ID does not find a material cause whenever it recognizes intelligence as a cause of a physical structure or event. Still, intelligence can be also the efficient cause. And the goal of science is to find a material cause not because it is material, but because the material cause in nature is typically the proper efficient cause. Hence, ID fulfills the goal of science by finding the efficient cause, even if it happens to be immaterial.

When it comes to the final cause, we need to distinguish two understandings of finality. The first is the immanent finality found in every physical being. In this sense, every being has an internal final cause, proportional to its nature. For example, a bird builds a nest in order to lay eggs and procreate, or the bacterial flagellum rotates in order to move the bacterium in a liquid. Another type of finality transcends the order of nature and points to the ultimate destination of things. In this sense human beings are called to eternal life in heaven and animals were created to enable humans to achieve their goal of biological life on earth. Science not only can, but indeed does, speak about the first type of finality, whereas the second type belongs to philosophy or theology.[32] For the theory of intelligent design it is enough to assume that intelligence is capable of acting within the limits of immanent finality, such as when intelligence puts together all parts of the flagellum in order to make it work in the bacterium. Hence, intelligent design does not violate the limits of science by imposing the type of finality that transcends the limits of science. In contrast, theistic evolution often postulates the second type of finality, because it postulates finality in the evolution of nature taken as a whole (the cosmos evolving toward the final stage of perfection, biology evolving toward a "noosphere" and such). For this reason theistic evolution is not scientific.

Finally, we need to address the objection that ID postulates a universal cause rather than particular causes and thus exceeds the scope of science. "Universal cause" may be understood in two ways. First, from the perspective of the cause, it means that the cause acts on many different things or everything. Second, from the perspective of the effect, it means that all effects of a given kind require one type of cause. Science is not interested in the first type of universal cause; however, it belongs to science to find the second type of universal cause.

---

[32] Many contemporary philosophers defend the appeal to final causality in modern biology. However, very few of them make the necessary distinctions. For example, R. Machuga criticizes biology for avoiding final causality, but his own examples of how final causality should be employed in modern biology show only the first of the two types of finality presented here. See R. Machuga, *In Defense of the Soul: What it Means to Be Human* (Grand Rapids: Brazos Press, 2002), p. 85.

Indeed, the more universal is the cause in the second sense, the more unifying and general the scientific theory that proposes it. For example, the movements of celestial bodies may be explained by Newtonian mechanics, but at great distances and at high speeds this theory fails, and then a more universal theory is needed, such as general relativity. ID postulates the universal cause only in the second sense, by claiming that all things bearing characteristics of being designed must be explained by the same type of cause, which is intelligence. Hence, ID does not transcend the scope of science.

Ad 9. The explanatory filter excludes explanation by chance and laws only when a given structure/event cannot be explained by them. It does not follow that nothing is explainable by chance or laws. Hence, ID does not exclude scientific explanations by chance and laws, but rather incorporates the explanation by intelligence into science. And broadening the scope of possible explanations in science by no means diminishes science.

Ad 10. This argument stems from the misunderstanding of the difference between philosophy and natural science. It is true that neo-Darwinism is reductionist, because it reduces the explanation of all biological structures to the interplay between chance (random genetic mutations) and necessity (natural selection). Intelligent design, however, opens biology to explanations by intelligence, which is the only known cause capable of producing specified and irreducible complexity. Still intelligent design should not look for natures or substantial forms of living beings, because this belongs to philosophy (metaphysics), not to science (biology), where ID is found. Since philosophical interpretations exceed the capacity of science, science is not reductionist simply because it does not provide philosophical interpretations. In contrast, neo-Darwinism is reductionist and locks the door against classical metaphysics, because mechanism can generate only compounds of particles and conglomerates of parts, but not specified natures or distinct substances. Therefore, according to neo-Darwinism nothing in biology can be a *true substance* or a *distinct nature*, and this conclusion forbids classical metaphysics. Intelligent design, however, does not provide any mechanism of how biological structures emerged, and thus it neither endorses reductionism nor excludes classical metaphysics.

Ad 11. According to Aquinas (see Chapter II, section 2 above), there are two stages in the history of the universe: the stage of formation, which ended with the creation of man, and the stage of operation, which lasts until now. At both stages there is the ordinary divine providence that guides all things to their natural ends. This includes things such as the movements of the heavenly bodies or the generation of living beings. However, the type of divine activity specific to the first stage is not ordinary providence but the supernatural formation of the universe, which happened by the direct action of God (by definition, any direct act of God must be supernatural). Divine intervention, from the Latin *inter-venio*, means that God enters between two events in a chain of causes and effects in order to change the outcome of these events. But this is not what was happening when God was forming the universe. In the supernatural formation something new was added to the order of nature without destroying anything that had existed. When forming the universe, God did not operate within the existing chains of causes and effects, but rather started new such chains by adding new beings (new distinct natures) to the entire order of creation. Therefore, supernatural and direct formation cannot be an intervention, because every intervention presupposes existence of things, whereas creation does not presuppose anything (or presupposes nothingness).

At the second stage (during the operation of the universe after the universe was formed), there is the ordinary and the extraordinary providence. The extraordinary providence takes place when God acts in the order of nature supernaturally. This may happen either directly, when God does something without any secondary causes, e.g., stopping the movements of celestial bodies (Joshua 10:13) or multiplying loaves (John 6:11–13), or indirectly, when God does something using supernatural secondary causes, e.g., sending the Angel to deliver the Annunciation to Mary. Ordinary providence does not imply any interventions, because this is how God guides all things to their natural ends according to the laws He established. Supernatural providence, however, includes interventions, because interventions take place when God changes the ordinary course of events.

Owing to the fact that the order of nature was brought about by God in the work of formation rather than in the work of providence, it is incorrect to call any divine action that results in the emergence of new things "intervention." Hence, the theological concept of creation adopted by Aquinas (and all orthodox Christianity) has nothing to do with interventionism—creation is not an intervention.

Calling intelligent design interventionism is mistaken for another reason. ID theory says that intelligence must have caused the design of the organic structures, or maybe even whole species, but it does not say *how* it was done. The question of *how* exceeds the competence of ID as much as it exceeds the competence of science. Therefore, many different "theories of origins" may be compatible with ID. It is irrelevant, therefore, for ID whether God, or any other being, introduced design into nature by intervention or not. And to prove the compatibility of ID and Aquinas (in this respect), it is enough to show that Thomas does not exclude that living beings have intelligence rather than chance or necessity as their origin. This is evident from the quotations provided in the *sed contras* earlier in this chapter. Hence, even if "Thomism provides a corrective to ID," Thomas himself provides a corrective to the Thomists who believe that the design of living beings came about according to the ordinary operations of nature, such as biological evolution. According to Thomas, species of living beings have a supernatural origin.

Ad 12. Since ID does not speak about how design was introduced into biology (see the previous answer), ID does not imply direct divine causality. In other words, direct divine causality may be the best theological interpretation of irreducible and specified complexity, but this interpretation, as well as any other "theory of creation," goes beyond the theory of ID.

Still, it is possible to ask a philosophical question: Could God have tuned all laws and constants in nature in such a way that nature would produce new design using the finely-tuned mechanisms? To answer this question, first we need again the distinction between the origin of design and its communication. Aquinas, for example, says that when a species is created, its design first comes directly from God, but once the design is present in nature, it is passed on to posterity through natural generation.[33] This is why an individual comes about through generation, but the power of generation does not explain the origin of the species or substantial form of the individual. Hence, saying that "[even though] blind causes can explain the production of an effect which is ordered, they cannot explain the order in the effect" boils down to saying that design may be passed on by the blind and automatic forces, but cannot be produced by them, which is contrary to Darwinism and theistic evolution.

Next, we need to see the three levels of order in natural things. The first is the level of things that happen by chance. Chance, properly speaking, does not generate order. The second level consists of structures/events that follow patterns and always happen in the same way. This is the domain of laws, mechanisms, and other regularities. The third level is that of specified complexity, which consists of a highly improbable assemblage of parts which additionally match an

---

[33] "As no pre-existing body has been formed whereby another body of the same species could be generated, the first human body was of necessity made immediately by God" (S.Th. I,91,2 co).

independent pattern. (For more about specified complexity see W. A. Dembski's book *The Design Revolution*.) Now, theistic evolutionists believe that God designed the first and the second order in such a way that they would bring about the third order. But this is impossible, because if chance could create order, it would not be chance any more, and if patterns and regularities, such as laws of nature, could create an independent specification, they would no longer be mere patterns or regularities. This assumption of theistic evolution leads to a contradiction, because if something is repetitive, it is not chaotic, and if something is specific, it is not repetitive or chaotic. A lower order does not contain the properties of the higher order, and if it did, it wouldn't be a lower order. For example, gravity, electromagnetism, etc. do not contain specified information about the workings of the cell. So it does not matter how finely these laws might be tuned; they are not enough to create specification. (For more explanation of this claim, see Excursus 2, at the end of Chapter VI below).

Of course, theistic evolutionists do not say that the laws of nature create specified complexity, but that God creates it by using them as an instrumental cause (as a sculptor uses a chisel). But this is also impossible, because every tool operates in a given manner and produces certain types of effect. God, working like an artist, chooses tools adequate to His intended goals. Physical laws, however, by their very nature cannot contain, let alone produce, specified complexity. The same is true about chance. Therefore, neither law nor chance is an adequate tool to create life and species. Specified information must come directly from an intellect. Whether it comes directly from the divine intellect, or an angelic one, is a separate question to be settled by philosophy and theology. Aquinas attributes the production of species directly to God, excluding any active cooperation of the angels. Since irreducibly complex biological systems constitute the substantial parts of living beings, following Aquinas, we concede that only God could have made species by his direct action. This conclusion, however, is philosophical and, while being in harmony with ID, it also transcends the explanatory power of the ID theory.

Ad 13. According to Aquinas, those natural things which do not have cognition are directed to their goals "from the outside," by an external agent: "The intellect ordering the means to the end is sometimes united to the agent or mover; such is man in his actions: sometimes it is separate, as in the case of the arrow whose flight in a definite direction is effected by an intellect united not to it but to the archer" (De Pot. q.1, art. 5, co). It follows that, according to Aquinas, not all order and design in nature is immanent, as the objection states. Things that do not have cognition receive direction from an outside agent, whereas things that have cognition give direction to those that don't have it. Still, even those things that have cognition are not the ultimate causes of their cognition. They receive it from God, because intellectual beings also come from God. Thus, there is nothing in nature that would have an "internal" design, not given from the outside; otherwise, there would be things in nature that do not come from the first intellect, which is impossible. However, some of the designs and goals in nature are passed on naturally, as happens with the propagation of animals in which every subsequent generation contains the original plan and arrangement of parts introduced in the beginning by God. Similarly, laws of nature, which are also designed, exist as long as matter exists, even though they are not created by matter, but rather arranged by the divine intellect. Hence, every design and order in nature is first externally imposed by God, and then it may be passed on by the inherent properties of nature. The objection, therefore, stems from the confusion between the origin of design and its transmission. The origin is always external, even if the propagation and persistence of design may happen thanks to the internal properties of nature. Besides, it is irrelevant for the argument for intelligent design what the origin of design is.

Ad 14. This objection stems from misunderstanding the difference between the design argument and design inference, which we explained in the body of this chapter (section 2 above). Design inference (used to detect design in the theory of ID) is not intended to prove the existence of a designer, let alone the God of Christianity.

Each of the three levels of knowledge has its own argument and possible conclusions regarding the existence of God. Theology proves not only that God exists, but also that God is triune, which cannot be proved by philosophy. Philosophy, in turn, proves the existence of God understood as the first omnipotent and eternal cause of all being, upon which everything that exists depends. We know that this cause is the Holy Trinity from faith, not philosophy. Intelligent design, which is in the domain of natural science, does not prove the existence of any god, but rather yields evidence that some elements of the universe cannot be produced by anything else but intelligence. This provides evidence for the existence of intelligence, but it does not prove anything about the nature of this intelligence. And this limitation of ID complies with the limits of science, which cannot prove God's existence, let alone the existence of the Trinity.

It does not follow, however, that ID excludes the existence of the Christian God. Neither does it replace or render impossible the philosophical and the theological arguments for God's existence. On the contrary, ID is perfectly compatible with natural theology as well as the theological treatise *On the Trinity*. It should not be surprising for any believer that scientific truths are compatible with the truths of philosophy and faith. After all, this is precisely what we would expect if Christianity were true.

Ad 15. ID provides tools to recognize which natural structures/events are best explained by chance, necessity, or intelligence. It does not follow that the nature of these three factors is the same. In science we look for the proper or more proximate causes of structures/events, not for ultimate explanations. Some natural things have chance as their immediate cause, while others are explicable by the laws operating in nature. Science assumes the existence of laws and chance events, but to ask where they come from is beyond science. Hence, if something may be explained by chance or laws, chance and laws constitute a full scientific explanation, even if philosophically and theologically this explanation would be unsatisfactory. There are, however, some things in nature that cannot be explained by chance and laws, but instead require an intellect as the causal factor. In such cases, science can recognize that physical objects must be attributed to intelligent causation. This does not mean that intelligence is just one among the natural causes. It is beyond the theory of intelligent design to inquire into the nature of the intelligence. Thus, the possibility that the intelligent cause transcends all of the natural causes remains open.

Ad 16. If "creationism" means that different natures of living beings were created directly by God, then it is a classic Catholic position shared by the greatest minds of Christianity, including Thomas Aquinas (see Chapter II, section 2). This position does not contradict any scientific evidence, because questions of origins, such as the origin of species, are not scientific. Science cannot explain the origin of distinct natures, even if it can say something about their history. This is consistent with with the fact that most founders of modern science, including Copernicus, Galileo, Kepler, and Newton, were creationists. Yet they were successful in their scientific endeavor because they asked how the universe is built and how it works, not where the forms of the universe came from. The first question belongs to science and is a matter of scientific inquiry; the second belongs to philosophy and theology.

If, however, "creationism" means "Young Earth Creationism" (YEC), it adds to the belief in the special creation of species two other beliefs: belief in the short time (six natural days) of the creative events, and belief in the short history of the universe (thousands rather than billions of years). But according to Augustine and Aquinas, the time-scale of creation is not essential to faith (see Chapter III, section 2 above). So the "Young Earth" position insists on more than Catholic teaching requires. Yet it is not in contradiction with Catholic teaching, for the Catholic Church on her part resolved that the word "day" (Hebrew *yôm*) from the Genesis account can be understood either as a natural day or any other period of time.[34] Hence, there is no obstacle coming from Church teaching to embracing Young Earth Creationism.

When it comes to science, as distinct from theology, the case is different, because there is overwhelming evidence that the universe is older than a few thousand years, and that it was formed over a longer time than six natural days. Hence, Young Earth Creationism—insofar as it defends the short history of the universe—is not against the faith, but it does appear to be against science or even against reason.

Intelligent design, however, is not creationism in either sense, for it neither claims the direct creation of species nor the short history of the universe. Young Earth Creationism is as much compatible with ID as are other concepts of creation, such as Old Earth (day-age) Creationism (OEC) and even theistic evolution. This is possible, because all concepts of creation (including theistic evolution) are on the level of theology, whereas ID remains within the limits of science.

---

[34] See the Decree of the Pontifical Biblical Commission *On the Historical Character of the First Three Chapters of Genesis* (June 30, 1909). *Enchiridion Biblicum*, EB 339.

CHAPTER VI:
THOMISTS VERSUS THOMAS

1. AQUINAS AND THE PROGRESS OF SCIENCE

Many Thomists have adopted theistic evolution because they believe that the theory of biological macroevolution is an accurate scientific explanation of the origin of species. However, this can be the case only if we *assume* that a scientific answer to the question of origins is at all possible. Christians believe that some things in the universe are not explicable by science. For example, Thomists agree that miracles cannot be scientifically explained, because they are beyond the capacity of nature; they happen by the supernatural causation of God, who sometimes chooses to act supernaturally in the natural order. Nevertheless, Thomistic evolutionists believe that this type of causality did not take place in the formation of the universe. Instead, God decided to create the universe using natural secondary causes alone. Thus, they exclude supernatural causality in the formation of the universe, but accept the multitude of supernatural and even direct divine acts in the history of salvation. Apparently, these scholars do not see any incoherence in this worldview.

If you ask a Thomistic evolutionist why Thomas defends the supernatural origin of species, and specifically the special creation of the human body, he will usually deny that Thomas teaches the supernatural origin of species and then claim that Thomas's teaching is compatible with theistic evolution. But when you demonstrate that Thomas indeed teaches the supernatural origin of species, the Thomist will typically change the line of argumentation. The new answer is that Thomas did not know many of the things discovered by modern science, and thus many of his teachings about nature are no longer valid. The examples usually put forward by the Thomistic evolutionist to substantiate this claim are Thomas's belief in the geocentric model of the solar system and in spontaneous generation. Thomists favoring evolution often refer to the analogy between Copernicus and Darwin: As Copernicus modified Thomas's understanding of the planetary system, so Darwin modified his understanding of biology.[1]

We agree that many of Aquinas's teachings regarding the material universe have been surpassed by the progress of science. However, we add, that this does not include the origin of life, species, and man. To see this clearly we need to distinguish between two types of question regarding the material universe. One concerns how the universe operates, the other where the universe with its forms came from (a distinction introduced above in Chapter V, section 2, ad 8). The latter question cannot be answered by science alone. For example, science cannot tell us how the universe began. Although modern data strongly favor the temporal beginning of the universe, scientists may still claim that it is eternal by proposing non-scientific theories such as the multiverse. That the universe actually had a temporal beginning we learn from theology (supernatural revelation). And if we look at the progress of science, only those truths that concern the operation of the universe have legitimately modified our worldview. Some ancient people believed that the earth was a flat disc,[2] but

---

[1] Some Thomistic evolutionists go as far as distancing themselves from Aquinas's doctrine when they cannot accommodate it to their evolutionary views. For example, B. Ashley suggests that Aquinas was wrong when teaching that there is no secondary causation in creation. M. George believes that "Aquinas would need to revise his critique of Empedocles" because his teaching excludes chance from formation of species. See B. Ashley, "Causality and Evolution," pp. 229–230, and M. George, *What Would Thomas Aquinas Say about Intelligent Design?*," p. 693.

[2] It is important to note that the belief in a flat Earth was significantly less common in the past than is usually thought today. Even in antiquity most educated people already favored the spherical shape of the Earth.

science proved that it was closer to a globe. Christians thought that the universe was a few thousand years old, but it turned out to be billions of years old. The Ptolemaic model of the cosmos placed Earth in the center of the universe, but science showed that this was not the case. Ancient and medieval people believed in a number of celestial spheres, but science showed that there were no spheres, but rather galaxies and many planetary systems similar to ours. People thought that there was a sphere of fixed stars, but science has shown that stars are distributed in space unevenly, in clusters, and revolve around centers of gravity other than the Sun. Thomas thought that planets did not change, were incorruptible, etc., but all of this was disproved by later discoveries. Aristotle thought that species of living beings were unchangeable and eternal, and Carl Linnaeus believed that species were not eternal, but were all created in the beginning as they are now, and that their number hadn't changed, but since then we have learned, contra both Aristotle and Linnaeus, that species appeared successively in great "explosions" of life, and that most of them went extinct. However, species did not change over the millions of years of their existence (*stasis*). So, has Darwin shown that species evolved from a single ancestor? Should his theory replace the belief in the separate creation?

The common point of all theories legitimately disproven by the progress of science is that all of them describe the universe, but do not say where its constitutive elements came from. And this is precisely why these theories could be overturned and replaced by new scientific explanations. Darwin's theory does not match the pattern. It is not a theory of nature, but rather a theory of the *origin* of nature. This becomes clear

---

Eratosthenes made impressively accurate calculations regarding its radius as early as the 3rd century B.C. By medieval times the globosity of the earth was an established conviction among educated people of Europe. J. B. Russell provides a good refutation of the claim that most medieval people believed in a flat Earth. See his book *Inventing the Flat Earth: Columbus and Modern Historians* (Westport, CT: Praeger, 1991).

when we compare the title of his book with that of Copernicus's. Darwin wrote a book *On the Origin of Species*. The Greek word for "origin" is "genesis." And this word was used in the Septuagint as the title of the first book of the Bible, precisely because the Book of Genesis is revealed by God to explain the origins of the universe and its various forms. Darwin thus proposed an alternative "Genesis." In contrast, Copernicus wrote *On the Revolutions of the Celestial Spheres*. He did not explain the origin of the celestial spheres, but their operations, how they work, interact. This is why Copernicus, Galileo, Newton, and others were true scientists, and why they could have been right in proposing new theories, whereas Darwin appropriated something that does not belong to science by its very nature.

Medieval people inherited most of their knowledge in physics and astronomy from antiquity. This includes Aquinas, who did not create any theory of nature. His views regarding physical reality come from preceding philosophers. Such views could be modified by new scientific discoveries. Truths belonging to faith, however, cannot be modified by new scientific discoveries because they speak about exceptional events that transcend the order of nature. When Aquinas teaches about the origins of the universe, he constantly refers to the Bible and maintains that even though natural philosophy (science) may have a different opinion, we believe in the Christian truth, because it is revealed in Holy Writ. For example, Aquinas recognizes that Aristotle and many other natural philosophers favor an eternal universe, and he even says that an eternal universe would be compatible with the Christian idea of a created universe. Nevertheless, he believes in a temporally created universe, because it is divinely revealed.

Aquinas's flexibility regarding theories about the operation (as opposed to the origin) of nature can be seen in this interesting remark about the planetary system:

> In astrology [i.e., astronomy] the theory of eccentrics and epicycles is considered as established, because thereby

the sensible appearances of the heavenly movements can be explained; not, however, as if this proof were sufficient, forasmuch as some other theory might explain them (S.Th. I,32,1, ad2).[3]

Hence, even in the thirteenth century, Aquinas knew that theories of nature are developed to explain the appearances (phenomena) of nature, but this does not mean that a given theory must be an ultimate explanation of a given appearance. It is, therefore, important to realize that what Aquinas assumes as a predominant scientific view of his times is one thing, whereas what he teaches as a matter of faith is another, especially when he speaks of something that a Christian is obliged to believe in and defend against the attacks of unbelievers. When speaking about the origin of man, Aquinas does not make any comments, such as "this is how philosophers of nature explain it today, but this may be explained in a different way in the future." No, he makes it clear that we adopt these truths from revelation and by faith. *Sufficit auctoritas Scripturae* ("The authority of Scripture suffices") is his refrain when speaking about origins. Those Thomists who believe that Darwin rightly modified Aquinas regarding the origin of species do not have the correct understanding of the nature of science and its limits. If Aquinas lived today, he would not adopt the scientifically unfounded and metaphysically nonsensical claims about universal common ancestry and transformation of species. Instead, he would adhere to Biblical faith and principles of sound philosophy. Based on this foundation he would develop firm arguments against biological macroevolution on each level—science, philosophy,

---

[3] See also Aquinas's statement in *De Caelo* II,17: "Yet it is not necessary that the various suppositions which they [ancient astronomers] hit upon be true—for although these suppositions save the appearances, we are nevertheless not obliged to say that these suppositions are true, because perhaps in some other way, that men have not yet comprehended, the appearances of stars may be saved."

and theology. And this is the task for contemporary scholars who want to be Aquinas's disciples and followers.

2. WHY DO THOMISTS ADOPT THEISTIC EVOLUTION?

Throughout this book we have presented substantial difficulties for Thomists who adopt the evolutionary origin of species and of the human body. We showed that even the Augustinian concept of seminal reasons is incompatible with macroevolutionary postulates of Darwin and his followers. Furthermore, we explained that the theory of intelligent design in modern science by no means diminishes—let alone excludes—Aquinas's metaphysical principles or his argument for God's existence. Despite all of this, many (perhaps most) contemporary Thomists adopt the ideas of universal common ancestry and the transformation of species. One should therefore ask, how is it possible that scholars quite faithful to Aquinas in all other areas would so clearly stray from their Master when it comes to this particular problem? Indeed, when reading contemporary books on Thomism or classical metaphysics, one has an impression that many of the authors understand metaphysical principles and are able to apply them to many aspects of the modern view of nature; yet when it comes to the origin of species some kind of blackout happens, and the authors forget all that they explained in previous chapters of their books. They take a break from *sana philosophia* to present a "Thomistic type of theistic evolution." Once they have finished discussing the origin of species, they return to the paths of healthy metaphysical reasoning. The incoherence observed in their enterprise must have some explanation. There must be a proportional reason why Thomists defend the naturalistic paradigm in explaining origins, even though the same Thomists wholeheartedly fight the naturalistic paradigm when teaching about miracles or articles of faith. In what follows we will try to explain why this happens.

A. THE ADOPTION OF THE NATURALISTIC PARADIGM

At the beginning of this book (Chapter I, section 1) we showed that the contemporary Thomistic consensus on evolution (which is theistic evolution) differs greatly from the consensus reached by the Thomists a hundred years ago. This 180-degree turn cannot be explained otherwise than by a change of paradigm in thinking about origins. Every culture favors particular concepts, beliefs, theories, or convictions. These may change and evolve according to new data, discoveries, or intellectual trends. Yet every culture also entertains some deeper, fundamental conviction that we can call a paradigm or a foundational myth. People of a given time are born into this cultural paradigm and see all theories and concepts through it. Particular ideas may be changed easily, but to change the paradigm takes generations of people and vast intellectual work.

The foundational myth is always expressed in a language attractive to the people of the time. For the ancients it was the language of unbelievable stories providing answers to the important questions, such as who the gods are, how the universe and the human race began, why there is suffering, etc. Mythologies provided the worldview and secured a unifying paradigm for culture. After Christianity prevailed in the West, mythologies were replaced with the Bible. The Book of Genesis was the source of the new, Christian worldview, and the new paradigm for culture. Genesis explained how the universe began. The language of fairy tales was replaced with the language of historical realism. The common conviction was that the Biblical narrative recounted events that actually took place, though they could not be verified by historical studies or physical experiments. This paradigm is clearly seen among the founders of modern science. None of them challenged the historical authenticity of the creative events described in Genesis.

However, in the eighteenth century the Biblical paradigm was put to the test by the new approach generally called "naturalism." First deism and mechanicism, then positivism, claimed that Christianity did not provide a viable worldview. The Bible was relegated to explaining only the invisible, moral, eschatological, or spiritual. Naturalists believed that everything concerning the material history of the universe must be explicable within a coherent set of natural causes. This *post-Christian* or *neo-Pagan* paradigm is the one dominating contemporary culture. Darwin's theory was not simply a result of this intellectual shift but greatly contributed to its advent. As long as Thomists, and more broadly—Christian intellectuals—remained within the Biblical paradigm they defended the classic Christian understanding of creation. Once they gave in to the naturalistic paradigm, their goal changed. From defending Christianity they moved to tinkering with Christian doctrine in order to make it "compatible" with naturalism. This is how theistic evolution came about.

This explains why it does not matter what particular arguments one presents in the debate on creation and evolution. Those who think according to the naturalistic paradigm see theistic evolution everywhere, and do not see anything contrary to it anywhere, neither in science, nor theology, nor philosophy. This also explains why so many Thomists adopt and eagerly defend a theory so plainly contradicting Aquinas's teachings. They do not do it for the sake of particular arguments, but because of the paradigm which they were taught at school and through popular culture. Moreover, no one (including catechists and theology professors) has ever told them that there is something wrong with this approach. Having grown up in a culture where naturalism is the paradigm, they have no reason to question natural explanations of origins—especially since the vast majority of their friends and peers from the academic community share the same opinions. And now that the naturalistic paradigm pervades Thomistic academia, the academic community ensures that no dissenter publishes anything clearly contradicting the established compromise between science and faith called theistic evolution. The question of compatibility between the faith and evolution has been resolved *a priori*, without even raising any serious objections. Academic papers in top journals are published not to explain the issue but to confirm the theistic-evolutionary paradigm, no matter how strikingly their theses stray from Aquinas.

Rev. Ignacio Carbajosa observes the same problem in Biblical studies. His description of how the documentary hypothesis colonized academia for over a century quite well fits our context. In his book *Faith, the Fount of Exegesis*, he reproduces the following words of David J. A. Clines:

> No longer is it the truth or falsity of a particular theory that determines whether it will find favor in the guild. Bad arguments will not be driven out by good arguments. Reason will not be the arbiter. Rational debate still happens in the academy, I allow, and issues are sometimes settled purely on their merits. But when it comes to grand theories like the documentary hypothesis there is too much investment in the power that worldviews and grand theories accumulate to themselves for that to happen. I do not mean that there is no longer any place for rational argument, but only that rationality is subordinate to the exercise of power. It is naïve to think otherwise, or to act as if our decisions on such matters were not bound up with where we stand in a world of power.

Carbajosa comments on this passage as follows:

> When Clines speaks of *power*, he has in mind, he makes clear, two types of power. On the one hand, the power of the people and institutions who adopt a certain point of view and, on the other hand, the power of theories and world views to convince a large number of followers.
>
> In the first case, some important exegetes with great influence, attached to institutions of great prestige, have supported, and continue to support, the documentary

hypothesis. As a consequence, it will be difficult for those who do not adopt the same position to get a position in those institutions; they will not be invited to contribute a presentation at seminars, and they will hardly be able to find recommendations to publish their research. It is not by chance that resistance to the documentary hypothesis has usually arisen outside the centers of power, often from young scholars who work in second- and third-ranked institutions...

In the second case, it cannot be denied that the documentary hypothesis triumphed because it offered some weighty arguments in its favor. However, it was not the existence of evidence in its favor that gave such a long life to Wellhausen's theory. It was, rather, its explanatory ability and its comprehensive claims. Indeed, the classic theory became a matrix in which all the questions about the history and literature of Israel found a place. In reality, it was a world view that deserved the name "paradigm." Whole generations of students have assimilated this world view and have developed their research projects about ancient Israel within this framework. Not to have done so would have entailed remaining outside the academic community.

Carbajosa again quotes Clines:

The intrinsic power of the theory gave authority to the community that adopted the theory, but in so doing made every new member of the scholarly community a victim of its power.[4]

---

[4] For this and the Clines and Carbajosa passages above, see I. Carbajosa, *Faith, The Fount of Exegesis* (San Francisco: Ignatius Press, 2013), pp. 77–78.

Carbajosa's description, *mutatis mutandis*, matches the situation in Thomistic studies: Biblical scholarship was pervaded by the evolutionary hypothesis of the origin of the Pentateuch, and Thomism by theistic evolution. In both cases the underlying assumption is that supernatural causes should not be allowed in explaining material and historical phenomena. Yet this works also in the opposite direction: Once we replace the naturalistic paradigm with the Christian one, we will not fail to notice obvious things such as the incompatibility between the facts of nature and Darwin's theory, or theistic evolution and Aquinas's metaphysics. Moreover, we will immediately see that the historical reading of Genesis does not contradict any facts of nature discovered by contemporary science. In the Biblical paradigm the whole science-faith synthesis makes sense and every concept of classical philosophy and theology finds its place. After re-adopting the Biblical paradigm in Thomistic studies one does not need to compromise Thomas to be a Thomist.

B. THE DEFICIENCY IN SCIENTIFIC KNOWLEDGE

The more knowledge humanity possesses the harder it is to be a polymath. Today even the greatest scholars of one discipline do not claim expertise in all its subfields. Even though philosophy and theology are more unified (because they look for wisdom and the ultimate cause of everything), still the sheer quantity of articles and books produced requires a significant time and attention to grasp even superficially everything that an expert should know. This prevents theologians and philosophers from knowing natural science well enough to be able to distinguish scientific facts from the materialistic interpretations. In contrast, the ancient and medieval theologians were usually well-versed in the natural knowledge of their times. Aquinas, for example, thanks to his knowledge of science (at the time philosophy of nature) was able to fight atomists and materialists whose views contradicted Christianity, because he knew that their theories of nature were wrong. Today, however, a large number of theologians, including many Thomists, simply do not know biology well enough to understand the deficiency of Darwinian explanations.

Unfortunately, the numerous science-faith conferences, discussions and programs, supposedly designed to enrich theologians' understanding of natural phenomena, miss the point, because the invited scientists are not interested in presenting the facts without naturalistic theories. Biologists and philosophers of nature typically defend their naturalistic worldview rather than ask real questions and present otherwise obvious difficulties. Dissenters from the Darwinian paradigm are, by default, ignored. Thomists organize those conferences not to look for true answers, but rather to buttress their conviction that their answers are true. Often at these meetings the theory of intelligent design takes up a significant amount of the discussion—but only to criticize it, not to hear from its proponents. Qualified critics of the dominant paradigm are rarely invited. Consequently, biological facts crucial for judging evolutionary theories remain unknown among these philosophers. How many know that genetics does not prove common ancestry? How many are aware that the fossil record (if it represents the genuine history of life) evidences *against* Darwin's theory or that the functional amino-acid sequences are too rare to emerge by chance? How many realize that the entire evolutionary project is based on a shaky assumption that the closer the similarity the closer must be the genealogical relation between two organisms? Remove this one assumption and the entire story collapses.

A striking example of the deficiency in biological knowledge among theologians is seen in their widespread acceptance of the central neo-Darwinian claim that by manipulating genes one can modify organisms virtually to any extent. But the evidence says something different. Genes, indeed, contain a lot of information. For example, they inform the cell as to what proteins to build. But they do not inform the cell how to arrange those proteins into three-dimensional structures. Therefore, there must be some other type of information in every organism that orchestrates the living being as a whole. As philosopher of science Stephen C. Meyer puts it:

> Other sources of information must help arrange individual proteins into systems of proteins, systems of proteins into distinctive cell types, cell types into tissues, and different tissues into organs. And different organs and tissues must be arranged to form body plans.[5]

And if this is the case, it does not matter how long we mutate the genome, nor does it even matter whether the mutations are random or guided by God, because by genetic mutations we will never get the epigenetic information necessary to build any form of life. Genes are indispensable, but they are not the whole story. To build an organism we need other sources of information.[6] And for this reason alone neo-Darwinism has reached a dead end. Does this fact affect theistic evolutionists?

Theistic evolutionists, even if confronted with all facts rendering neo-Darwinism impossible, say something like this: "Darwin might be wrong and his theory definitely had very negative influence on our understanding of morality. But a non-Darwinian evolution is possible. We need to distinguish between the Darwinian ideology and the theory itself. The theory does not carry any social or moral baggage. God could have used evolution." The fact that many Thomists defend

---

[5] S. C. Meyer, *Darwin's Doubt* (HarperOne, 2013), pp. 276–277.

[6] Good examples of metaphysicians' complete unawareness of this problem are Ric Machuga's chapter on evolutionary biology in his book *In Defense of the Soul: What it Means to Be Human* (Grand Rapids, MI: Brazos Press, 2002, pp. 80–99) and Stephen J. Pope's paper "Familial Love and Human Nature: Thomas Aquinas and Neo-Darwinism" (*American Catholic Philosophical Quarterly*, Vol. LXIX, 1995, No. 3, pp. 447–469).

evolution even against the scientific facts should cause reflection. These Thomists do not defend a mere biological theory but a theological and metaphysical paradigm. Evolution is essential to their larger (naturalistic) worldview or framework for thought. And this is why many continue to believe it regardless of the evidence.

It is possible that some Thomists adopted biological macroevolution because they were honestly convinced that there is "overwhelming scientific evidence" in its favor. Of course, scientists supporting neo-Darwinism are not interested in informing philosophers about the difficulties of the theory. Biologists like to believe that they have resolved the riddle of life—something that philosophers attempted for centuries. At the end of the day, Thomists adopting theistic evolution lose this debate twice: once when they accept just-so stories about reptiles evolving into birds or apes evolving into humans, and a second time when they do everything to show that these stories are compatible with Aquinas and classical metaphysics. Our goal here is not to condemn these thinkers but rather to point out the unsatisfactory state of the matter in our times. We encourage Thomists to consider the biological evidence anew and square it with the best of classical Christian philosophy and theology.

C. THE FEAR OF THE "SCIENTIFIC COMMUNITY"

Whether we like it or not, the fact is that modern science was born through a conflict within philosophy, and specifically over the philosophy of nature. Even today, both scientists and philosophers of nature do not exactly understand the competencies of both disciplines. It is not our goal here to elaborate upon this problem. It is enough to notice that in modernity philosophers of nature, those who unreservedly relied on Aristotelian explanations, were proved wrong many times regarding theories of nature. The Galileo affair was used by materialists to convince theologians that the Bible should not be used to explain anything in the physical realm. Very rarely in this debate would either of the parties make crucial distinctions, such as the one between questions about the origin of the universe and questions about its operations. First deism, and later positivism, Marxism, and Darwinism challenged the role of Christianity in forming people's worldview. All of these ideologies strove to remove religion from explaining anything visible or material and relegate it to the invisible realm. This also, especially in positivism, resulted in denying theology the status of a science, or even of a rational mode of inquiry. Communists in the East and liberal materialists in the West removed theology from universities based on the "charge" that she is not scientific. By scientific, however, they understood only what is experimental and measurable. And, indeed, theology and philosophy are not scientific in the same sense as natural science. It does not follow, however, that they are not valuable cognitive disciplines, do not explain anything, or do not provide true knowledge.

The multifaceted attack of modern scientism on philosophy and theology produced two responses. One response was to isolate theology from modern discoveries, as if our understanding of the universe had not progressed since the sixteenth century. This (partially) explains things like Young Earth Creationism, or some new attempts to defend geocentrism. The more common response, however, consisted in an attempt to prove at any price that philosophy and theology are scientific. This (partially) explains the rationalism in theology that came about as either the "extreme" form of neo-Thomism or critical exegesis in Biblical scholarship. In both cases theologians tried to mimic scientific methods and thus present theology as "hard science."

Theistic evolution is the fruit of the same approach, according to which theologians try to accommodate theology to the predominant views among scientists. However, among theistic evolutionists the predominant strategy of avoiding the conflict usually is not to mimic the scientific method in theology, but to limit theological prerogatives, to the point of making theology an insignificant enterprise for those who "simply do not know science." When an apparent conflict between the Bible and a scientific theory arises, theologians remove religion from the visible realm and propose that divine action left no marks in nature. Both strategies—revamping theology and philosophy on the model of natural science, and depriving it from any realistic physical meaning—are mistaken from the start, because these disciplines simply are not scientific in the same sense. Somewhere deep at the core of theistic evolution is the dread theologians and philosophers feel of being called "anti-scientific." This is why the main objective of their science-faith dialogue is not to establish the proper limits of both realms but rather to modify theology in such a way that it does not upset scientific materialists.

Unfortunately, not being well-versed in science, theologians have difficulties in distinguishing science from what is just a materialistic philosophy presented as a scientific theory. Their exaggerated esteem or even fear of the "scientific community" makes them unable to question the so-called "scientific consensus." Some theologians and philosophers are aware of the disagreement in the scientific community regarding Darwinian theory. They know that scientists supporting intelligent design are challenging the "scientific consensus" and thus have opened the way for non-reductionist science. However, the same fear of being called "anti-scientific" drives those theologians to go along with the consensus anyway, in order to preserve the modicum of respect they enjoy in academia.

When Aquinas came out with his plan of using a pagan philosopher to buttress Christian thought he was definitely in the *avant-garde* and he risked condemnation by the Church and ridicule by unbelievers. Yet, the commitment to the truth along with deep personal faith made his academic endeavor a beacon of ecclesiastical thought for centuries. Today's debate over origins requires from Thomists the same courage to speak out for Christian faith. Thomists are invited to resist modern evolutionary mythology on the one hand and to recover the authentic belief in creation on the other. This twofold task cannot be achieved by studies alone. It requires voluntary engagement, moral commitment and, most of all, courage to challenge the neo-Pagan worldview.

D. ARTISTS AND CRAFTSMEN

The present situation cannot be resolved without doctrinal decisions from the Church. The Church has to clearly establish the limits of naturalism by explaining and confirming the Christian doctrine on creation. Meanwhile, Thomists could prepare the way for the resurrection of the Catholic and Christian understanding of creation. For example, they could show the metaphysical impossibility of biological macroevolution. In fact, they should be the leading apologists of Christianity, especially in areas where reason and faith encounter each other so directly as in the science-faith dialogue.

There is currently something like a science-faith synthesis dominating ecclesiastical thought. At the scientific level it adopts biological macroevolution (usually along with the neo-Darwinian mechanism) as the best scientific theory of origins. At the theological level it rejects the literal and historical reading of Genesis and, instead, proposes theistic evolution as the best theological account of creation. In our opinion, this predominant view is mistaken in what it adopts from science as well as how it treats the Bible. Moreover, this approach is substantially incompatible with sound philosophy as developed by Aquinas. Therefore, it should be replaced with a new synthesis, based on a different paradigm. This includes adoption of intelligent design at the scientific level (as the best available scientific theory of origins) and, at the theological level, the return to the historical reading of Genesis, which was the Christian approach from the beginning of the Church. This new science-faith synthesis, unlike the one currently dominating, is perfectly compatible with all physical data, the Bible, and classical metaphysics.

The task of Thomists is to develop this new approach to the question of origins. However, to build a new synthesis, one needs to be more like an artist rather than a craftsman. Artists are those who create new things. If their creation is excellent, it becomes a blueprint for craftsmen. Craftsmen, in contrast, are those who recreate things according to patterns they have learned. They rarely come up with anything new. No doubt, Aquinas was a very talented artist of theology and philosophy. This is why he created "the greatest synthesis ever attained by human thought."[7] But Thomists are merely craftsmen. They limit themselves to repetition. In this sense, Thomists, by definition, cannot be faithful to Thomas, because they, contrary to him, choose to be craftsmen instead of artists. To build the new science-faith synthesis it is not enough to be a craftsman. This requires another step, something that very few Thomists are able to do, namely, accommodating something entirely new from culture and science. This novelty is the modern theory of intelligent design which was not attainable for any ancient or medieval scholar. Aquinas was able to build a synthesis because he reached out to the pagan philosopher Aristotle and robbed him of whatever good he proposed. Today Aquinas would do the same—he would reach out to science and take the best of it to develop his theological teachings about origins.

The problem with Thomistic evolutionists is that in the name of Thomism they reject Aquinas's method of

---

[7] John Paul II, *Fides et Ratio*, no. 78. Another Pope, Leo XIII, said of Aquinas that: "clearly distinguishing, as is fitting, reason from faith, while happily associating the one with the other, he both preserved the rights and had regard for the dignity of each; so much so, indeed, that reason, borne on the wings of Thomas to its human height, can scarcely rise higher, while faith could scarcely expect more or stronger aids from reason than those which she has already obtained through Thomas" (*Aeterni Patris*, no. 18).

synthesizing and incorporating new powerful ideas. Instead, they stick to theistic evolution which is bad science and even worse theology. By doing so, they become guilty of the old charge that has been recurring in ecclesiastical debates since the neo-Thomistic renewal in the nineteenth century—that Thomists use Aquinas to support ideas which have little to do with Thomas himself. Unfortunately, contemporary Thomistic evolutionists do little to render this accusation false. In fact, their belief in evolution, which they project onto Aquinas, leads them to a distortion of the teachings of the Angelic Doctor to a degree unprecedented in the history of Thomistic thought. Never before has Aquinas's philosophy been abused as blatantly as happens in theistic evolution.

By saying this we do not intend to forbid anyone to believe in theistic evolution. There are different worldviews and philosophies out there, and every man has right to choose what he believes. However, no one should use Aquinas to support evolutionary views or any other ideological commitments. We showed in this book that Aquinas's philosophy is not just incompatible with theistic evolution, but excludes it in principle. Aquinas believed literally in Genesis, in the separate creation of species, and the formation of the first human body directly by God. Was he right? This is a separate question. But even if he was wrong (and we do not think this is the case) his teaching remains irreconcilable with biological macroevolution. This cannot be changed by tinkering with some of his secondary doctrines. The incompatibility enters the very foundations of his philosophy and theology, because these two worldviews are built upon two different paradigms—the Christian paradigm based on the Bible and faith, and the evolutionary paradigm based on naturalism and materialism. Aquinas chose to work within the Christian paradigm. Our hope is that this book, as imperfect as it is, will become a source of new inspiration for Thomistic thought and encourage scholars to work for the renewal of the Christian worldview in contemporary culture.

EXCURSUS 2: COULD GOD HAVE USED EVOLUTION?[8]

The question of whether God could have used evolution in forming the universe boils down to whether God could have caused nature, working only through its own inherent properties, to bring about all species of living beings. If in biological evolution there were any supernatural causation, i.e., the type of causation that exceeds the natural operation of the universe, then evolution would not be a natural process, but rather some form of creation. This type of divine activity would not be compatible with naturalism and could not be explained scientifically. In other words, natural processes would appear discontinuous to science and would require theological explanation. Hence, the question is whether God could have inserted into the natural order such properties and laws that would make matter produce life, and make living beings develop into higher and higher (i.e., more complex, more diverse and biologically advanced) forms.

This problem has many philosophical, theological, and scientific aspects. Taking into account classical Christian theology, which is based on revealed sources, we cannot say that God used evolution to form species. In Genesis we find clear teaching that the formation of the universe was due to some extraordinary and peculiar type of divine causality which transcended the order of nature and was finished once for all with the creation of man. Genesis speaks about divine "orders" given to nature which instantaneously cause effects in the form of plant and animal life distinguished according to their kinds.

It is true that many contemporary theologians (including Biblical scholars) reject this classic Christian interpretation. They say that the Bible teaches only *that* God created, but not

---

[8] This part should be read as a supplement to our previous article, "Could God Have Used Evolution?," published in *More than Myth?: Seeking the Full Truth about Genesis, Creation, and Evolution*, ed. R. Stackpole and P. D. Brown (The Chartwell Press, 2014), pp. 228–245.

how He did it. This opinion, however, stands in opposition to the major principle of Catholic exegesis saying that the Bible should be interpreted in accordance with tradition. None of the orthodox authors from the past, such as the Church Fathers and holy Doctors, would agree that the formation of the universe and the origin of species were caused by a natural process acting from *within* nature. Again, the fact of their limited knowledge in biology has nothing to do with the problem of origins, because the origin of species cannot be explained by natural investigation. Divine supernatural causation is a matter of faith (not science) and must be accepted on the divine authority of Scripture.

Hence, in accordance with the Scriptures and holy tradition we must hold that God did not use biological macroevolution to create species. Accordingly, theistic evolution is rendered false by the classical Christian theology of creation for theological reasons. This brings us to an important conclusion: The question of whether God could have used evolution is entirely hypothetical, and even if the answer was "yes," we could not claim that in fact He did it. It is important to keep this distinction in mind, because the logic of the argument as presented by theistic evolutionists is exactly the opposite: They usually think that since God "could have used evolution" therefore, He must have done it, or at least, it is quite certain He did it.[9] In fact, there is no such necessity or logical

---

[9] For example, M. George believes: "If a human being can design a dishwa[sh]er to go through a variety of different cycles without needing someone to step in and nudge it along, and this pertains to his perfection as engineer, *it seems unfitting* that God would choose not to design a universe in which new kinds of beings can develop as a result of natural causes within that universe" [emphasis added]. See M. George, "What Would Thomas Aquinas Say about Intelligent Design?," p. 684. J. S. Wilkins thinks that if using evolution is possible for a "limited deity" then "it is *even more the case* that an omniscient, omnipotent, and omnibenevolent deity would be able to select the best of all possible worlds in which natural selection realizes his plan." See Wilkins's previously cited "Could God Create Darwinian Accidents?," p. 38.

transition. God could have done many things, in many different ways, yet He chose the ways He wanted, and in many cases these are not the ways humans would choose or expect.

The proponents of theistic evolution also claim that since God is omnipotent He could have produced species using natural processes. This argument puts anyone who would dare to doubt this possibility in a difficult position, because saying that God could not have used evolution seems to limit his power and deprive God of His divine attributes. Saying that *God could not have done something* sounds like a grave heresy. However, many classical Christian writers, including Aquinas, say that even though God is omnipotent it does not follow He can do anything whatsoever. According to Aquinas, God cannot make a circular square or straight curve. He cannot make something that has happened not to have happened, and He cannot make something greater than Himself, or make Himself cease to exist. In each of these instances God's "inability" does not stem from a lack of power on His part, but from the contradiction in terms present in those examples. They contain logical contradictions, they cannot be thought of, they cannot exist, because they are self-contradictory.

Although it may be harder to realize, saying that God used evolution to create species leads to the same problem—it requires God to engage in logical contradictions. For example, in evolution there are only accidental changes, whereas creation of a new species requires creation of a new complete nature. Accidental change alters the accidents of a substance, but not the substance itself. Hence, accidental change may be defined as any change that is not substantial. If, therefore, accidental changes led to creation of new complete natures, this would mean that the accidental change was at the same time a substantial change, which is a contradiction in terms—God would need to make the accidental change a substantial change at the same time. This is one of the reasons why the older Thomists called theistic evolution "metaphysically absurd" and "contradicting common sense" (see Ch. I, sect. 1).

This argument is valid under three conditions: first, that we understand and accept the principles of classical metaphysics; second, that we understand notions such as "God," "creation," and "nature" in a classical Christian way; and third, that we accept *moderate realism* as our epistemological position. All of these, however, are adopted and defended by Aquinas. Thus, a Thomist cannot say that God could have used evolution without making Him the author of a logical contradiction.

Another reason why God could not have used evolution is that evolution is not a sufficient cause of the effects it is supposed to have produced. According to the evolutionary story, there are in nature some emergent tendencies or laws of self-organization that lead to the production of new species. However, even if there are some instances of self-organization (as in the production of crystals) they are not the type of change that could bring about completely new species and higher levels of life. Laws create regularities in nature, but regularities are not enough to build a new form of life. For this reason, saying that God used evolution amounts to saying that God made something emerge from nothing without His immediate (or at least supernatural) act. God, of course, can make something out of nothing, but he cannot make nothing to create something by itself. Otherwise something could turn spontaneously into nothing just as easily as nothing could change into something. Moreover, this would mean that a higher effect (such as a higher form of life) can be generated by a lower cause, which again boils down to saying that nothing makes something. This scenario would also contravene the metaphysical distinction between potency and act; it would mean that something in potency can move into act without previous act, which is like saying that something makes itself, or acts without a cause, which is another absurdity.

We see therefore that saying "God could have used evolution" leaves us with a number of metaphysical problems that end in logical contradictions. In any case, before saying that God could have used evolution, a Christian scholar should first attempt to resolve these problems. Otherwise, it is not possible (even hypothetically) that God used evolution. Despite a number of books that address the topic of metaphysics and evolution, no convincing answers to the objections presented here have been delivered.[10]

These logical and metaphysical problems find their counterpart on the empirical level. In order to believe that God used a natural process of evolution to assemble the whole diversity of creatures we first need to realize what this scenario really involves. If one believes that natural (material) processes generate new species one cannot believe that living beings have an immaterial principle or a soul. Otherwise, one needs to assume that matter can generate immaterial forms, which again is metaphysically impossible. Hence, if one believes in God using natural evolution to create species, one needs first to reduce biological reality to a combination of particles and arrangements of atoms. (By the way, it is surprising that many Catholic philosophers who fight this type of reductionism among biologists accept theistic evolution, which necessitates this type of reductionism.)

Let's assume for the sake of the argument that life indeed can be reduced to physical and chemical mechanisms and interactions. Now we need to ask what it actually takes to build a mechanism. If life were assembled by evolution pursuant to physical mechanisms, there should be a recognizable law or path which nature followed. Some biologists believe that this is the neo-Darwinian mechanism of genetic mutations and natural selection. To see the problem with this proposal we need to refer to much simpler and well-known examples, such as mechanisms built by humans. To some degree engines and other devices created by humans resemble living beings. (For non-reductionist metaphysicians, mechanisms can account only for some aspects, or parts, of living beings, whereas for

---

[10] Some examples showing how those attempts are unsatisfactory have been presented throughout this book (see, for example, Ch. II, sect. 3).

reductionists, including those who believe in the ability of the evolutionary mechanism to produce species, everything found in living beings, indeed, life itself, must be reducible to mechanism.)

For example, to produce a watch a watchmaker is needed. A watchmaker first designs and then crafts the watch using different tools. To make another watch, he simply takes another piece of metal and crafts it into another watch according to the previously conceived design. Even at this point the analogy between a watch and a living being fails. In nature one living being produces another similar to itself. For example, a cat generates a cat, and a snake generates a snake. If, therefore, animal generation were comparable to human craftsmanship, a craftsman should be able to make a watch that could make another watch, which could make another watch and so on. Humans can make a factory that would make watches by itself, but not watches that make other watches. Car production lines are nearly entirely automated. We can say that humans design mechanisms that can produce another mechanism (such as cars and watches) automatically (i.e., without any additional purposeful activity on the part of the engineers). Blind machines produce machines. But is that the same as cat generating cat?

And what about the ability of living beings to regenerate themselves after being wounded or sick? This is another place where the analogy fails. We see that machines (such as cars and watches) cannot regenerate themselves. Moreover, automatic production of mechanisms requires a factory, a set of many machines, which is a huge resource compared to the mechanism of a car itself. A living being, such as a cat, is not essentially different from another living being (e.g., another cat) that it generates, whereas the factory making cars differs dramatically from a single car. All of this leads us to conclude that a living being as such (as a certain whole) differs from any known mechanism, either natural (such as waves mechanically produced in the oceans) or created by humans (such as cars and watches).

This difference is caused by the immaterial principle that allows a living being to act beyond what is attainable by purely physical and chemical mechanisms. Living beings cannot be reduced to material reactions and processes alone, even if those processes and reactions constitute some part of their basic (and empirical) level of operation.

Now, the fact that living beings transcend the level of physics and chemistry has led some philosophers to believe in some extraordinary "potencies" embedded in the animated world. They think that if such amazing phenomena as generation and regeneration happen on a regular basis then there must be some other hidden powers in nature that account for macroevolutionary transformations and the alleged development of the whole biosphere to the higher and higher levels of life. In philosophy this approach to nature is called *vitalism*. In fact, vitalism is what (consciously or unconsciously) inspires many philosophers to adopt theistic evolution.[11] They are correct in their anti-reductionist understanding of biology, but this paradoxically leads them to the opposite error, namely, attributing to nature spiritual powers, consciousness, or a common soul. Thus, theistic evolution ends up either in mechanistic reductionism (this happens when one wants to

---

[11] For example, Jacques Maritain believes that biological macroevolution is driven by "a power of self-regulation" awakening when "the tendentiality of matter passes over into act in higher forms." Maritain introduces himself as a critic of Teilhard de Chardin, but we have no clue how his own concept of theistic evolution differs from that of Teilhard. Even on the level of the language alone Maritain fails to avoid the *ad hoc* imaginative and esoteric concepts that are so abundant in Teilhard. Besides believing in "evolutive tendentiality" and "tendentiality of matter," Maritain resorts to surrealistic ideas such as "a power of finalized invention," the "superelevating and superforming motion of God," the "transnatural ontological tendency," and even the "élan of expansion"—a notion strikingly similar to the Bergsonian "élan vital" (whose orthodoxy was questioned by the Church a few decades earlier). In all of this Maritain believes he represents and defends the realistic philosophy of Thomas Aquinas! See his previously cited paper, "Toward a Thomist Idea of Evolution."

explain the origin of species by a biological mechanism), or in the spiritualization of nature in the form of vitalism (when one seeks for some mysterious powers of self-organization hidden in the biosphere). Classical Christian philosophy sees the non-mechanical character of life, recognizes the immaterial principle in every living being (particular souls), but at the same time does not fall into fantastic visions of reptiles capable of transforming into birds or apes evolving into humans. In the Christian approach, immaterial principles in nature account for generation and regeneration, but these powers are limited to established species and cannot bring about completely new living natures or higher orders of being.

Leaving behind the problem of vitalism, let's return to the problem of evolution as a mechanism that God would use to create species. Some scholars believe that God could have front-loaded the evolutionary process in the beginning of creation in such a way that the ensemble of constants and forces would ultimately produce species such as lions, horses, and apes.[12] If this were truly the case, it would follow that a tiny change in one of the variables would bring about a different species at the end. So, if gravitation, for instance, were slightly stronger or weaker, then after billions of years, instead of a bear we might get a sphinx or an elf (a species imagined but not existing). This approach, besides the fact that it again reduces life to physical

---

[12] B. Ashley's solution, presented in his 1972 paper in *The Thomist*, boils down to a front-loaded type of theistic evolution: "Nuclear, chemical, and biological evolution, although involving very different kinds of events, have this in common: atom, molecule, and organism are products of historical events no less complex and sequentially ordered than the entities which they produce. The new species is not a "greater emerging from the less," because the amount of information it contains in *integrated* form is no greater than the amount of information present in the historical evolutionary process. What is spread out in history is condensed, as it were, in the emerging new species." "Evolution in all its phases requires no other forces in nature than the fundamental cosmic forces of gravitation, electromagnetism, and the nuclear forces." See Ashley, "Causality and Evolution," pp. 215, 227.

motions, is extremely naïve, because it does not recognize anything like different orders in nature. Obtaining life from non-life, and new species from utterly different species, takes more than just different initial conditions. It requires design.

To be sure, the proponents of front-loaded evolution believe that God could have inserted design into simple properties of matter and physical laws He created at the beginning of the universe. Then, over the course of immense time, that original design would develop and become apparent in the form of different species. This thinking attracts many scholars who want to save biological macroevolution, but who also doubt that any blind process could account for it; yet this thinking stems from a fundamental misunderstanding of what design is and what it takes to communicate it.

In order to show the problem of "front-loaded" evolution, first we need to build an abstract mathematical tool (A) and then confront it with reality (B).

(A). Let's imagine we draw ten cards from a pool of twenty-six cards, each with a different natural number from 1 to 26. We return a card after each draw. We do it three times, thus obtaining three chains of digits:

a. 3,5,23,7,10,12,3,15,20,2
b. 3,3,3,3,3,3,3,3,3,3
c. 8,1,22,5,1,16,9,26,26,1

Anyone conscious of what is going on would immediately question the randomness (and fairness) of the second draw (b). Drawing a "3" ten times in a row is so extremely improbable that we have reason to doubt that the draws were fair. The mathematical probability of obtaining this result is like 1 in 26^{10} (or roughly 1 in 10^{14})—far too low to expect it to happen randomly. Yet, the mathematical probability of obtaining the first and the third chain is exactly the same. Indeed, any chain of ten digits from the pool of twenty-six is equally improbable. Therefore, there must be something other than just the extremely low mathematical probability which makes us doubt the randomness of the second chain while trusting the randomness of the two others. This "something" is the presence of the repetitive pattern in the second chain. We know that random events do not create patterns, whereas the second chain clearly represents a pattern—each number in the chain is just a repetition of the previous number. This fact makes us doubt that the second chain is random. Thus, we can distinguish between random events and those that follow patterns. Patterns, i.e., highly improbable structures that can be described by a simple formula, cannot be produced by chance.

Now let's imagine that on the reverse of each of the cards with a number there is a subsequent letter of the alphabet corresponding to the number. We turn the cards around and we see three chains:

1. c,e,w,g,j,l,c,o,t,b
2. c,c,c,c,c,c,c,c,c,c
3. h,a,v,e,a,p,i,z,z,a

The first chain is just gibberish; the second follows a pattern and thus cannot be random. The third, however, contains information, i.e., an understandable (intelligible) message. Many people would doubt the randomness of the third chain. Again, the common experience is that messages come from humans (intellectual beings) not from tossing cards randomly. This also makes us think that the third chain was not picked up randomly. Can our common intuition that the second and the third chains are not generated randomly be rigorously confirmed by mathematical and empirical sciences?

The first chain can be random because there is no pattern that would describe it. This complies with the nature of random events. However, in the physical universe very few events are truly random. (See our previous discussion of randomness and necessity in Chapter V, section 2, subsection

A.) For example, if we throw a die, the outcome is determined by the direction we impose and the forces of nature (gravity, friction, impetus). If we could know all of the forces involved, we could predict the exact outcome of each throw. This is why, if the die is fair, each digit should turn up in roughly one-sixth of the total number of the throws. If we do just six (or fewer) throws, the outcome is undetermined. But if we throw a die a thousand times, each digit should appear roughly 166 times (1000/6). If the outcome significantly deviates from this number (for example one digit appears more than 200 times at the cost of other digits), we have reason to doubt the fairness of the die. In this case a simple statistical test for randomness will reveal that the event is not random. The same is true about the three chains described above. The second cannot be random, because it represents a pattern. If the draws of the cards were random, there should not be a pattern in the outcome. And the more draws of the card we try, the less probable a pattern becomes. In fact, if the events are random, an increase in attempts (i.e., increased probabilistic resources) will tend to destroy any pattern. This is why on a large scale truly random events will not generate patterns, whereas necessary events (such as throwing a die) will tend to create patterns in what is determined (the appearance of each digit should constitute roughly 1/6 of the total number of throws) and ruin patterns in what is random. (Random in this case is the order of digits. This is why throwing a die will not *generate* but *ruin* patterns such as 111,222,333,444,555,666,111…).

There are two reasons why the third chain of letters cannot be obtained by drawing cards randomly. Both reasons stem from the fact that this chain contains information. Information must be expressed (communicated) in an intelligible language. And every language contains some patterns (though no language is reducible to patterns). For example, in English there are 26 letters, five vowels and twenty-one consonants. Vowels constitute roughly 20% of the letters (5/26). However, in an average English text, vowels account for about 40% of the total number of letters.¹³ If letters were chosen randomly, vowels would constitute only 20% instead of the required 40%. Another example is the "space key" which should randomly appear one time in 27 (26 letters plus space constitute the pool). But in any text spaces appear much more often (like one time in three or four hits of the keyboard). And there are many other rules in different languages (such as that punctuation marks come always before spaces, that in Polish "l" never appears after "r," etc.) that cannot be reproduced by a random selection of letters. We can say that every language contains rules and that rules create a framework for freedom which fills the linguistic framework with meaning. For this reason, a random choice of letters on a larger scale will never create an intelligible text, even if some short words (e.g., "you" or "to") may randomly appear.

The second reason why information cannot be generated randomly is *specification*. In the third chain of letters we see three words: "have," "a," and "pizza." The arrangement of the letters is not only quite improbable but also *specified*. We understand these chains of letters because they match independent ideas in our minds. This is why texts are intelligible. A text can be understood because it refers us to abstract concepts which we already store in our minds. In contrast, random chains of letters are unintelligible, they cannot be described by a simple formula (like patterns in necessary events), and they do not match an independent pattern.¹⁴

In sum, our mathematical model contains three types of events: random, necessary (i.e., repetitive), and purposeful (i.e., designed). It is important to realize that one type of event is not reducible to another. For example, a designed event

---

[13] See "Consonants," *Encyclopedia Americana*, Vol. 3, edited by E. Wigglesworth (Philadelphia: Blanchard and Lea, 1857), pp. 449–453, 452.

[14] This is also the reason why ID is not just a probabilistic argument, as some critics misrepresent it. See, for example, W. Newton, op. cit., pp. 573, 577.

cannot be represented by a pattern, because a pattern does not contain specification.[15] A pattern cannot be represented by randomness, because randomness is not repetitive and cannot be described by a simple formula. Indeed, a random event is defined as a non-necessary event, and a necessary event is something that does not come from a free choice, like information.[16]

(B). Now we will confront this mathematical model with the problem of biological origins and the idea of "front-loaded" evolution. In nature we find three types of events and structures that are generally described by one of our model's events. There are things that are random (like movements of the particles on the quantum level), things that are necessary (for instance, any object thrown up will fall down owing to gravity), and things that contain specification. A good example lies in the genomes of living organisms. Genetic information resembles sentences of a human language or a computer program. It gives instructions to the cell about how to build proteins and perform various functions. As in the human text specification comes from the meaning of a particular arrangement of letters, in genes specification comes from the function the gene

---

[15] It is also possible that an event that looks random or necessary was actually produced by intelligence. An intelligent cause can imitate the effects typically produced by chance or laws. The detection of intelligent design is possible only where intelligence has produced an effect typical for its workings, that is, characterized by specified or irreducible complexity.

[16] M. George believes that random mutations could be ultimately non-random and thus could generate design. They could result from the operation of some preprogrammed necessities in genomes. George presents this as an argument against W. Dembski's argument for ID from specified complexity. But George's argument does not differ from saying that design is simply pre-loaded in the laws of nature. Why this is impossible is shown here and in what follows. George does not seem to understand the difference between patterns and specification. This is where her criticism of Dembski's argument fails. M. George, "What Would Thomas Aquinas Say about Intelligent Design?," pp. 676–700, 678–679, 685.

performs. A particular arrangement of base pairs (A–T, T–A, C–G, G–C) in the double helix of the DNA makes the gene perform this and not another function.[17] In effect we see that a particular linear arrangement of the base pairs (1-D structure) causes the production of a particular protein (3-D structure) which performs a particular function. The function and the three-dimensional structure of the protein specifies the gene in the same way as the meaning (the function) of the word "pizza" specifies the set of characters p-i-z-z-a. On the large scale in biology we find different organs and whole living beings that perform characteristic functions and behaviors. The functions of the organs and those of the whole organisms constitute the specification of the genetic information.

The problem with front-loaded evolution is that we do not find specified information anywhere in nature but in living beings. Hence, if specified information is present there must be living organisms around. But this was not the case even eight to nine billion years after the Big Bang. The fine-tuning of the many laws and constants governing the universe brought many physicists to the conclusion that they were purposefully designed. However, the fact that the laws are designed does not mean that they can create design. They account for repetitive patterns. Yet life requires specified information. So, it does not matter how finely the laws are tuned; they cannot produce a new type of order, namely, the order characterized by specification. Laws can pass on design, but they cannot create it. The passing on of design happens, for example, in the natural generation of subsequent animals. Still, we cannot say that the law of generation creates the information. It only passes on what is already present in the parent.

---

[17] We are talking here about the standard model. Today we know that cells read many sequences of base pairs on many levels, and this is why one string of information—a "gene"—can perform many different functions. The standard model was exceeded by modern discoveries; however, the standard model remains valid to the degree required by the argument presented here.

Some theistic evolutionists would say, therefore, that the first life must have been created, but once life was present it could have developed into all species. But this scenario encounters the same problem: One living being contains only a minuscule percentage of the specified information required for millions of different species. The evolutionary scenario requires that one organism, subject to evolution, give rise to new genetic information. But the information contained in the first living being is subject to the laws of nature, such as random mutations and natural selection. So, again, the new specified information would need to come from the operation of the laws (mutation, variation, selection), which, as we said, is impossible.

Another solution is that all information was packed into the first living being and then developed in a natural process of generation, thus creating all biodiversity. But this idea is counterfactual. If we scrutinize the most primitive organisms (which do not substantially differ from the first living beings), we do not find in them the whole of the genetic information present in all species. And even if such superfluous information had been present in the earliest organisms, according to the very logic of Darwinian evolution, it would have been eliminated by mutations and/or natural selection. Thus, the superfluous information most probably would have been lost in the very beginning as something useless and hindering efficient operation of the cell. Moreover, we know that DNA is not the only carrier of biological information present in cells. There are different sources of information absolutely necessary for an organism to live. For example, the physical structure of the cell itself constitutes a three-dimensional pattern that tells the cell how to arrange proteins into a body plan. Since this kind of information determines the body plan of an embryo it cannot at the same time provide the information needed to build an organism with entirely different body plan (determination toward one physical form excludes determination toward another). Thus, as a matter of fact, we do not find front-loaded information in primitive organisms that would allow them to develop into all species. Believing that *God could have used evolution* by front-loading biological information boils down to saying that all genetic and epigenetic information present in all biodiversity (including the extinct species) could have been packed into the first primitive cell. I do not know of any actual experiments that would demonstrate that this is impossible. Still, I believe that anyone who understands the problem cannot think otherwise. And if this is impossible, then front-loaded evolution is also impossible.

We said above that one type of structure/event is not reducible to another. This means that random events cannot generate patterns present in necessary events. Further, random and necessary events combined cannot generate specification. This is a problem of an ascending hierarchy of organization—a lower type of event (random and necessary) cannot generate the higher type (intelligible, or informative). In this sense chaotic movements of particles cannot produce the same type of effect as is typically produced by a mind, and necessity in the form of laws of nature cannot act freely, i.e., in the way that minds work (for example, by free choice of alphabetic characters producing intelligible texts containing specified information).

But the same is true in the opposite direction: A higher order of events is not reducible to the lower order without annihilation of the higher order. If specification is present, it cannot be presented in the form of random or necessary events without destroying information. If a pattern is present it cannot be transformed into randomness without destroying the pattern. In other words, one type of event/structure cannot be expressed or contained in another without ruining what is essential for that type. A good example of an attempt to hide specification under randomness or repetitive patterns is found in coding machines such as Enigma. The goal of codes is to hide meaning (specification). The authors of codes try to make a meaningful text look like a random string of characters, or like a simple repetitive pattern. Yet, specification is never removed from the encrypted text, but only hidden in it. If it were removed, the message (meaning) could never be recovered.

This fact has fatal consequences for anything like front-loaded biological evolution. Neither random events, nor laws of nature, nor primitive genomes contain the specification needed to build the proteins or the body plans of all living beings. At the same time we conclude that specification is not just quantitatively but qualitatively different from randomness and repetitive patterns. Hence, natural evolution would require production of something (information) from nothing (unspecified patterns and chaos) and this contradicts common sense. Indeed, something cannot emerge from nothing except for direct divine causation. But theistic evolution excludes direct divine causation and for this reason it contradicts common sense. This is why God could not have used evolution as a way of producing all species.

Thomas Aquinas did not know most of what was brought up in the argument above. Yet, based on healthy metaphysical reasoning alone, he came to the same conclusion when he wrote:

> Therefore, as no pre-existing body has been formed whereby another body of the same species could be generated, the first human body was *of necessity* made *immediately* by God (S.Th. I,91,2, co).

BIBLIOGRAPHY

Acta et decreta Concilii Provinciae Coloniensis (Coloniae: 1862).
Adler, M. J. *Problems for Thomists: The Problem of Species*. New York: Sheed & Ward, 1940.
Artigas, M., T. F. Glick, and R. A. Martínez. *Negotiating Darwin: The Vatican Confronts Evolution 1877–1902*. Baltimore: Johns Hopkins University Press, 2006.
Ashley, B. "Causality and Evolution." *The Thomist*, 36(2), pp. 199–230.
Augustine, St. *Confessions*. http://www.newadvent.org/fathers/1101.htm.
Augustine, St. *De Civitate Dei*. http://www.newadvent.org/fathers/1201.htm.
Augustine, St. *De Genesi ad Litteram*. In *On Genesis*. Volume I/13 of *The Works of St. Augustine: A Translation for the 21st Century*. Edited by J. E. Rotelle, O.S.A. Translated by E. Hill, O.P. Hyde Park, NY: New City Press, 2002.
Augustine, St. *On the Trinity*. http://www.newadvent.org/fathers/1301.htm.
Austriaco, N. P. G., J. Brent, Th. Davenport, and J. B. Ku. *Thomistic Evolution: A Catholic Approach to Understanding Evolution in the Light of Faith*. Tacoma, WA: Cluny Media, 2016.
Axe, D. *Undeniable: How Biology Confirms Our Intuition that Life Is Designed*. New York: HarperOne, 2016.
Baldner, S. E., and W. E. Carroll. *Aquinas on Creation*. Toronto: Pontifical Institute of Mediaeval Studies, 1997.
Barr, S. "The End of Intelligent Design?" *First Things*, 2 October 2010. http://www.firstthings.com/web-exclusives/2010/02/the-end-of-intelligent-design.

Barr, S. M. "Chance, by Design." *First Things*, December 2012, pp. 25–30.

Beckwith, F. "Intelligent Design and Me, Part 2: Confessions of a Doting Thomist." BioLogos, 10 March 2010. http://biologos.org/blogs/archive/intelligent-design-and-me-part-2-confessions-of-a-doting-thomist#sthash.1g2YeG6H.UvejmyAX.dpuf.

Beckwith, F. J. "Intelligent Design, Thomas Aquinas, and the Ubiquity of Final Causes." The Biologos Foundation. http://biologos.org/uploads/projects/beckwith_scholarly_essay.pdf.

Behe, M. *Darwin's Black Box: The Biochemical Challenge to Evolution*. New York: Touchstone, 1996.

Bohm, D. *Causality and Chance in Modern Physics*. Philadelphia: University of Pennsylvania Press, 1971.

Carbajosa, I. *Faith, The Fount of Exegesis*. San Francisco: Ignatius Press, 2013.

Carroll, W. E. "Creation, Evolution, and Thomas Aquinas." http://www.catholiceducation.org/articles/sc0035.html.

Cessario, R. *A Short History of Thomism*. Washington, DC: The Catholic University of America Press, 2005.

Chaberek, M. "Could God Have Used Evolution?" In pp. 228–245 of *More than Myth?: Seeking the Full Truth about Genesis, Creation, and Evolution*. Edited by R. Stackpole and P. D. Brown. The Chartwell Press, 2014.

Chaberek, M. *Catholicism and Evolution: From Darwin to Pope Francis*. Angelico Press, 2015.

Condic, M. L., and K. L. Flannery. "A Contemporary Aristotelian Embryology." *Nova et Vetera*, Vol. 12, No. 2(2014), pp. 495–508.

"Consonants." *Encyclopedia Americana*, Vol. 3. Edited by E. Wigglesworth. Philadelphia: Blanchard and Lea, 1857.

Darwin, Charles. *On the Origin of Species*. London: John Murray, 1859.

Dei Filius. Dogmatic Constitution of the First Vatican Council. DS 3002. http://inters.org/Vatican-Council-I-Dei-Filius.

Dembski, W. A. *The Design Inference: Eliminating Chance Through Small Probabilities*. New York: Cambridge University Press, 1998.
Dembski, W.A. *The Design Revolution*. IVP Press, 2010.
Dodds, M. *Unlocking Divine Action*. CUA Press, 2012.
Enchiridion Symbolorum Definitionum et Declarationum. Denzinger-Schönmetzer, ed. 34. Freiburg: Herder, 1967.
Euvé, F. *Darwin i chrzescijanstwo*. Krakow: WAM, 2010.
Feser, E. "'Intelligent Design' theory and mechanism." 10 April 2010. http://edwardfeser.blogspot.com/2010/04/intelligent-design-theory-and-mechanism.html.
Feser, E. "Between Aristotle and William Paley: Aquinas's Fifth Way." *Nova et Vetera*, Vol. 11, No. 3(Summer 2013), pp. 740–749.
Feser, E. "The Trouble with William Paley." November 4, 2009. http://edwardfeser.blogspot.com/2009/11/trouble-with-william-paley.html.
Feser, E. *Scholastic Metaphysics*. Editiones Scholasticae. Piscataway NJ: Transaction Books, 2014.
Feser, E. *The Last Superstition*. South Bend, Indiana: Saint Augustine's Press, 2008.
Forrest, B. "The Non-Epistemology of Intelligent Design: Its Implications for Public Policy." *Synthese* (2011), 178, pp. 331–379.
George, M. "On Attempts to Salvage Paley's Argument from Design." In *Science, Philosophy, Theology*. Edited by J. O'Callaghan. South Bend, Indiana: St. Augustine's Press, 2002.
George, M. "Thomistic Rebuttal of Some Common Objections to Paley's Argument From Design." *New Blackfriars*, Vol. 97, No. 1069, May 2016, pp. 266–288.
George, M. "What Would Thomas Aquinas Say about Intelligent Design?" *New Blackfriars*, Vol. 94, No. 1054, Nov. 2013, pp. 676–700.

Gilson, E. *From Aristotle to Darwin and Back Again*. Translated by J. Lyon. Notre Dame: Notre Dame Press, 1984.

God and Evolution: Protestants, Catholics, and Jews Explore Darwin's Challenge to Faith. Edited by J. W. Richards. Seattle: Discovery Institute Press, 2010.

Hardon, J. A. *The Catholic Catechism: A Contemporary Catechism of the Teachings of the Catholic Church*. New York: Image Book, 1981.

Haught, J. F. *God After Darwin*. Westview Press, 2008.

Heller, M., and J. Zycinski. *Dylematy ewolucji*. Tarnow: Biblos, 1996.

International Theological Commission. *Communion and Stewardship: Human Persons Created in the Image of God*. July 23, 2004. http://www.vatican.va/roman_curia/congregations/cfaith/cti_documents/rc_con_cfaith_doc_20040723_communion-stewardship_en.html.

Irenaeus, St. *Adversus haereses*. http://www.newadvent.org/fathers/0103.htm.

John Paul II. Address to the Pontifical Academy of Science, October 22, 1996. https://www.ewtn.com/library/PAPALDOC/JP961022.HTM.

John Paul II. *Evangelium Vitae*. http://w2.vatican.va/content/john-paul-ii/en/encyclicals/documents/hf_jp-ii_enc_25031995_evangelium-vitae.html.

John Paul II. *Fides et Ratio,* https://w2.vatican.va/content/john-paul-ii/en/encyclicals/documents/hf_jp-ii_enc_14091998_fides-et-ratio.html.

Johnson, Ph. E. *Darwin on Trial*. Second edition. Downers Grove, IL: InterVarsity Press, 1993.

Klubertanz, G. P. "Causality and Evolution." *The Modern Schoolman*, 19(1), Nov. 1941, pp. 11–14.

Koninck, Ch. De. "The Cosmos. The Philosophic Point of View." In pp. 256–321 of *The Writings of Charles De Koninck*, Vol. 1. Edited and translated by R. McInerny. Indiana: University of Notre Dame Press, 2008.

Koons, R. C., and L. P. Gage. "St. Thomas Aquinas on Intelligent Design." *Proceedings of the American Catholic Philosophical Association*, Vol. 85 (2011), pp. 79–97.

Krapiec, M. A. *Wprowadzenie do filozofii*. Lublin: RW KUL, 1996.

Kuhn, Th. S. *The Structure of Scientific Revolutions*. Chicago: University of Chicago Press, 1962.

Larmer, B. "Is There Anything Wrong With 'God of the Gaps' Reasoning?" *International Journal for Philosophy of Religion*, Vol. 52, 2002, pp. 129–142.

Leo XIII. *Aeterni Patris*, https://w2.vatican.va/content/leo-xiii/en/encyclicals/documents/hf_l-xiii_enc_04081879_aeterni-patris.html.

Leo XIII. *Arcanum divinae sapientiae*. Acta Sanctae Sedis, 12. Romae: 1879; reprint, 1968.

Lichacz, P. "Czy stworzenie wyklucza ewolucje?" In pp. 71–94 of *Teologia sw. Tomasza z Akwinu dzisiaj*. Poznan: Uniwersytet Adama Mickiewicza, Wydzial Teologiczny, 2010.

Luyten, N. "Philosophical Implications of Evolution." *New Scholasticism*, 25(1951), pp. 290–312.

Machuga, R. *In Defense of the Soul: What it Means to Be Human*. Grand Rapids: Brazos Press, 2002.

Mayr, E. *Systematics and the Origin of Species from the Viewpoint of a Zoologist*. New York: Columbia University Press, 1942.

Maritain, J. "Toward A Thomist Idea of Evolution." In pp. 85–131 of *Untrammeled Approaches. The Collected Works of Jacques Maritain*, Vol. 20. South Bend: University of Notre Dame Press, 1977.

McKeough, M. "The Meaning of the *Rationes Seminales* in St. Augustine." Ph.D. dissertation, Catholic University of America, 1926.

McMullin, E. "Darwin and the Other Christian Tradition." *Zygon*, Vol. 46, No. 2 (June 2011), pp. 291–316.

Messenger, E. C. *Evolution and Theology*. NY: The Macmillan Company, 1932.

Meyer, St. C. *Darwin's Doubt*. New York: HarperOne, 2013.

Meyer, St. C. *Signature in the Cell: DNA and the Evidence for Intelligent Design*. New York: HarperOne, 2009.

Newton, W. "A Case of Mistaken Identity: Aquinas's Fifth Way and Arguments of Intelligent Design." *New Blackfriars*, Vol. 95, Issue 1059, Sept. 2014, pp. 569–578.

Nogar, R. J. *The Wisdom of Evolution*. New York: Mentor-Omega Book, 1966.

On the Historical Character of the First Three Chapters of Genesis. A Decree of the Pontifical Biblical Commission (June 30, 1909). *Enchiridion Biblicum*, 99 (EB 335–39). http://www.catholicscripture.net/enchiridion/genesis.html.

Pius XII. Address to the Pontifical Academy of Sciences of November 30, 1941. *AAS* 33 (1941). In *Papal Addresses to the Pontifical Academy of Sciences 1917–2002*. Vatican: The Pontifical Academy of Sciences, 2003.

Pope, J. "Familial Love and Human Nature: Thomas Aquinas and Neo-Darwinism." *American Catholic Philosophical Quarterly*, Vol. LXIX, 1995, No. 3, pp. 447–469.

Ratzinger, J. *Creation and Evolution: A Conference with Pope Benedict XVI in Castel Gandolfo*. Edited by S. O. Horn and S. Wiedenhofer. San Francisco: Ignatius Press, 2008.

Russell, J. B. *Inventing the Flat Earth: Columbus and Modern Historians*. Westport, CT: Praeger Publishers, 1991.

Ryan, F. "Aquinas and Darwin." In *Darwin and Catholicism*. Edited by L. Caruana. NY: T&T Clark, 2009.

Ryland, M. "What is Intelligent Design Theory?" *Second Spring*, 2012(15), pp. 46–57.

Salij, J. *Pochodzenie czlowieka w swietle wiary i nauki*. In pp. 277–286 of *Kontrowersje wokol poczatkow czlowieka*. Edited by G. Bugajak and J. Tomczyk. Katowice: Ksiegarnia Swietego Jacka, 2007.

Saltet, L. "St. Jerome." *Catholic Encyclopedia*, Vol. 8. New York: The Encyclopedia Press, 1909. http://www.newadvent.org/cathen/08341a.htm.

Schneider, R. J. "Essay II: Theology of Creation: Historical Perspectives and Fundamental Concepts." http://community.berea.edu/scienceandfaith/essay02.asp.

Shea, M. "Intelligent Design vs. the Argument from Design." http://www.ncregister.com/blog/mark-shea/intelligent-design-vs.-the-argument-from-design/#ixzz4DE85uK6v.

The Council of Vienne, 1311–1312. *Decision against Pietro Olivi*. http://www.ewtn.com/library/COUNCILS/VIENNE.HTM#09.

The Fifth Lateran Council. Session 8, December 19, 1513. http://www.papalencyclicals.net/Councils/ecum18.htm.

Thomas Aquinas: Selected Writings. Edited by R. McInerny. London: Penguin Books, 1998.

Till, H. van. "Basil, Augustine, and the Doctrine of Creation's Functional Integrity." *Science & Christian Belief* 8, No. 1 (1996), pp. 21–38. http://www.asa3.org/ASA/topics/Evolution/S&CB4-96VanTill.html#1.

Till, H. van. "Is the Creation a 'Right Stuff' Universe?" *Perspectives on Science and Christian Faith*, Volume 54, No 4 (December 2002), pp. 232–239.

Tkacz, M. W. "Aquinas vs. Intelligent Design." *This Rock*, Nov. 2008. http://www.catholic.com/magazine/articles/aquinas-vs-intelligent-design.

Verschuuren, G. M. *Aquinas and Modern Science: A New Synthesis of Faith and Reason*. Angelico Press, 2016.

Wilhelm, J., and T. B. Scannell. *Manual of Catholic Theology based on Scheeben's Dogmatik*, Vol. 1. 4th ed. London: Kegan Paul, Trench, Trübner, 1909.

Wilkins, J. S. "Could God Create Darwinian Accidents?" *Zygon*, Vol. 47, No. 1, March 2012, pp. 30–41.

Wippel, J. F. "Aquinas on Creation and Preambles of Faith." *The Thomist*, Vol. 78, No. 1, Jan. 2014, pp. 1–36.

Zycinski, J., and M. Heller. *Dylematy ewolucji*. Tarnow: Biblos, 1996.

AQUINAS'S WORKS QUOTED IN THE BOOK:

Commentary to Metaphysics, In Met.
De Caelo
De Decem Praeceptis
De Ente et Essentia
De Potentia Dei, De Pot.
De Veritate
In Libros Physicorum
Questio de Anima
Scriptum super Sententiis, Super Sent.
Sentencia De anima
Sententia Libri Politicorum, Sent. Politic.
Summa contra Gentiles, ScG
Summa Theologiae, S.Th.
Super de Trinitate
Super II Corinthios, In II Cor.
Super Ioannem, Super Io.

"A large number of contemporary Thomists insist that theistic evolutionism - understood as the claim that the origin and development of all living things can be explained wholly in terms of the operation of secondary causes with no reference to divine intervention in the course of nature - is altogether consistent with their master's philosophy and theology. Fr. Michael Chaberek amply demonstrates in this timely work that this is not the case, that theistic evolutionism is, in fact, inescapably at odds with fundamental elements of Thomas' thought."

Robert Larmer, PhD,
Professor and Chair, Department of Philosophy,
University of New Brunswick

"Fr. Michael Chaberek makes an excellent textual, philosophical, and theological case that the teaching of St. Thomas Aquinas on human origins is incompatible with macroscopic evolutionary theory, even so-called 'theistic evolution.' A must read for Thomists and non-Thomists alike."

David Arias, Ph.D.,
Professor of Philosophy,
Our Lady of Guadalupe Seminary

"Father Michael Chaberek's book is surely the most precise treatment of the relationship between the thought of St. Thomas and Darwinian evolution ever written. When Darwin first proposed his theory, most Thomists rejected it. In contrast, most contemporary Thomists not only accommodate it, but dismiss alternatives such as intelligent design, which would seem to represent a positive step forward. What can explain this shift? Chaberek shows convincingly that Thomists who claim that Darwinism and Thomistic thought are compatible have been satisfied with a glossy reading of Darwinism and St. Thomas, and a naive reading of the scientific evidence. In some cases, this represents a repudiation of Thomism itself. All future writing on the subject will have to take account of Fr. Chaberek's trenchant critique."

Jay W. Richards PhD,
analytic philosopher, Fellow at Discovery Institute,
Co-ounder of Institute for Faith, Work and Economics

"Much ink has been spilled of late trying to reconcile the principles of Thomas Aquinas with Darwinian evolution. Fr. Chaberek has finally given the issue the book-length treatment it deserves, and things don't look good for Thomistic evolutionists. His arguments are fresh and challenging. All further discussion will need to take account of this important work."

Logan P. Gage PhD,
professor of philosophy,
Franciscan University of Steubenville

"Fr. Michael Chaberek's book is one of few that require both courage and competence. As Thomas Aquinas had to face the common opinion denying the possibility of creatio ex nihilo back in the 13th century, Fr. Chaberek today questions theistic evolution. His book is worth reading because it teaches honest and straightforward thinking and it shows readers how to respond to theistic evolutionists who commonly impose their views in Christian circles."

Rev. Prof. Andrzej Maryniarczyk S.D.B.,
philosopher, Chairman of the Department of Metaphysics,
Catholic University of Lublin, Poland

ABOUT THE AUTHOR

FR. MICHAEL CHABEREK O.P., S.T.D. is a member of the Polish Dominican Province, with a Doctorate in Fundamental Theology from Cardinal Stefan Wyszynski University in Warsaw. His academic focus includes science and faith dialogue, theology of creation and the theory of intelligent design. Fr. Chaberek is the author of *Catholicism and Evolution* (Angelico Press, 2015) and a contributor to *More than Myth?: Seeking the Full Truth about Genesis, Creation and Evolution* (Chartwell Press, 2014). He authored the website AquinasandEvolution.org.

www.ingramcontent.com/pod-product-compliance
Lightning Source LLC
Chambersburg PA
CBHW071656090426
42738CB00009B/1543